TO THE MEMORY OF KAREN HORNEY

"Gentle-rebel" of psychoanalysis
who was the first to see through what many
are today discovering and who is alive in
this book through her insight
into character and her faith in self-analysis.
Through her indirect influence I began to become an
effective psychotherapist and to her I am
grateful for bringing us Fritz Perls to America.

Books by Claudio Naranjo

Enneatypes in Psychotherapy

*The End of Patriarchy
and the Dawning of a Tri-une Society*

El Niño Divino y el Héroe

*Gestalt Therapy: The Attitude and Practice
of an Atheoretical Experientialism*

Gestalt sin Fronteras

Ennea-Type Structures

La Vieja y Novísima Gestalt: Actitud y Práctica

How to Be

Techniques of Gestalt Therapy

The Healing Journey

The One Quest

The Psychology of Meditatio

Earth, bas-relief sculpture by Totila Albert, 1962

Artistic Rendering by Kelly Rivera

CHARACTER AND NEUROSIS
An Integrative View

CLAUDIO NARANJO, M.D.

GATEWAYS/IDHHB, INC.
PUBLISHERS

ISBN: 0-89556-066-6

©1994 by Claudio Naranjo
All Rights Reserved. Printed in the U.S.A.
First Printing: July, 1994.
Second Printing: June, 1996.
Interior pages printed on recycled paper.

Published by:
GATEWAYS/IDHHB, INC.
PO Box 370
Nevada City, CA 95959
(800) 869-0658 or (916) 272-0180

Library of Congress Cataloging-in-Publication Data

Naranjo, Claudio
  Character and neurosis : an integrative view / Claudio Naranjo.
      p.   cm.
  Includes bibliographical references and index.
  ISBN 0-89556-066-6 : $21.95
    1. Enneagram.   I. Title.
BF698.35.E54N37   1994   94-21263
155.2'6--dc20   CIP

Acknowledgments

Portions of this book have been published previously in the following Gateways Books editions:

Ennea-type Structures: Self-Analysis for the Seeker ©1990, 1991 by Claudio Naranjo.

"Protoanalysis" is a registered service mark of the Arica Institute, Inc.

Editor and Project Manager for Gateways: Iven Lourie
Cover design by Nancy Christie.
Cover art: Drawing by Kelly Rivera after bas-relief sculpture "Earth" by Totila Albert, 1962.

Quotations of Karen Horney reprinted from *Neurosis and Human Growth* by Karen Horney, by permission of W.W. Norton & Co., Inc. Copyright 1950 by W.W. Norton & Co., Inc., renewed © 1991 by Jeffrey Rubin and Stephanie Steinfeld. Quotations of Theodore Millon from *Disorders of Personality, DSM-III: Axis II*, reprinted by permission of John Wiley & Sons, Inc., © 1981 by John Wiley & Sons, Inc. Quotations of Catherine R. Coulter from *Portraits of Homoeopathic Medicines*, Vol. 1, © 1986, by Catherine R. Coulter, and Vol. 2, © 1988 by Catherine R. Coulter, both published by North Atlantic Books, reprinted by permission of Catherine R. Coulter.

TABLE OF CONTENTS

Preface by Frank Barron ....*xv*
Author's Foreword ....*xxi*

By Way of Introduction:
   A Theoretical Panorama 1
1. Anger and Perfectionism (Type 1) 39
2. Avarice and Pathological
   Detachment (Type 5) 65
3. Envy and Depressive Masochistic
   Character (Type 4) 96
4. Sadistic Character and Lust (Type 8) 127
5. Gluttony, Fraudulence, and "Narcissistic
   Personality" (Type 7) 151
6. Pride and the Histrionic Personality
   (Type 2)..174
7. Vanity, Inauthenticity, and "the
   Marketing Orientation" (Type 3) 199
8. Cowardice, Paranoid Character,
   and Accusation (Type 6) 222
9. Psychospiritual Inertia and the
   Over-adjusted Disposition (Type 9)....................245
10. Suggestions for Further Work on Self 269

Appendix-Remarks for Differential Diagnosis 282
Biographical Notes...290
Index 293

"These are the hindrances: the darkness of unwisdom, self-assertion, lust, hate, attachment. The darkness of unwisdom is the field of the others... The burden of bondage to sorrow has its root in these hindrances."

PATANJALI -- BOOK II

"So, oft it chances in particular men,
That for some vicious mole of nature in them,
As, in their birth, -wherein they are not guilty,
Since nature cannot choose his origin,-
By the o'ergrowth of some complexion,
Oft breaking down the pales and forts of reason,
Or by some habit that too much o'er-leavens
The form of plausive manners; that these men,
Carrying, I say, the stamp of one defect
Being nature's livery, or fortune's star,
Their virtues else, be they as pure as grace,
As infinite as man may undergo,
Shall in the general censure take corruption
For that particular fault: the dram of eale
Doth all the noble substance of a doubt,
To his own scandal."

SHAKESPEARE (HAMLET - ACT I - SCENE IV)

"Introspection is the first step toward transformation, and I understand that, after knowing himself, nobody can continue being the same."

THOMAS MANN - ON HIMSELF

PREFACE
by Frank Barron

Claudio Naranjo has always been associated in my mind with surprise and a touch of mystery. In the beginning I simply knew that someone existed in far-off Chile who was responsible for visits I would receive at the Institute of Personality Assessment and Research in Berkeley. The visitors were, invariably non-psychologists and Chileans, and they would ring the front doorbell at the Institute and ask to see me, saying it had been suggested to them to do so by Dr. Claudio Naranjo. Invariably they would turn out to be interested in my ideas about simplicity and complexity, symmetry and asymmetry. Some were artists, some were architects, none were psychologists or psychiatrists. They arrived steadily enough, one by one, that it became customary fro the receptionists to call me on the inter-com and say, "It's another architect from Chile."

So I knew Claudio simply as the source of some very entertaining and intelligent interested parties who had a curiosity about the same sorts of things that interested me. Then one day, when I was teaching at Harvard, Claudio himself appeared, unannounced, at my door in the Center for the Study of Personality. He seemed very shy, introduced himself diffidently, and almost immediately we became friends. I knew him immediately to be unique and uncategorizable. Several years later, when he was staying in Berkeley himself, I asked him to be a subject in a double-blind experiment I was doing, comparing the effects of alcohol, psylocybin, and mescaline on various behaviors, including finger-painting. Claudio was one of the lucky ones, and he was soon deeply engrossed in his paintings, an occupation new to him. (He also made some piano compositions and played them while under the same beneficent influence.) A bit later I was preparing an article on this and other experiments for *Scientific American*, and I asked him whether I might use his painting as one of the illustrations, perhaps with identification of the subject. He laughed and replied, "Frank, yes of course, and you can print my MMPI profile next to it if you wish."

In the light of the formidable effort Dr. Naranjo has made in integrating typological approaches to personality, I think this a telling anecdote. He takes typology very seriously, as one should, but attaches no onus to any group membership. He is a typologist who does not think in terms of groups or diagnoses, though he will do so as necessary. His typologies, I should add, are dynamic not static; his framework is appropriately simple and symmetrical, but the inner differentiation is complex and somehow open-ended, or what I might call asymmetrical.

I am tempted to go on with anecdotes about Claudio, but perhaps I should stick to a narrative of his comings and goings in the service of his remarkable work as a psychologist of personality. He stayed at Harvard only a few days on that first visit, and his reason for being there was that he had brought his mother to Boston for some specialized eye surgery at the Phipps Clinic. My wife and I got to know her quite well in the course of her hospitalization and convalescence, and I learned something of Claudio's educational history and the distinctions and honors he had been accorded: a year in Paris on a musical fellowship, won by his early piano compositions, his field work in anthropological medicine in South America, his place as a cultural leader in democratic Chile before the authoritarian darkness descended. Mrs. Naranjo herself was a lady of the highest degree, a true pleasure to know.

Claudio himself next appeared in my life space when he came to Berkeley in 1962 on a Fulbright scholarship. He had begun it at Harvard, where he was Gordon Allport's student and received the influences of David McClelland and the noted botanist and authority on natural psychedelics, Richard Schultes; then he had gone to the University of Illinois to spend several months learning factor analysis with Raymond B. Cattell and carrying out his own first studies of the dimensions of personality. He was interested in spending a bit of time with us at the Institute, and we were pleased to accommodate him. He was very much involved with computer technology and the promise of this new technology for the study of personality, and, in fact, he had obtained from the University of Illinois the donation of the now-superceded Illiac II to the University of Chile. Later, in 1965, when Claudio returned on a Guggenheim Fellowship, I was working on my Inventory of Personal Philosophy, a 200-item questionnaire built in part from Cattell's summary of factors in values (in the early volume Description and Measurement of Personality). I had samples of some 400 males and 400 females, and Claudio undertook a collaboration with me on factor analysis of these data. This has remained unpublished, alas, partly because he had to leave before we could get it all together. And he was off in search perhaps of bigger game. He had decided to visit the Indians in the jungles of the Colombian Andes in search of knowledge about their ritual religious practices based on the use of banisteriopsis caapi (yage).

Typically mysteriously, Dr. Naranjo flew to Bogota and set off toward the jungle. A week's trek took him to the Putumayo River where he hired a dugout canoe with an outboard motor and a guide and made his way to the Kofan Indians, carrying little in the way of gifts but a vial of LSD I had given him (a gift to me from Timothy Leary) before he left. I know he became a friend of the chief shaman there, and exchanged some of that product of civilized chemical technology for a crateful of banisteriopsis caapi. I know, I say, because among other things there arrived one day at my office in Berkeley a quite large crate of dried cuttings of the plant, which I quickly took to the Center for Biochemical Dynamics at the University. There the chemists Tony Sargent and Alexander

Schulgin did the proper chemical analyses. Later, Sargent, Shulgin, and Naranjo published a theoretical paper of great importance in the British scientific journal, *Nature (1969: 221, 537)*. Later, *The Lancet* (March 8, 1969) was to hail this on its editorial page as an important breakthrough in our understanding of the biochemistry of schizophrenia.

Following his stay with the Colombian Indians, Claudio went on, after whatever adventures of soul and body, to his home in Santiago, where he used yage in some remarkable studies of its effects on white European subjects (now published in Harner's *Hallucinogens and Shamanism*). I say remarkable, for he discovered that archetypal images of exotic flora and fauna, such as tropical plants and jaguars and snakes, well enough known to the Indians but quite unknown to the whites, made their appearance in the hallucinogenic reveries of his subjects. This technique remains largely unexplored since then, but I think it is a promising avenue of research on the problem of ancestral memory and the relationship of this-life experience to latent unexperienced potentials for archetypal imagery (see Barron, Frank, "Towards an Ecology of Consciousness," *Inquiry*, 15, 95-113, 1972).

In our next chapter, for this begins to seem more a novella than an introduction to a most serious intellectual effort by a leading typological psychologist and psychiatrist, Dr. Naranjo returns to Berkeley to continue his work. But I will skip over some fascinating events to arrive at what was to be the beginning of the great effort presented in this book. One day Claudio came into my office and announced that he was leaving Berkeley a bit earlier than he had planned, because a call...in the sense of a spiritual demand...had come to him to study with a Sufi master who had surfaced in Chile and who was gathering people together for his teaching in the desert town of Arica. It was, Dr. Naranjo told me, the most important thing in life for him at that time to go there to learn from the Sufi master. By then I had learned not to be surprised, so I simply asked whether I could help in any way. Yes, he told me, there was no appropriate housing in Arica, and a couple of dozen people from the United States were going there. I do not remember now whether it was he or I who came up with the idea of the geodesic domes of Buckminster Fuller, which could be shipped in compact form and easily re-assembled in the desert. I succeeded in tracking down a Fuller dome nearby, fully occupied and providing shelter for students in an experimental school hidden in the woods somewhere between Berkeley and Santa Cruz, and we set off for the woodlands by a route I imagine must have been in some ways as tangled as the path from Colombia to the Kofan. We were cordially received (Claudio appearing at anyone's door is always welcomed), and soon enough he had arranged for the purchase and shipment of six domes to Chile.

Arica was to become famous in ways more than geographic, but that is another story, and it is time I said something about character and neurosis in relation to the integrative typological approach Dr. Naranjo here adopts. He himself has made the argument for its necessity very well indeed in the text, and I need not repeat it in any detail here. The point is, I believe, that factor analysis on the one side and psychiatric diagnosis on the other have brought us to a point where correspondences between the two sets of results cry out for understanding. And more than that, the spun-out clinical theories of therapists who subscribe to neither approach call out too for recognition. Put simply, there is need for a new conceptual structure. The increasingly popular cognitive approach must be fused with the psychodynamic and affective perspectives. A proper conceptual structure must open new paths to the understanding of persons in relationship with one another, so that the beleaguered self obtains at least a glimpse of what is happening in the other person. In my own doctoral dissertation at Berkeley ("Psychotherapy as a Special Case of Personal Interaction") I had made efforts in this direction by pairing results on the same dimensions for both patient and therapist, and Timothy Leary was soon to attempt the same sort of synthesis through his idea of the interpersonal reflex at multiple levels of communication (*The Interpersonal Diagnosis of Personality*, Ronald Press, 1957). But these efforts fell short of an established dyadic characterology, and that is precisely what is needed. In the present work, Dr. Naranjo not only has the interpersonal clearly before him, but he also puts the motivation to personal relationship in the forefront. He sees the importance of deficit motivation in determining neurotic stances. And motivation, after all, however omitted it may be in the common factorial interpretation of personality, is the *sine qua non* of a comprehensive view of individual as well as social reality.

I find this book, which is professional and difficult and not simply one of the popular efforts at using the insights suggested by the System of the Enneagram, to be exciting and challenging. Dr. Naranjo is qualified, qualified indeed as no one else is, to deal with the depths of the mind, its measurable manifestations, the psychiatric-diagnostic social necessities, and the variety of approaches that may be called therapeutic (or individuating, or aiming at behavioral change, or at bringing about a new, deeper, and broader experience of the self). He has brought his abilities and experience to bear on the difficult task of integrating the various partial approaches whose lack we all feel, and he has seen new connections that make his work an outstandingly creative contribution.

I think I can promise the careful reader of this book some surprises, with no more mysteries than are necessary and fitting. It is a work in which a lifetime of courageous and skillful exploration and mapping comes to fruition and is communicated in a manner both simple and complex, symmetrical and asymmetrical: complexly symmetrical as an Enneagram and utterly asymmetrical as life and time.

FOREWORD

He who knows, and knows that he is: he is wise.
Let him be followed.
By his presence alone man may be transformed.

(Sarmouni Recital)

I owe Frank Barron the idea of the book's sub-title, and I anticipate that my readers will find its appropriateness obvious even though its spirit has not been that of focusing on controversial issues. I have been an open minded explorer of many schools, and I think my most specific contribution is of an integrative nature. The view that I outline throughout the book's chapters may just as well be called cognitive as psychodynamic, and is also one in which personality is viewed as a system of traits. I think that we can only artificially separate traits from motives and from modes of seeing things[1], just as I also think that it is artificial to separate a social learning view of these traits from an object relational view that considers the internalization of parental figures and early feelings towards them.

---

[1]Though sometimes I emphasize the behavioral or the cognitive or the affective, an implicit point of view, to the effect that every behavioral trait is associated to a cognitive aspect and a motivational aspect, will pervade this book.

Together with constituting a clinical exploration of the same domain usually investigated by personality theorists embracing the mathematical approach and also a psychodynamic exploration of personality traits and their interconnections, and together with including a consideration of character orientations as styles of defense and styles of valuing that are linked to particular illusions concerning fulfillment, the understanding that I present here may also be called a transpersonal or spiritual view of character and neurosis or, alternatively, an existential view—inasmuch as it equates (as will be seen) spiritual "endarkenment" with loss of being.

Perhaps it may be of interest, in view of the ambition of such an encompassing synthesis, to state that the view in these pages has not come about as a consequence of an ambitious intent, but, rather, has been the result of a spontaneous integration of the views with which I have become familiar in the course of my personal intellectual adventure in personality research, upon my exposure to an influence outside academic psychology. In retrospect I can see that the issues of personality and human types have constituted an ongoing love affair during the last twenty years of my life, and in this an element of vocation seems to have converged with another of fate—most striking for the fact that after abandoning the field it seems to have drawn me into itself again, from the back, so to speak, without a deliberate intention on my part, as a consequence of the spontaneous maturation of an understanding derived from a living influence from a Sufi teacher in the so called "Fourth Way" tradition.

From the beginning of my psychological studies I was strongly interested in human types. Though my original interest in becoming a medical student was purely scientific and it was the discovery of Jung that moved me to remain there after I was disappointed in the search for wisdom through neuro-physiology, my real plunging into the spheres of psychotherapy and psychology occurred a year later, when I came to Ignacio Matte-Blanco's psychiatry course. Matte-Blanco[2]—founder of the

---

[2]Who migrated at the outset of Chilean dictatorship and has become, internationally respected, both for his psychoanalytic teaching and for his innovative work in the symbolic logic of schizophrenic thinking.

Psychoanalytic Institute in Santiago and head of the psychoanalytically oriented Psychiatric Clinic at the University of Chile—was a man of wide interests whom I must thank not only for an inspiring psychoanalytic education but also for an acquaintance with existential psychiatry and, no less pertinently to this book, for a familiarization with William Sheldon's ideas and research. In this, as in other matters, his personal interest resonated with the work conducted at the Clinic, where not only was Sheldon on everybody's lips but also patients were somatotyped.

Sheldon's notion that three dimensions of human temperament are intimately related to the body structures that derive from the original three layers of the human embryo had a profound impact on my understanding of things at that time. This was for me the time of exploring threefoldnesses and trinities. The inspiration for this lifelong particular interest of mine was the simultaneous impact of Gurdjieff, an initiate of a little known esoteric school, whose thinking was originally divulged through the Russian journalist, Ouspensky,[3] and Totila Albert, Chilean-German man of knowledge and artist. While Gurdjieff (founder of the Institute for the Harmonious Development of Man) spoke of "The Law of Three"—a cosmic principle according to which it is possible to distinguish an active force, a negative force, and a neutralizing force in all manner of phenomena in the process of becoming—Totila Albert envisioned Father, Mother, and Child as "three components" in the human being and in the cosmos and sought to warn his contemporaries concerning the dangerous obsolescence of our patriarchal society.

Given the ring of deeply-lived truth in the statements of both Gurdjieff and Totila Albert, it was natural for me to feel attracted to Sheldon's vision; for just as the notions transmitted by the former two—proceeding from tradition and personal revelation respectively—seemed to validate each other reciprocally, so this joint visionary background seemed to validate and be validated, in turn, by Sheldon's scientific findings. The coherence between Sheldon's findings and Totila's

---

[3]Ouspensky, P.D., *In Search of the Miraculous* (New York: Harcourt, Brace & World, 1949).

vision, further, included the fact that Totila Albert's statements included the envisioning of the three layers of the embryo as biologic expression of the universal "Components" or "Principles."

"Already the fecundated egg contains its three components in a latent form. In the outer sheath, the ectoderm, which gives rise to the skin, the sense organs of the central nervous and establishes the link to the macro-cosmos, we may find the father principle. In the inner layer, the endoderm, out of which develop most inner organs and constitutes the link to the earth, we find the mother principle. In the middle layer, the mesoderm, which is constituted of one sheath facing the ectoderm and the other facing the endoderm from which will proceed the future support system (skeleton), the action system (muscles), the source of impulses and circulation (the heart), the responsibility in the preservation of the species (generative tissue) we find the child principle."[4]

For a Sheldon enthusiast such as I was, it could not fail to be a concern that after the publication of Sheldon's *The Varieties of Temperament*[5], criticism was voiced concerning both arithmetic mistakes and methodology. In regard to the latter, it was the opinion of some that factor analysis would have been a better method for the handling of his data than the earlier technique of cluster analysis that Sheldon had used. It will not be difficult to understand that I became a student of factor analysis and avidly read the research performed by the two foremost experts in its applications to personality research at the time— Hans Eysenk in England and Raymond Cattell in the U.S. The wide divergence of their answers as to the underlying dimensions of personality amounted to a further stimulus to continue investigating the issue. Eysenk's results appeared excessively simple for, according to his claim, personality could be described in terms of only three variables: intelligence, neuroticism and extroversion/introversion. There was no room

---

[4]Totila Albert quotations from an unpublished manuscript. For a more extensive account, see Claudio Naranjo, *The End of Patriarchy and The Dawn of a Tri-une Society* (Berkeley: Amber Lotus, 1994).

[5]Sheldon, W.H., and S.S. Stevens, *The Varieties of Temperament : A Psychology of Constitutional Differences* (New York: Harper & Brothers, 1942).

here for Sheldon's distinction between an active and an emotional (or expressive) extroversion, which seemed so true to life. Cattell, on the other hand, obtained 16 factors from the analysis of questionnaire material, and one formed the impression that these could have just as well been 15 or 18, for their ensemble lacked an intrinsic coherence that might be comparable to mathematical elegance.

My interest in a more active engagement in personality research happened to coincide with a period of discomfort as an apprentice of psychoanalytic psychotherapy (when I felt that what I was able to offer did not meet the needs and high expectations of my clients) and it coincided, too, with an availability of research help in the form of psychology students who were interested in carrying out projects under my direction on occasion of their required dissertations. Since my engagement at the Institute of Medical Anthropology at the time involved a commitment to study the dehumanization process that had become apparent as an aspect of medical "education," and this involved, in turn, the development of adequate testing instruments, this also contributed to a part-time professional shift.

The opportunity of coming to the U.S. in 1962 when the need to accompany my mother to an eye surgeon in the U.S. was kindly seen by the University of Chile as an occasion to give me a short commission, and visits to Harvard and Ohio State University in Columbus (concerning findings in the field of perceptual training) whetted my appetite for a more extended academic pilgrimage—which I subsequently had the good fortune of being able to carry out.

A Fulbright scholarship, in 1963, allowed me to spend more than half the year at Harvard University again as a student of Gordon Allport, David McClelland, and others. I was, most specially, a "visiting scholar" at the Center for Studies of Personality, where Henry Murray's heritage was strong, and meeting Murray in person was surely an additional incentive to become acquainted with his contributions.

I visited during the next months (as originally planned) with Dr. Raymond B. Cattell at the University of Illinois at Urbana. I had been in correspondence with Dr. Cattell for some time (since I had consulted him in regard to the re-factoring of the 16PF in South America) and had been a sort of disciple of his at a distance, even before coming to establish contact with him through correspondence—since after reading his book on factor analysis I became immersed in it as a true believer seeking deeper understanding of the mind through statistics. The months at Urbana were busily spent learning and pondering further my own research and visiting people like Drs. Osgood and Mowrer. Before leaving I accepted Dr. Cattell's invitation to become a partner of his private enterprise, IPAT (Institute of Personality and Ability Testing), as representative for South America. It seemed an appropriate mantle to the work I had been carrying out on my own accord thus far, though little new came of it in view of my falling in love with California soon after. This came about following a letter of invitation from Dr. Frank Barron, then at the Berkeley campus, when I was nearing the end of my stay at Harvard.

I had met Dr. Frank Barron when I first set foot through the door of the Center for Studies of Personality, on the Harvard campus, during my earlier trip to the U.S., when I initiated my brief academic visiting tour and he was filling in for Gordon Allport, who was at the time on sabbatical. I was familiar with Barron's work on creativity and had even used an adaptation of his simplicity/complexity test (which I had learned of through the *Scientific American*), so when I saw his name on the board opposite the entrance door I inquired about the possibility of a visit. An immediate rapport and the discovery of many areas of affinity were to mature into a friendship that was a background factor to both his invitation to spend some time at the Institute for Personality Assessment and Research in Berkeley before returning to Chile and to my truly fate-full decision to accept it.

But Berkeley was not to be only one more academic adventure: I fell in love with the place and its atmosphere and decided to return to it. This I had occasion to do about a year later as a Guggenheim Fellow, and once more IPAR opened its doors to me, this time as a Research Associate.

Though my stay at IPAR during the time I was a Guggenheim Fellow (1965 to 1966) was the tail end of a two year long scholarly pilgrimage, my search for truth had never been completely intellectual and a thirst for a more experiential answer perhaps could not fail to be stimulated when one visited the Altered State of California in the early sixties.[6] Of particular relevance among the influences coming from the realm of the "consciousness revolution" (first embodied in the realm of psychology by the humanistic movement) was that of Fritz Perls —founder of Gestalt Therapy and disciple of Karen Horney— who insisted on calling his approach both holistic and existential. In spite of being principally a clinical phenomenologist with a rather anti-theoretical slant (at the time), I gained much understanding from the imprint of his living presence. In similar manner I could say that my thinking is existential to the extent that my clinical practice has been implicitly existential as a consequence of the way I was most significantly helped.

Of Horney I need to make special mention since Horneyan therapy was the most influential in my healing before gestalt and also it was the most influential in my way of practicing psychotherapy (also before gestalt). It came to me through Hector Fernandez, Provost, of whom I was a first experimental subject in the matter of a supervised and systematic self-analysis that was more meaningful than my earlier Kleinian analysis at the Chilean Psychoanalytic Institute. Some years before our meeting Hector Fernandez had undergone a process of profound change—a process which he called "self-analysis" but which could be said to have been to a considerable degree spontaneous and inspired. Since Horney had been for him the catalyst, he became a Horney apostle who lucidly elaborated on her ideas as he commented on the ongoing journals of a group of some ten of us in the late fifties.

I can say of myself what I have never heard of anybody else saying: Karen Horney is my favorite psychological author. True, Freud was a prophet—a socio-cultural change agent of great magnitude—yet he, who for years shone in my intellectual heavens like a father figure, is someone whose works I cannot read today without some embarrassment. Perls has written that "From Fenichel I got confusion; from Reich brazenness; from Horney human involvement without terminology."[7]

---

[6]I am borrowing the term of Dr.Roland Fischer, former editor of the *Journal of Altered States of Consciousness*.

[7]Perls, Fritz, *In and Out the Garbage Pail* (New York: Bantam Books, 1969).

I think the fact that Horney has the simplicity speaks something of her subtle and certainly not grandiose greatness. I am glad to see, now that psychoanalysis is revising some of its earlier views, that she is beginning to be remembered again to some extent, but I think that the true value of her work is still to be discovered. In calling attention to her with the dedication of this book, I not only want to point toward her in general, but to acknowledge the extent to which she has made a spontaneous appearance throughout the pages of this book. But to continue my story: there came a time, at last, in 1969, when the experiential seeker in me took precedence over the intellectual investigator. As I prepared to embark on my life's pilgrimage I felt drawn to share in the form of various books what I had learned until then[8], but I did not feel drawn to make any statements concerning my work on personality or human types. My search seemed in this field at that moment abortive.

I suppose it will come as a surprise to my readers if I say at this point that in spite of the broad curriculum described above, the main influence in this book comes from none of the sources that I have mentioned thus far. It came, on the contrary, from where I least expected it: from somebody who was first pointed out to me as a Sufi master and in whose experiential guidance I became interested enough to leave my academic life behind—perhaps, it seemed, forever.

I should interpolate here for the sake of context that, as many who were deeply affected by the Gurdjieff heritage, I had been disappointed in the extent to which Gurdjieff's school entailed a living lineage. I had turned in my search towards Sufism and had become part of a group under the guidance of Idries Shah by the time that friends from my home country invited me to meet a spiritual teacher steeped in the sources of that "esoteric Christianity" that Gurdjieff called "The Fourth Way." They wrote me about their experiences after meeting Oscar Ichazo and suggested that I meet him during one of my

---

[8]I wrote *The One Quest, The Psychology of Meditation* and *The Healing Journey* which were published in the seventies. I recently published *Gestalt Therapy: The Attitude and Practice of an Atheoretical Experientialism* (Nevada City, CA.: Gateways Books, 1993), and my book *The Divine Child and The Hero* is now in preparation.

intermittent visits. So I did, and I was excited to find somebody who declared himself, like Gurdjieff, an emissary of the specific school towards which my search had been polarized in recent years, the school about which Gurdjieff wrote at the end of *Meetings with Remarkable Men* and Roy Davidson wrote in his traveler's report on a visit to a Sarmoun community in the Hindu Kush[9]. I keep for an eventual autobiography the story of my private apprenticeship from then on, and will only say here what is most relevant to the subject of this book: during a series of open lectures sponsored by the Chilean Psychological Association, then under the direction of my friend and former supervisor Hector Fernandez, I heard Ichazo present a view of personality that seemed congruent with Gurdjieff's but went beyond it in detail.

During these lectures on what he called "protoanalysis," Ichazo agreed with Dr. Fernandez's request that he give us a practical demonstration of the method. He interviewed Dr. Fernandez's patients for a few minutes and gave such an accurate and detailed report that we were impressed, while unable to understand, however, the leap from Ichazo's brief interrogatory to his elaborate perceptions. It seems to me now that if my contact with Ichazo had broken off at this point I would never have learned to do the same through a sharpening of characterological intuition and characterological information. I came into this ability nearly a year later mostly as a spontaneous by-product of the deeply transforming experience undergone when I returned to Chile for a long retreat under Ichazo's direction in Arica.[10]

Though no further theory was presented in the course of the time spent in Arica during the second half of 1970, the intimate knowledge of more than forty companions surely contributed to the fact that in the aftermath of a deeply transformative solitary retreat inserted during that period, I

---

[9]Davidson, Roy Weaver, in *Documents on Contemporary Dervish Communities* (London: Society for Organising Unified Research in Cultural Education,1966).

[10]This personal invitation to join Ichazo in Arica in time extended, upon my suggestion, to include some friends and further extended by increments until more than forty Americans joined me, a group who would in turn originate the Arica Institute.

suddenly became able to see the structure of others' personalities as a good caricaturist sees the essential traits in a person's physical features. To this awakening of a "clinical eye" I owe everything that I was able to learn about personality types and personality in general from then on, and for the intellectual experience of an increasing coalescence of what information on the subject I acquired. I could say that the enneagram of the Sarmouni[11] acted as a magnet in my mind to bring together the pieces of psychological lore that, until then, were separate, an organizing catalytic factor causing the relative chaos of the information to come into a more precise pattern.[12]

When the time of my Arica pilgrimage gave way to a time of intense involvement in a combination of therapy, teaching, and spiritual guidance that began for me in 1971, it was only natural for me to seek to integrate my earlier backgrounds with the recent learnings. In the context of what might be called a meditation-and-psychotherapy group, I had occasion to find out how the central ideas of protoanalysis, and more specifically its nine-fold characterology, served as a first point of spontaneous crystallization for earlier understandings and for a gradual drawing of associations between my ongoing observations (in light of protoanalysis) and the standard classical observations of the psychological literature.[13]

Later, the work with a group that became the beginning of SAT Institute, in California, constituted a more prolonged opportunity both to observe character and to draw the bridges between the "Fourth Way" view and academic psychology. In view of the secrecy with which these psychological ideas were being presented by Ichazo after my own involvement with him,

---

[11]For more on the Sarmoun or Sarman tradition see J.G. Bennett's *Masters of Wisdom*.

[12]Ichazo did not provide descriptors of character types, but only diagnosis and the concepts reported by Lilly and Hart (in Tart's *Transpersonal Psychologies*).

[13]Thus, for instance, recognizing that both Fromm's Marketing Orientation and the personality labeled by Lowen as narcissistic allows me to see that both authors are employing different vocabulary and high-lighting different aspects of the same character. It is remarkable to note that Horney, too, gave the word "narcissistic" a similar denotation. In spite of their friendship and affinity, Fromm and Horney don't seem to have realized that they were talking about the same thing.

I, too, made such secrecy a requirement for admission to the groups that I taught—either directly or through delegates—in the decade following 1970. Not deeming a verbal agreement binding enough, I went so far as to obtain from every participant a signed contract, one item of which addressed itself to an agreement not to disclose some of the ideas and the spiritual practices taught in SAT. Toward the end of the seventies, however, several among those who were committed to keep these teachings for themselves and to draw only implicitly from this vision into their own work began offering "Enneagram Courses," first in the Berkeley area, then more widely.

Just as the coming of enneagram courses to the marketplace was a stimulus to begin thinking of publishing my observations, the publication of the first book on the subject made my intention definite. As in the case of several doctoral dissertations and enneagram course notes that had already come into my hands, the essential content of this echoed my own teaching in 1972, yet there was much in it I disagreed with. Furthermore, I thought that it was in bad taste for its authors to take the initiative of publishing something that would have been of negligible interest to its readers or publishers without its non-original component. Since this Foreword was written, many popular books on the enneagram types have appeared, and I have only sampled the more important ones: Palmer's, Riso's, and Molina's. Palmer's I find the most informative, though I would have expected a greater original contribution; Riso's is more original, but less accurate, so there is much he claims that I disagree with; Molina's axiological slant has represented the most substantial contribution, I think, and he provides more nourishing reading matter than other authors on the subject. I disagree, though, with his claim that ego-types are fully constitutional and instinct-related states are only pathological complications. Just as I disapproved of the freedom that some of my ex-students took to offer enneagram courses outside of the SAT context (however justified they may have felt), I have felt critical toward the freedom that the first popularizers have taken to publish material that is part of a more comprehensive body of understanding and which neither Ichazo nor myself chose to bring into the open.

I can only hope that a time comes when it may be said of their eagerness to teach and publish that "the devil does not know for whom he works"—as Oscar used to say. For it is easy to imagine that in retrospect we may come to admire the artistry through which divine providence has created out of their excitement an enneagram movement of enough significance to attract the interest of an all-too-conservative establishment for which esoteric wisdom and such things as the enneagram are suspect if not reprehensible.

Since the coming of the personality enneagrams into the public light and since the announcement of workshops on protoanalysis to the wider public by Arica Institute, I have resumed my teaching venture, both refining the application of the ideas presented by Ichazo—not only in regard to the analytic but also the behavior modification stages—this time in the Latin world. Throughout these years of experience, I have received increasing confirmation for the traditional view to the effect that, indeed, the interpretations suggested by this "Fourth Way" map are objectively the central ones for the people of each character type. At the same time I don't want to ignore that the process of assisting insight is an artistic one where an intuitive therapist or guide speaks not from the book but from a direct perception of aberration. The process of insight is of course not one of coming to accept a label or even knowing something in particular about one's psyche but the process of coming to know something *really* —which means to know it most of the time and in a way coherent with the rest of one's knowing. Yet when we work with a specific individual we do find a specific facet of personality in the foreground amidst its universally shared structure. The traditional contention that the recognition of a ruling passion has a great therapeutic power is echoed in my experience which tells me that, while alternative interpretations can be equally true, interpretations oriented according to a perception of the ruling passion and ruling fixation are *particularly* important to accept and heed.

While Gurdjieff worked through his injunction to insight and his masterful confrontation, and Ichazo worked with authoritative (or perhaps authoritarian) diagnosis, I have increasingly emphasized throughout my work the facilitation of a self-diagnostic process supported by a good grasp of the typology. While writing the nine chapters that constitute the main body of this book I have implicitly conceived of them, among other things, as a basis for self-diagnosis, and I take for granted that already the self-perception deriving from the intermittent recognition of this will be of therapeutic consequence.

The immediate trigger for the writing was the offer from my friend Marta Huepe to give me her full time during her summer vacation in January and February of 1988. Besides being a wonderful host in her beautiful spot of countryside in El Arrayan (Santiago-Chile), her keen interest in the subject and her empathetic participation made her an ideal listener as I dictated the cassettes that she then transcribed.

Though already the task of packing my papers for the writing journey to Chile in 1988 had constituted an incentive to formulate an outline of the book, this original outline rapidly changed into a spontaneously emerging one as I dictated, and only the overall structure remained. The book begins with a theoretical overview. Nine successive chapters deal with nine different character structures, none of which is new to psychology, but each here is presented in a new light: as a "specialization of the psyche" in one of nine possible directions according to the emphasis of one or other of nine interrelated motivational dispositions. A final chapter contains suggestions for further work with the material.

While I originally expected to draw mostly on memories for the illustration of the characters that are the focus of nine of the chapters of this book, I have instead drawn on classical character portraits, and I have also undertaken a review of the main psychological and medical sources. Among these I have not only included the perceptions of psychiatrists and clinical psychologists but included some of homeopaths as well. Without wanting to make a pronouncement for or against the validity of homeopathic treatment, in which I have no experience, I wanted to include the rich descriptions of human types that are part of homeopathic lore and approximate quite closely the character types with which I am personally acquainted. I have drawn these chiefly from the masterful synthesis on the subject by Catherine R. Coulter in *Portraits of Homoeopathic Medicines*.

While throughout my early teaching experience I described characters through a sequential commentary of their main traits, now I have wanted to base my reflections on some further elaboration of these trait lists[14]. Just as in that paper I sought to chart these "traits behind the traits" in a way that reflected their mutual inter-relationship in a psychodynamic pattern, here, too, I am basing my "psychodynamic reflections" on the consideration of hypothetical source traits and their inter-relationship more than on isolated descriptors. In the part of each chapter devoted to trait analysis I have interwoven description of character in terms of traits with a discussion of underlying motives and psychodynamic connections between traits as well as a spelling out of the traditional view to the effect that *at the center of each character there stands—in reciprocal relation to each other—a form of deficiency-motivation and a cognitive mistake.*[15]

The survey contributed by psychological and psychiatric literature is self-explanatory, and perhaps I only need to say here that I have concentrated on descriptive (over speculative) material, and that for each of the types of personality mapped by the enneagram I have found appropriate documentation— though one of them is strikingly missing in today's widely-used DSM III, and another poorly reflected among its repertoire of personality disturbances. A project that developed as I produced this book was a systematic explanation of the correspondence of the ennea-types to the psychological types in Jungian typology (the eight types in Jung's original observation and the description of typical respondents to questionnaires based on Jung's concepts).

I originally thought I would exclude an etiologic consideration from the present volume and relegate it instead to a future publication in view of the fact that a large proportion of

---

[14]As I already explored in my paper "On Puritanical Character" where I undertook a conceptual clustering of the observed traits in a character in order to better hypothesize the underlying, fundamental ones. (In *American Journal of Psychoanalysis*, Vol. XLII, no. 2, New York: Agathon Press, 1982).

[15]The notion of "the capital sins" are in the nature of both passions and destructive ideas can be found already in the first writer on the subject, Evagrius Ponticus in the IVth century.

my copious recordings prove to be for technical reasons too difficult to transcribe and that I am far from having analyzed the self-report data contained in them. I hope that my poor records may be compensated to some extent by the fact of having listened to some two hundred life histories per year for the last ten years. Perhaps I should apologize for not attempting to discuss the vast body of psychoanalytic speculation concerning the subject. My limited interest in doing so is not only a function of competing life tasks but also of my agreement with Peterfreund's view to the effect that psychoanalytic views of infancy are "adultomorphic."[16]

Once completed, the original manuscript included a review of the personality types in the special form of literature devoted to character description before the dawn of scientific psychology and still today. After Kösel Verlag (the German publisher) insisted on a simplification of the book, however, I have simplified the English version as well, and shifted my retrospective diagnoses and commentaries on Theophrastus, La Bruyère, et. al. for further publications.

A traditional emphasis on the view that a cognitive mistake constitutes the bottom-line of personality in the Middle Eastern oral tradition antedates and matches the increasing attention to a cognitive focus in contemporary psychology— through the work of people such as George Klein and Shapiro, Ellis, and Beck. Out of a personal conviction concerning the importance of the cognitive domain I have paid special attention to the subject of defense mechanisms (i.e., the selective ways of sustaining unconsciousness) that may be regarded as interdependent with the different interpersonal styles, and also to a search for a cognitive formulation of the interpersonal strategy itself. I am also claiming that every character entails a particular "metaphysical illusion": a wrong assumption in regard to Being—or, more precisely, to the possibility or *promise* of Being, as will be seen.

Besides the psychodynamic connections pointed out in each chapter between its "ruling passion," core strategy, and other substructures, I outline in successive installments an

---

[16]Peterfreund, E., *International Journal of Psychoanalysis*, 1978, 59, pp. 427-441.

existential interpretation of character, and, through that, a theory of neurosis as a search and loss of Being.

In this book I discuss the subject of *illusions* in conjunction with the issue of "ontic obscuration"[17]: how "Being scarcity" is experienced in each of the "psychological hells," how the individual is responsible in sustaining it, and how the *loss of being* is, in each case, sustained by a misguided thirst for *being*, which seeks its object not in being but in appearance: viz., not where it may be found, but where it is believed to be in view of a self-deceptive substitution, a mirage, an illusion, a trap, and a loop in a knot. For:

> conditioned personality leads to organismic interference,
> organismic interference leads to loss of the experience of being,
> loss of the experience of being leads to illusions, the"passions,"
> and the perpetuation of the conditioned personality;
> and so on and so forth.

In carrying out this last analysis I have followed the lead of Guntrip,[18] who posited that, just as the Kleinian psychotic layer of interpretation underlies the psychodynamic proper (in which libido is the source interpretation), we must seek a deeper "Winnicottian" or existential layer that acknowledges "loss of self" or "ego-weakness" as a deeper stratum than oral, anal, and genital (i.e., biological) libido.

Guntrip tells us that when he showed Fairbairn in 1957 his first draft of his paper "On Ego Weakness," Fairbairn said: "I am glad you have written this. If I could write now, this is the problem I would be writing about." Yet Fairbairn's health failed him before he could fully explore, as he wished, a patient's statement: "I've gone to the rock bottom where I feel I have not got an ego at all." In demonstrating that all psychopathology is

---

[17]An issue similar but perhaps broader than that alluded by R.D.Laing through the expression "ontic insecurity."

[18]Guntrip, Harry, in *Schizoid Phenomena, Object Relations and the Self* (New York: International Universities Press, Inc., 1969).

supported upon the skeleton of one particular character structure and that each character is animated by a specific "passional" motive, and in claiming that the nine passions constitute as many ways of seeking Being (interdependent with as many illusions concerning Being) that perpetuate ontic obscuration, I feel that I have fulfilled Fairbairn's dream.

It is through the exploration of a loss of being or self as the core of character that I have seen the book develop beyond a compact treatise on character types into the development of a comprehensive tenet. The contention that all psychopathology entails an "existential vacuum," an obscuration of being, in which it is supported and which it also supports, entails an obvious corollary: the inseparability of the enlightenment process from the healing of our inter-personal ills.

When I first named this book at the time of its dictation I called it *Character-structure and Dynamics (in Light of the Enneagram of the Sarmouni)*. After finishing it, however, I thought it appropriate to change the first part of the title to *Character and Neurosis*, for it is pervaded by the view that *the core of neurosis is characterological* and thus a comprehensive theory of character necessarily implies a theory of neurosis. Accordingly, I believe that in spelling out the structure and dynamics of the basic components of human character I have dealt (descriptively, dynamically, and existentially) with the whole gamut of neurotic styles.

Needless to say, I disagree with those who continue to hold character pathologies as complications, and fully endorse Wilhelm Reich's contention that the character constitutes the fundamental mode of defense. I find a most eloquent expression of my own conviction in Horney's claim:[19] "In the psychoanalytic concept of neuroses a shift of emphasis has taken place: whereas originally interest was focused on the dramatic symptomatic picture, it is now being realized more and more that the real source of these psychic disorders lies in character disturbances, that the symptoms are a manifest result of conflicting character traits, and that without uncovering and straightening out the neurotic character structure we cannot cure a neurosis. When

---

[19]Horney, Karen, *Neurosis and Human Growth* (New York: W.W. Norton & Co., 1990).

analyzing these character traits, in a great many cases one is struck by the observation that, in marked contrast to the divergency of the symptomatic pictures, character difficulties invariably center upon the same basic conflicts."

In recent weeks I have had the pleasure to see this attitude echoed by David Shapiro in his recent book *Psychotherapy of Neurotic Character*, where he says: [20]"I mean by this term that neurosis consists not of a nuclear conflict within the person—such as between particular unconscious impulse and defense—but of a distortion of the whole personality. Neurosis consists of certain restrictive and conflict generating ways in which the personality works...certain ways in which, as I put it earlier, the personality reacts against itself. I have used the term neurotic style in the same sense. From this standpoint, the old distinctions between 'symptom neurosis' and 'character disorder' each disappear; all neurosis is characterological."

I have found myself speaking to three audiences as I dictated the chapters of this book.

Firstly, the audience that I primarily had in mind as I incubated the project, when I envisaged the book as a guided self-insight process by remote control and an extension of the kind of work I have done with groups. For such readers I have written an additional chapter with suggestions as to how to put the information in the book to further use.

Secondly, as I have dictated the book, I have found myself speaking, with special interest, to theoretically-minded students of personality, and thirdly, to psychotherapists. I have sought to reconcile the conflict of speaking to laymen and specialists at the same time much as I would have done in speaking to both in the same room, by seeking mostly not to become too "academic," through avoidance of jargon and—I do this now—by asking my lay readers to be forbearing if some of my quotations and bibliographic references fail to interest them. As I stand before the nearly finished product I feel the satisfaction of anticipating that it will be both interesting and nourishing to its readers and that, through them, it may

---

[20]Shapiro, David, *Psychotherapy of Neurotic Character* (New York: Basic Books, 1989).

contribute to a generalized understanding of human fallenness at a time when we sorely need it.

CHARACTER AND NEUROSIS

An Integrative View

BY WAY OF INTRODUCTION: A THEORETICAL PANORAMA

"Like any field of scientific study, personality psychology needs a descriptive model or taxonomy of its subject matter...a taxonomy would permit researchers to study specified domains of personality characteristics...Moreover, a generally accepted taxonomy would greatly facilitate the accumulation and communication of empirical findings by offering a standard vocabulary or nomenclature.... Most every researcher in the field hopes, at one level or another, to be the one who devises the structure that will transform the present Babel into a community that speaks a common language."

Oliver P. John
*(Institute of Personality Assessment and Research,
University of California)*

1. A VIEW OF NEUROSIS, ENDARKENMENT, AND CHARACTER

I will speak here about personality in general and also about the process of what we may call the degradation of consciousness—what is technically called the "theory of neurosis"—and which finds symbolic echo in the spiritual traditions in the mythical stories of the "fall from paradise." I will not make a distinction between the spiritual "fall" of consciousness and the psychological process of aberrated development.

Let me just point out, as a beginning, that this degradation of consciousness is such that in the end the affected individual does not know the difference, i.e., does not know that there has been such a thing as a loss, a limitation, or a failure to develop his full potential. The fall is such that awareness comes to be blind in regard to its own blindness, and limited to the point of believing itself free. It is in view of this that Oriental traditions frequently use, in connection with the ordinary condition of humankind, the analogy of a person who is asleep—an analogy that invites us to conceive that the difference between our potential condition and our present state is as great as the condition between ordinary wakefulness and dreaming.

To speak of a degradation of consciousness, of course, implies the idea that the process of the "fall" is one of becoming less aware or relatively unconscious; yet the "fall" is not only a fall in "consciousness" proper; it is also, concomitantly, a degradation in the emotional life, a degradation in the quality of our motivation. We may say that our psychological energy flows differently in the healthy/enlightened condition and in the condition that we call "normal." We may say, echoing Maslow, that the fully functioning human being is motivated out of abundance, while in a sub-optimal condition, motivations have the quality of "deficiency": a quality which may be described as a desire to fill up a lack rather than as an over-flowing out of a basic satisfaction.

We may say that the distinction between the "higher" and the "lower" conditions is not only one of abundant love vs. deficient desiring. Still a more complete formulation is that which we find in Buddhism as an explanation of human fallenness in terms of what is called the "three poisons." In the triangular diagram below we may see depicted an inter-dependence of an active unconsciousness on one hand (commonly called ignorance in Buddhist terminology) and on the other a pair of opposites that constitute alternative forms of deficiency motivation: unconsciousness, aversion, and craving.

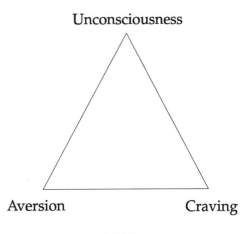

FIGURE 1

We are all acquainted with the Freudian view that neurosis consists basically in an interference with instinctual life. It was Freud's contention that this basic frustration of the infant in relation to his parents was a "libidinal" frustration, i.e., an interference with early manifestations of a sexual desire, mainly toward the parent of the opposite sex. Today few are willing to endorse this original view of psychoanalysis, and the so-called libido theory has fallen into question, to say the least. Modern psychoanalysts, such as Fairbairn and Winnicot, agree that the origin of neurosis is to be found in an imperfect mothering and, more generally speaking, in problems of parenting. More importance is given today to the lack of love than to the idea of instinctual frustration or, at least we may say, more importance is given to the frustration of a contact and relationship need than to pre-genital or genital manifestations of sexuality. However it may be, Freud had the great merit of realizing that neurosis was a nearly universal thing, and that it is transmitted generation after generation through the process of parenting. It took a heroic attitude to assert it in his time, yet now it is a platitude to say that the world, as a whole, is crazy, since it has become so obvious.

In the view of some spiritual documents such as the Gospel of Saint John, we find the view that truth is, so to speak, upside down in the world: "The light was in the world, but darkness did not comprehend it." In the Sufi tradition there is a widespread recognition of how a "true man" is also as if upside down, so that he seems to ordinary people an idiot. Yet we may say that not only in the case of heroic beings is truth crucified: it is also in the case of each one of us.

It is not difficult to conceive of the notion that we have all been hurt and, perhaps unconsciously, martyred by the world in the process of our childhood, and in this way we have become a link in the trasmission of what Wilhelm Reich used to call an "emotional plague" infecting society as a whole. This is not only a modern psychoanalytic vision: a curse visiting generation after generation is something that has been known since antiquity. The notion of a sick society is the essence of the old Indian and Greek conceptions of our time as that of a "dark age," a "Kaliyuga"—an age of great fallenness from our original spiritual condition.

I am not saying that mothering is everything; fathering is important too, and later events may have influenced our future development such as is evident in the traumatic war neuroses. Also early events, such as the extent of birth trauma, can have debilitating effects on the individual. Certainly the way in which children are brought into the world in hospitals constitutes an unnecessary shock, and we may conjecture that one born in the twilight and not slapped on the back to stimulate breathing may be better prepared to resist later traumatic conditions in life—just as a child who has been adequately mothered at the beginning of life may be better prepared to take on the traumatic situation of poor fathering.

Let us say, using Horney's metaphor, that we come into the world like the seed of a plant which carries in it certain potentialities and also instinctively awaits certain elements in its environment, such as good earth, water, and sun.

Harlow's experiment with chimpanzees, decades ago, demonstrated, for instance, that a baby monkey needs not only milk, but something furry to hang on to, and that it may develop into a somewhat normal adult given a terry cloth covered dummy of a mother, but not with an artificial mother made of wire, even if it has a bottle in its breast.

Surely the human needs, in order to develop into a fully functioning adult, are more complex, and there are many things that may go wrong, or saying it in an alternative way: there are many ways in which the requirement for good enough parental love is frustrated or betrayed. In some cases parental self-involvement may result in neglect, for instance, while in others too strong a need to lie on the part of the grown-ups may result in the invalidation of the child's experience; still, in other instances, tenderness may be over-shadowed by the expression of violence, and so on.

Let us say that the way we have come to be in this lower world that we inhabit after the fall from Eden—the personality that we identify with and implicitly refer to when we say "I"—is a way of being that we adopted as a way of defending our life and welfare through an "adjustment," in a broad sense of the term, and that usually is more a rebellion than a going along.

In the face of the lack of what he or she needs, the growing child has needed to manipulate, and we may say that character is, from one point of view, a counter-manipulative apparatus.

In this state of affairs, then, life is not guided by instinct but through the persistence of an earlier adaptational strategy that competes with instinct and interferes with the "wisdom" of the organism in the widest sense of the expression. The persistance of such early adaptational strategy may be understood in view of the painful context in which it arose and the special kind of learning which sustains it: not the kind of learning that occurs gratuitously in the developing organism, but a learning under duress characterized by a special fixity or rigidity of what behavior was resorted to in the initial situation as an emergency response. We may say that the individual is not free anymore to apply or not the results of his new learning, but has gone "on automatic," putting into operation a certain response set without "consulting" the totality of his mind, or considering the situation creatively in the present. It is this fixity of obsolete responses and the loss of the ability to respond creatively in the present that is most characteristic of psychopathological functioning.

While the sum total of such pseudo adaptive learning as I have described is commonly designated in the spiritual traditions as "ego" or "personality" (as distinct from the person's "essence" or soul), I think it is most appropriate to give it also the name of "character."

A derivative from the Greek *charaxo*, meaning to engrave, "character" makes reference to what is constant in a person, because it has been engraved upon one, and thus to behavioral, emotional and cognitive conditionings.

While in psychoanalysis the basic model of neurosis is one of instinctual life hemmed in by activity of a super-ego internalized from the outer world, I am here proposing that our basic conflict and our fundamental way of being at odds with ourselves consists in an interference with organismic self-regulation through our character. It is within character, as a parcel of it, that we can find a super-ego with its values and demands, and also a counter-super-ego (an "under-dog" as Fritz Perls used to call it) who is the object of the super-ego's demands and accusations and who pleads for its acceptance. It is in this "under-dog" that we find the phenomenological referent for the Freudian "id," yet it is a questionable thing to interpret its animating drives as instinctual. For it is not only instinct that is the object of inhibition within us—as a result of ingrained self-rejection and the wish to be something other than what we are: it is also our neurotic needs. The various forms of deficiency motivation, that I will propose that we call our passions, are forbidden to us, both in respect to their greed aspect and in their aspect of hate.

We may describe character as a composite of traits, and understand how each of these traits arose as either an identification with a parental trait or, conversely, out of a desire to not be like a parent in that particular regard. (Many of our traits correspond to an identification with a parent, and at the same time, an act of rebellion in regard to the opposite trait of the other parent.) Other traits can be understood in terms of more complex adaptations and counter-manipulations. Yet character is more than a chaotic array of traits. It is a complex structure that may be mapped as an arborization, where discrete behaviors are aspects of the more general behaviors and where even the various traits of a broader nature can be understood as the expression of something more fundamental.

The fundamental core of character I will be formulating here is twofold in nature: as a motivational aspect in interplay with a cognitive bias—a "passion" associated to a "fixation." We may picture the position of the ruling passion and a dominant cognitive style in personality by comparing them to the two foci of an elipse, and we may now amplify our earlier statement on character vs. nature, by speaking of the process in greater detail as *an interference with instinct by passion under the sustaining influence of distorting cognition.*

The map of the psyche offered on the following page is a graphic variant of the view of personality offered by Oscar Ichazo and is, in several ways, similar to that offered by Gurdjieff. According to both views, human personality (in the sense of character) comprises five "centers." Yet a fully developed human being has awakened in himself the functioning of two higher centers, that are given the names of "higher emotional" and "higher intellectual." While Gurdjieff spoke of a lower or ordinary intellectual center, a lower feeling center, and a lower movement center, Ichazo frequently called this movement center "instinctual," and according to the view that he claimed to transmit, this instinct center is, in turn, divided into three.

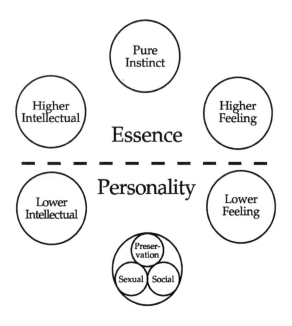

FIGURE 2

As of today, Freud's instinct theory of behavior has received severe criticism in psychology. First, the rise of etiology was an inducement to distinguish between instinct as is manifest in animal behavior (with its release mechanisms and highly fixed pattern of expression) and anything that could be called instinct in human life. Then the perceptions of Adler, Horney, Klein and later object relations theorists ended up causing part of the psychoanalytic world to turn not only against Freud's biologism but away from libido theory in particular.[1] Fritz Perls, who may be considered a new Freudian in view of his training with Reich, Horney, and Fenichel, seemed to be following the spirit of the

---

[1]Though Guntrip does not look upon drive for relationship as an instinct, others do. Model, for instance, speaks of two classes of instinct, while he speaks of the sexual and aggressive instincts of the id in addition to the newly recognized object relational instinct of the ego.

times as he switched from instinct language to cybernetic language in his concept of organismic self-regulation.

In contrast to such a tendency to drop the notion of instinct in the interpretation of human behavior, the view presented here not only involves an instinct theory—at least it gives instinct one third of the psychological arena—but also coincides with the psychoanalytic notion of neurosis as a perturbation of instinct—and, conversely, healing as a process of instinctual liberation. Unlike Freud's two instinct theories and also unlike Dollard and Miller's view of behavior in terms of a great multiplicity of drives, the theory proposed here acknowledges three basic instincts and goals behind the multiplicity of human motivation (purely spiritual motivation excluded): survival, pleasure, and relationship. I think that though some today (such as Gestaltists) may prefer to employ cybernetic language and say that neurosis implies a perturbation of organismic self-regulation, few would question the great importance of sex, preservation, and the relationship drive and their joint centrality as pervasive goals of behavior. Though Marx's interpretation of human life emphasized the first, Freud's the second, and present day Object-Relations theorists the third, I do not think that anybody has embraced a view that explicitly integrates these three fundamental drives.

Unlike traditional religions, which implicitly equate the instinctual domain with the sphere of the passions, the present view of the optimal mental state as one of free or liberated instinct, is one for which the true enemy in the "Holy War" traditionally prescribed against the false or lower self is not the animal within, but the realm of deficiency motivation: that of the "passionate" drives that contaminate, repress, and stand in place of instinct (as well as the cognitive aspects of the ego which, in turn, sustain the passions).

As may be seen in the map, the cognitive and emotional aspects of the personality are represented as operating in two alternative modalities, according to the level of awareness, while the instinctual center is represented only once. This may be viewed as a questionable convention, for there is the understanding that instinct can also manifest in two contrasting ways, either as bound instinct within the channels provided by

the ego or in a state of freedom where instinct is regarded as
belonging to the essence proper.[2]

One who is acquainted with the use of "essence" in
Sufism will understand the referent of this word to be that
deepest aspect of human consciousness, which exists "in God"
and becomes manifest to the individual after an annihilation
("faná"), but may find this meaning inconsistent with the present
mapping of discrete attributes of the essence such as the states
belonging in the sphere of higher intellect, higher feeling, and
instinct. The contradiction disappears if we make a distinction
between consciousness proper and the workings of the mind in
the conscious state (as distinct from the egoic states). When used
in this sense, however, we must beware of reifying essence, and I
can repeat here what I wrote in *Ennea-type Structures*:

"The broadest distinction in the body of Fourth Way
Psychology that I seek to outline, is between 'essence' and
'personality'—between the real being and the conditioned being
with which we ordinarily identify; between the greater and the
lesser mind. Where Gurdjieff spoke of personality, Ichazo spoke
of ego—more in line with recent usage (ego trip, ego death, ego
transcendence, and so on) than with the meaning given to 'ego'
in today's ego psychology. The distinction is similar to that
proposed today by Winnicott between the 'real self' and the 'false
self,' yet it may be misleading to speak of essence, soul, true self
or atman as if the reference were something fixed and
identifiable. Rather than speak of essence as a thing, then, we
should think of it as a process, an ego-less, unobscured, and free
manner of *functioning* of the integrated human wholeness."

Thus we can say that the "map of the psyche" offered
above is only complete if we claim that it also maps the space in
which the centers of personality and essence exist—a space that
may be taken as an apt symbol of consciousness itself. Since the
awareness in the context of which "the lower centers" may be

---

[2]Though I have said in *Ennea-type Structures* that pure instinct can be mapped as
three dots in contrast to the representation of bound instinct as three
enneagrams, I should quote Ichazo as claiming that while in meditative
absorption this is so, in the workings of expression of the essence in life it can be
mapped as an enneagram in which are combined the three central triangles of
the instinct enneagrams.

said to exist is degraded, I have shaded it in the modified map in Figure 3, while the three "higher centers," in contrast, are mapped within a white circle, to convey the notion of trinity in unity, characteristic of the Fourth Way and the Christian tradition in general.

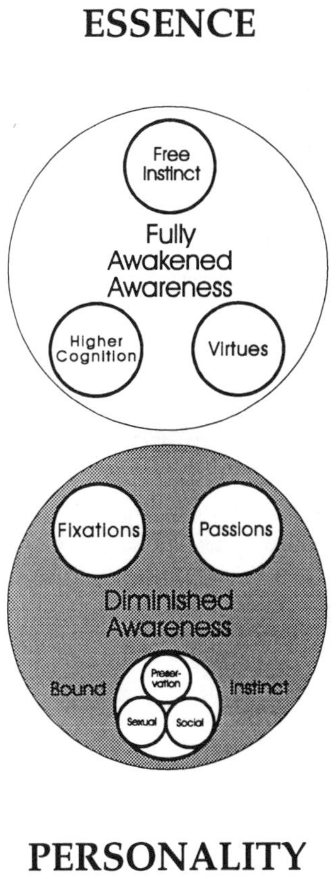

ESSENCE

PERSONALITY

FIGURE 3

2. THE CHARACTERS

Those acquainted with Gurdjieff's work will know how important in this approach to "awakening" was that aspect of self-knowledge consisting in the discernment of one's "chief feature," i.e., a pervasive characteristic of the personality that might be understood as a center of it (much as Cattell and others conceive of "source traits," each of which is conceived as the root of a trait tree). The view presented here goes further in claiming that the number of possible "chief features" are not unlimited—but the same as the number of basic personality syndromes. Additionally, we will be speaking of two central features in each character structure, as intimated above: one, the chief feature proper, consisting in a peculiar way of distorting reality, i.e. a "cognitive defect"; the other, in the nature of a motivational bias, a "ruling passion."

We may think that character can be structured along a distinct number of basic ways, that result in the relative emphasis of one or another aspect of our common mental structure. We may say that the "mental skeleton" that we all share is like a structure that can, like a crystal, break in a certain number of ways that are pre-determined, so that among the set of main structural features any given individual (as a result of the interaction between constitutional and situational factors) ends up with one or the other in the foreground of his personality—while the remaining features are in a more proximate or more remote background. We might also use the analogy of a geometric body that rests on one or another of its facets; we all share a personality, with the same "faces," sides, and vertices, but (in the language of the analogy) differently oriented in space.

According to this view there are nine basic characters (in contrast to Sheldon's three, Hypocrates' four temperaments, Lowen's five bioenergetic types, and the five dimensions of some modern factorialists, for instance). Each of these exists, in turn, in three varieties according to the dominant intensity of the self-preservation, sexual, or social drives (and the presence of specific traits that are a consequence of a "passional" distortion of corresponding instinct, which is "channelled" and "bound" under the influence of the individual's dominant passion)[3]. There are, of course, nine possible dominant passions and each is associated to a characteristic cognitive distortion, as well as with one, two, or three mental characteristics derived from the instinctual sphere, as just described.

The nine characters in the view presented here do not constitute simply a collection of personality styles: it is, rather, that of an *organized* set of character structures, in that specific neighborhood relationships, contrast, polarities, and other relations are observed between them. These relations are mapped according to the traditional geometric structure called an "enneagram."[4] Correspondingly, I will speak of ennea-types— short for "personality type according to the enneagram."

---

[3] I will not go into the 27 subtypes in the present volume, except to some extent, in the case of the varieties of suspicious character—since the forms of ennea-type VI are so differentiated that to speak of them in general would obscure their no less striking differential characteristics.

[4] In *In Search of the Miraculous*, Ouspensky quotes Gurdjieff saying that the teaching that he presented was completely autonomous, independent from any other paths (such as Theosophy or Western Occultism), and that it has remained hidden to this day. He continues to say that as other teachings use symbolic method, this one does too, and that one of its main symbols is the enneagram. This symbol consisting in a circle divided in nine parts by points that are connected between themselves by nine lines in a certain pattern expresses the "law of seven" and its connection with the "law of three." Also in the same book Ouspensky quotes Gurdjieff as saying that in a general way the enneagram must be distilled as a universal symbol and that each science may be interpreted through it, and that, for somebody who knows how to use it, the enneagram makes books and libraries useless. If an isolated person in the desert drew the enneagram on the sand, he could read the eternal laws of the universe, and he would learn each time something new that he had ignored completely thus far. He also says that the science of the enneagram has been kept a secret during a long time, and now it is more in the reach of all, yet only in an incomplete and theoretical way that is almost useless to one who has not been instructed in this science by one who has mastered it.

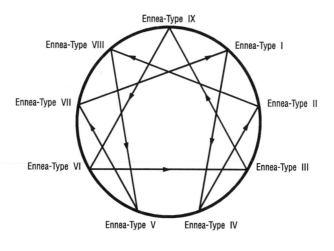

Figure 4

It has been an aspiration of modern psychology to organize the known characterological syndromes in what has been called a circumplex model. "Over approximately the past 30 years, various investigators have endeavored to demonstrate that the structure of personality traits, when defined by an individual's interpersonal behavior, may best be represented in terms of this circumplex model."[5] This is a circular continuum (shown in Figure 5) with adjoining characters being most similar to each other, while oppositions along the circle correspond to bipolarities; in contrast, the enneagram emphasizes tripolarity. One circumplex model was proposed by Leary in connection with his interpersonal system, another by Schaefer as the way to organize data resulting from his study of parent-child interactions. Lorr and MacNair in 1963 reported an "interpersonal behavior circle," resulting from a factor analysis of clinicians' ratings on various kinds of interpersonal behavior— which was interpreted as reflecting nine clusters of variables. In

---

[5]Cooper, Arnold M., Allen J. Frances, and Michael H. Sacks, *Psychiatry, Volume I, The Personality Disorder and Neurosis* (New York: Basic Books, 1990). Literature on the circumplex models cited in this paragraph, as well as the model in Figure 5, may be found in this same collection.

addition to these theoretically-derived circumplex models, Conte and Plutchik demonstrated that a circumplex model maps the main domain of interpersonal personality traits. By two different methods, one an analysis of similarity ratings of terms, another an application of factor analysis to semantic differential ratings of terms, they produced an identical empiric circular ordering of terms on the basis of their loading of the first two factors. A later study by the same authors examines the diagnostic concepts of DSM-II personality disorders. They found that these could also be arranged in a circumplex order fairly similar to that resulting from the 1967 study.

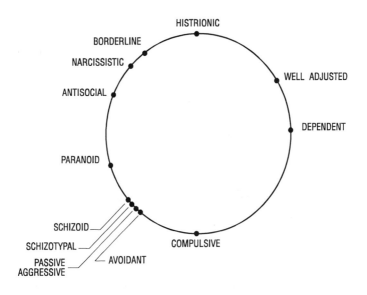

A circumplex structure of DSM III, Axis II personality disorders based on direct similarity scaling and semantic differential profile similarity.

Figure 5

Perhaps the scheme pictured in Figure 6 below is the most convincing circumplex model thus far. Agreeing also with current opinion in terms of the grouping of DSM III syndromes, the present characterology recognizes three fundamental groups: the schizoid group, with an orientation to thinking (that I will here designate as ennea-types V, VI, and VII), the hysteroid group, with an orientation to feeling (ennea-types II, III, and IV) and another group (which Kretschmer might have called collectively epileptoid) the members of which are constitutionally the lowest in ectomorphia and are predominantly oriented to action.

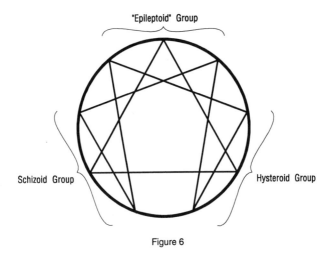

Figure 6

I now turn to a briefest description of the nine basic characters following the standard numbering given to points along the enneagram circle.

The first kind of personality style (and neurotic style, of course) is, in this view, both resentful and well intentioned, correct and formal, with little spontaneity and an orientation to duty rather than pleasure. Such people are demanding and critical towards themselves and others, and I will call them perfectionistic rather than branding them with a psychiatric label —though the syndrome corresponds to the obsessive personality in DSM III. While in the case of each one of the ennea-types we find that it coincides with a known clinical syndrome, it is also true that everybody may be regarded as the bearer of one personality orientation or another, and that each may be seen in specific levels ranging from that of psychotic complication to that of the subtlest residues of childhood conditioning in the life of saints.

Ennea-type II, in this Fourth Way characterology is one that I have characterized through the paradox of an egocentric generosity and corresponds to the histrionic personality of DSM III. Representative individuals are usually hedonistic, light-hearted and rebellious in the face of anything rigid or restrictions on their freedom. Early in the life of my first group in Berkeley a student, Dr. Larry Efron, summarized the characters in a collage of caricatures from William Steig, which he gave me on occasion of a birthday party. In the collage of Steig's caricatures, type II is represented by a clownish figure that contrasts with the struggling mountain climber that represents the hardworking and obsessional type I.

Enneatype III is interestingly not to be found in DSM III in spite of constituting the most American of characters (as Fromm observes, in connection with what he called the "marketing orientation"). I agree with Kernberg's dissatisfaction concerning the non inclusion of a form of hysterical personality not identical to the histrionic, in that the representative individual is not inconsistent or unpredictable in his emotional reactions and displays much more control as well as loyalty and the capacity for sustained emotional involvements. If the term hysterical were not also employed colloquially to designate the overly-dramatic and impulsive personality of type IV, it could be recommended to include both hysterical and histrionic in a future revision of the American *Diagnostic and Statistical Manual*. I find that most of Lowen's clinical examples in his book on *Narcissism* are type III individuals—yet the word "narcissistic" which has also been employed by Horney to describe the character, seems inappropriate because of alternative usage. This is the characterological disposition observed by Riesman, who discussed it in terms of other-direction. In the enneagram of caricatures, type III is represented by a medical doctor, emblematic of professional success and respectability, as well as professional know-how. Type III individuals seek appreciation in the eyes of others through achievement, effectiveness, and social graces, are both controlling and controlled, and constitute one of the happier characters in the enneagram.

Type IV is represented in the Steig caricature through an image that evokes the suffering victim of life circumstances and people. This corresponds to the self-defeating personality included in the revision of DSM III. It also corresponds to what Horney used to call masochistic character, in which there is a poor self-image, a disposition to suffer more than is necessary, a great dependency on the love of others, a chronic sense of rejection, and a tendency to discontent.[6]

The caricature of isolation in point 5 is appropriate for a disposition that may be regarded as the interpersonal style that emerges from and sustains retentiveness. This corresponds to the schizoid personality of DSM III and to individuals that not only have few relations but fail to feel solitary in their aloneness, who seek to minimize their needs, who are shy and have great difficulty in expressing their anger.

The warrior in point 6 again conveys a connotation apparently very different from fear, and yet alludes to a belligerence arisen from fear of authority and sustained through a (counterphobic) avoidance of the experience of fear. The warrior image is an appropriate caricature of only some ennea-type VI individuals, however, and not of the overtly weak and fearful. The subtypes are very differentiated in ennea-type VI, so that it embraces, along with the avoidant personality of DSM III, also the paranoid, still another form of suspicious character with more obsessive characteristics, as will be discussed in the appropriate chapter.

Type VII corresponds to Karl Abraham's oral-receptive or oral-optimistic character and is echoed today in DSM III by the narcissistic syndrome. The typical individual is one displaying nonchalence, a sense of entitlement, an orientation to pleasure and a more consciously strategic attitude in life than in most characters. The caricature figure in point 7 has, instead of a head, what seems to be wiring. It suggests living in fantasy and a

---

[6]As will be seen, I believe that the borderline personality *sensu strictu* corresponds to a complication of the same.

tendency to forget the real world through an absorption in planning and scheming.

Type VIII corresponds to Reich's phallic-narcissistic type and is echoed today in DSM III in the anti-social and sadistic personalities. It is that of a person oriented to power, domination, and also violence. At point 8 we see a caricature of somebody who stands on a platform in order to talk down to people or rather to harangue them with powerful voice and demeanor. It is appropriate, though it leaves out a representation of sadistic behavior.

At point 9 the human figure is sitting as fits a depiction of laziness, and the whole drawing suggests vacationing under the shade of a palm tree on a tropical beach. While appropriate to the depiction of laziness in the conventional sense, it does not allude to the psychological laziness of one who does not want to look at himself, nor to the characteristic of resigned over-adaptation of type IX. In the DSM III classification type IX corresponds to the dependent personality—though the name is not very appropriate since dependency is shared by a number of personalities and I do not think that it constitutes the core of the type IX character structure, that is also resigned, self-postponing, gregarious, and conforming.[7]

Rather than illustrating the characters with the above-described caricatures, the essence of which can be translated into words, I have shown in Figure 7—as additional information—a drawing by Margarita Fernandez that conveys some of the constitutional and gestural characteristics of the ennea-types.

Mapping the characterological syndromes onto a circle implies the claim that there are neighborhood relationships between them—and this may be readily observed—yet it would not describe the situation completely, since adjoining characters are also contrasting in some ways. While type I is rigid, type II is intolerant to rigidity, for instance, and while type II is impulsive, type III is controlled. Type III, in turn, is happy and type IV sad, type IV emotional and clinging and type V intellectual and detached; and so on. When we consider the realm of passions alone, however, each of them may be understood as a hybrid of the two adjoining ones.

---

[7]DSM-III-R.

FIGURE 7

Generally speaking, a person who embodies any one of the nine characters can easily see in himself the two adjoining ones in the map. Thus, an ennea-type III individual, whose life is geared to pleasing and succeeding, can coherently understand his behavior in life from the perspective of type II and type IV respectively; likewise, an ennea-type IV person can understand his experience as one of frustrated type III or interpret his actions and feelings from the vantage point of clinging and a sense of impoverishment as in the schizoid individual.

More generally, of course, each person's life or experience may be interpreted from any of the nine perspectives, and so it is that the perspective that sees fear behind everything —so central to psychoanalytical thinking—has been regarded as universally applicable throughout decades of experience. Yet, surely, some interpretations strike home more easily in some characters, while others are comparatively more remote.

While the interpretation that emphasizes the ruling passion and cognitive perspective typical to each one of the points in the enneagram is the most fitting, we may say that the adjoining ones come second—particularly that one among them that happens to be in the corner of the central triangle in the map. Thus, concern with self-image or narcissism is even closer than the schizoid characteristic, as an interpretational background for type IV. Likewise in the case of ennea-type VII we may say that it is essentially a fear-based character belonging in the schizoid group.[8] Yet, it is also strongly related to vindictive character in its impulsive, rebellious, and hedonistic characteristics.

Ennea-type VIII, on the other hand, is essentially lazy-minded (type IX), though its characteristic odd inwardness-avoidance is covered up with the typical intensity with which the individual seeks to make himself feel alive, escaping the sense of deadness attendant upon his or her lack of interiority.

The characters mapped in the six and nine corners of the enneagram stand, each of them, like in point three, between a polarity. While it is a polarity of sadness and happiness at the right side corner (IV-II), it is a polarity of aloofness and expressiveness at the left side (V-VII), and one of amoral or anti-moral and over-moral at the top (VIII-I).

The relations indicated by the arrows connecting the points in the inner triangle of the enneagram, and also those connecting the rest of the points in the sequence 1, 4, 2, 8, 5, 7, 1 may be said to correspond to psycho-dynamic relations, when the enneagram is understood as a map of the individual's mind, as will be explained in connection with the enneagram of passions. When the map stands for a set of characters we may take them to point out the covert presence in each of the one preceding it in the flow, as is not obvious when we consider the enneagram of the passions that constitute the motivational dispositions behind the characters (see below).

In addition to the relationships of neighborhood and those mapped by the lines in the enneagram's "inner-flow," we may see also relations of opposition in the enneagram: just as types I and V stand at opposite ends on a straight line, so do the characters type VIII and type IV, and along the horizontal axis, type VII and type II.

---

[8]In the broader sense of the term—distinct from the use of schizoid for ennea-type V specifically.

I am calling the I-V axis the "anal" axis of the enneagram, inasmuch as both the schizoid character and the obsessive-compulsive character may be said to be "anal" in terms of the descriptions of Freud and Jones, as I am discussing in the first and second chapters of this book respectively.

The IV-VIII axis, on the other hand, I am calling, in memory of Karl Abraham, the oral-aggressive axis; for true as it may be that it is mostly the frustrated and complaining type IV character that has been called oral-aggressive, the characteristics of ennea-type VIII are deserving enough of the appellation.[9]

The II-VII axis I am, analogously, calling oral-receptive, for true as it may be that it is type VII that best corresponds to Abraham's oral-optimist, histrionics are not only "oedipal" but oral-receptive as well.

In contra-distinction to the characters discussed thus far, I think that ennea-type VI and ennea-type III may be called phallic—though all but the counter-phobic type VI can also be regarded as inhibited phallic, while type III is, in its cockiness, a form of a converse, "excited" version of the phallic disposition.

I have said nothing about ennea-type IX in terms of what echoes there may be of the pre-genital syndromes and early genital orientations. This is a character that may well be called pseudo-genital for in most instances it seems less pathological than others, essentially adjusted, contented, loving, and hard-working. It is a character that mimics mental health (and thus what the word "genital" was originally meant to mean). The story of type IX is that of an individual who grew up too fast, who matured under pressure, losing his or her childhood. Along with this over-maturity, however, there lingers in the individual's experience, just under the threshold of ordinary awareness, a regressive disposition deeper and more archaic than that of the pre-genital stages—a deep wish on the person's part to stay in his or her mother's womb and the sense of never having come out. Types I and VIII also belong together in the enneagram as mirror images of each other, at each side of point IX. I have characterized them, when speaking of the characters adjoining type IX, as anti-moral and over-moral, but it remains to

---

[9]It may be noted that Fritz Perls, who placed so much stress on deliberation and on oral-aggression, was himself of the phallic-narcissistic, vindictive type.

say of them that otherwise they share an active disposition. In the same way ennea-type V and ennea-type IV at the bottom of the enneagram offer a sharp contrast (intense and phlegmatic, we may call them) and yet are also similar in their fragility, hyper-sensitivity, and withdrawnness. Ennea-type II and ennea-type VII, which we discussed as two forms of an oral-receptive disposition, can also be regarded as a third pair, along with I-VIII and V-IV, in that they are mainly expressive (rather than active and introversive).

On the whole we may speak of a right side and a left side of the enneagram in symmetry around point 9, and we see that the right side is more social, and the left side anti-social; or, in other terms: there is more seduction on the right and more rebellion on the left. I have no doubt that, at least in the Western world, there is a predominance of men on the left and women on the right, though some characters are more differentiated in terms of the sex ratio. While I and III are more common among women, they are not nearly as feminine in terms of membership as type II and type IV. On the left side the most distinctly masculine character is VIII.

Sharp contrast can be seen between the characters in the pair of VII-IV as well as that of V-II. In the former case this is a contrast between happy character and sad character, and in the latter a contrast between cold aloofness and warm intimacy.

Finally, there is a contrast to be observed between the top and the bottom of the enneagram. While type IX, at the top, represents a maximum of what I have called a defensive extraversion—i.e., an avoidance of inwardness—that goes hand-in-hand with contentedness, the bottom of the enneagram represents a maximum of inwardness and also discontentedness. We may say that those at the bottom of the enneagram never feel good enough or satisfied enough, regard themselves a problem, and are also identified as pathological by the outside world, while type IX is a position where the individual is least likely to make a problem of himself or appear pathological to others. A common feature links type IX to both type IV and type V, however: depression. Between type IX and type IV depression proper is the common element.[10] Ennea-type V may be regarded as depressed too, in terms of apathy and unhappiness, yet the most visible commonality between type IX and type V is that of resignation: a giving up of relationship in V, a resignation without the outer loss of relationship in IX (a resignation in participation), that gives the character its self-postponing and abnegated disposition.

3. THE DYNAMIC CORE OF NEUROSIS

Taking for granted that emotional deterioration is supported by a hidden cognitive disturbance (fixation), I will now examine this realm of passions, i.e., the sphere of the main deficiency-motivated drives that animate the psyche. It is logical to begin with them since, tradition tells us, they constitute the earliest manifestation of our fallenness process in early childhood. While it is possible to recognize the predominance of one or another of these attitudes in children between five and seven, it is not until an age of about seven years (a stage well known to developmental pscyhologists from Gesell to Piaget) that there crystallizes in the psyche a cognitive support for that emotional bias.

The word passion has long carried a connotation of sickness. Thus in his *Anthropologie*, Kant says that: "An emotion is like water that breaks through a dike, passion like a torrent that makes its bed deeper and deeper. An emotion is like a drunkenness that puts you to sleep; passion is like a disease that results from a faulty constitution or a poison."

I think that one of the grounds on which passions have been regarded as unhealthy has been an observation of the pain and destructiveness that they entail—in turn consequences of their craving nature. We may say that they are facets of one basic "deficiency motivation." The use of the Maslowian language, however, need not blind us to the appropriateness of the

---

[10]Ennea-type IX being the most common background of endogenous depression, ennea-type IV more often manifests as neurotic depression.

psychoanalytic notion of orality: passions may be seen as a result of our retaining as adults too much of the attitudes that we all shared as infants at the breast: of a being stuck in a position of excessive sucking and biting in face of the world.

Not only is the word "passion" appropriate for the lower emotions in that they exist in interdependence with pain (pathos), but also because of its connotation of passivity. It may be said that we are subject to them as passive agents rather than free agents—as Aristotle predicated of virtuous behavior and modern psychology of mental health. Spiritual traditions mostly agree in regard to a potential disidentification from the passionate realm made possible by the intuition of transcendence.[11]

Inspection of the enneagram of the passions in figure 8 shows that three of them (at points 9, 6, and 3) occupy a position more central than the others. Also, because of the symbolism of the enneagram, according to which the different points along it correspond to degrees and intervals in the musical scale, psychospiritual laziness, at the top, stands as the most basic of all —being, as it were, the "do" of the passions.

The fact that these three mental states are mapped at the corners of the triangle in the enneagram of passions conveys a statement to the effect that they are cornerstones of the whole emotional edifice, and that the states mapped between them can be explained as interactions in different proportions of these three.

---

[11]While it is a goal of this tradition of "work-on-self" to bring about a shift in the control of behavior from the lower emotional center of the passions to a higher center, a still further stage is envisioned: a shift from the "lower intellectual center" of ordinary cognition—pervaded by wrong views of reality formed in childhood (fixations)—to the higher intellectual center of contemplative-intuitive understanding.

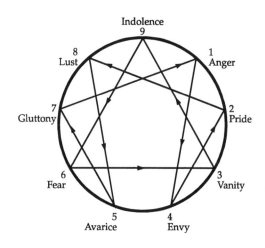

FIGURE 8 - ENNEAGRAM OF PASSIONS

It may be observed that the proposition of a psychological inertia as a cornerstone of neurosis (9) echoes the learning theory of neurosis as conditioning, while the other two points in the inner triangle echo, in turn, the Freudian view of neurosis as a transformation of childhood anxiety (6), and the existential one (3), which envisions inauthentic being and "bad faith" as the basis of pathology.

The interconnections shown between these three points (in the form of sides of the triangle) constitute what we may call psychodynamic connections, so that each may be said to underlie the next in a sequence mapped by arrows between them in a counter-clockwise direction. If we read this psychodynamic sequence starting at the top, we may say that a lack of the sense of being (implicit in the psychological inertia or "robotization" of sloth) deprives the individual of a basis from which to act, and thus leads to fear. Since we must act in the world, however, as much as we may fear it, we feel prompted to solve this contradiction by acting from a false self rather than (courageously) being who we are. We build, then, a mask between ourselves and the world, and with this mask we identify. To the extent that while we do this, we forget who we truly are, however, we perpetuate the ontic obscuration that, in turn, supports fear, and so on, keeping us in the vicious circle.

Just as the sides of the "inner triangle" indicate psychodynamic connections between the mental states mapped at points nine - six - three - nine (in that sequence), it remains to be said that the lines connecting points 1 - 4 - 2 - 8 - 5 - 7 - 1 likewise indicate psychodynamic relations and that each passion may be understood as grounded in the previous one.

Let us consider the case of pride. It is easy to see that just as the individual's expression of pride constitutes an attempt to compensate an insecurity in respect to self-worth, prideful people, as a group, have in common a repression and over-compensation for the sense of inferiority and lack that is dominant in envy. In envy, in turn, we may speak of anger that has turned inward in an act of psychological self-destruction. While in the case of angry and disciplinarian character we may see an attempt to defend oneself from the oral-receptive, spoiled, or self-indulgent attitude of gluttony.

Ennea-type VII, in turn, in its expressive skill, persuasiveness, and charm seems the very opposite of the laconical awkwardness of ennea-type V and yet can also be seen as the way out of it, an over-compensation of deficiency to false-abundance, similar to that through which envy is transformed into pride. Type V or schizoid character, again, is as opposite as can be from the confrontative, impulsive, gross, and aggressive character of the lusty, rebellious type VIII, yet it is possible to understand that moving away from people and the world as an alternative form of expression of vindictiveness—a vindictive decision to not give one's love to others as well as a vindictive willingness to erase the other from one's inner life. When we consider the tough, bullying, and over-masculine ennea-type VIII, finally, we find again that it is the very opposite of the tender, sensitive, and over-feminine histrionic type II. Yet lust may be seen as an exaltation and transformation of pride, in which dependency is not only denied but transformed into a predatory, exploitative, or overwhelming attitude toward others.

As for the relation between passions mapped as adjacent along the circle, it is possible to view each as a hybrid between those on each side. Thus pride may be regarded as a hybrid of vanity (an excessive concern with the self-image) and anger—

where anger is implicit as an assertive self-elevation vis-a-vis others; envy, in turn, may be understood as a hybrid of vanity with the sense of impoverishment of avarice, which combination results in a sense of not being able to live up to the requirements of vanity.

Rather than characterizing the passions—which I expect to be doing in the successive chapters of this book as I describe the characterological disposition in which they predominate—I will only say that we need to return to an original meaning for the traditional words. "Anger," for instance, will be used here as a more inward and basic antagonism in the face of reality than an explosive irritation; "lust" as more than an inclination to sex or even pleasure: a passion for excess or an excessive passionateness to which sexual satisfaction is only one possible source of gratification; likewise "gluttony" will be understood here not in its narrow sense of a passion for food, but the wider sense of a hedonistic bias and an insatiability; and "avarice" may or may not include avarice in its literal meaning and will designate a fearful and greedy holding on, a withdrawn alternative to the outreaching attachment out of lust, gluttony, envy, and other emotions.

Though the enneagram of passions graphically displays a statement to the effect that in each individual, nine basic forms of deficiency motivation exist as a system of interdependent components, the view of character elaborated in this book involves a complementary postulate—to the effect that in each individual one or another of the passions (and the corresponding fixation) is dominant. Yet in contrast to the view of some Christian theologians that there is a hierarchy of seriousness among the capital sins—and also in contrast to the view of contemporary psychology that the characters (in which these different mental states are most distinct) not only arise from different stages in development but are more or less serious or pathological than others—this "Fourth Way" view asserts that the passions are equivalent both in ethico-theological and in prognostic terms. This statement may be translated to imply that while some characters may be more successfully treated than others by present-day psychotherapy and interpretations of mind, the path of transformation is not radically better or worse for the different personalities in terms of the traditional approaches of work-on-self and meditation.

4. COGNITIVE DISTORTION STYLES

Though not identical to what Freud meant by it, the word "fixation" brings to mind that it is through cognitive disturbance that we are most "stuck"—each fixation constituting, as it were, a rationalization for a corresponding passion. While the passions are the early core of psychopathology out of which the realm of the fixations has emerged, according to this view the fixations are the ones that structurally underlie the passions in the present.

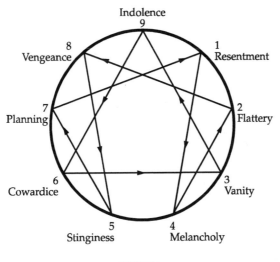

FIGURE 9

Ichazo defined the fixations as specific cognitive defects —facets of a delusional system in the ego—yet the names he gave to them sometimes reflect either the same notion as the dominant passions do or associated characteristics that failed to satisfy his own definition. I reproduce in Figure 9 the enneagram of fixations according to Ichazo as reported by Lilly in Tart's *Transpersonal Psychologies*.[12]

Here it may be seen that the reference to resentment in point 1 is nearly redundant with "anger," and in the case of point 2, flattery refers mostly to "self-flattery," which is inseparable from the self-aggrandizement of pride. In the case of point 3, Ichazo did provide words with significantly different meanings for the emotional and the cognitive aspects of a character, and yet I have questioned his ascribing of restlessness in the pursuit of achievement to the fixation realm and of deceit to the emotional realm of the passions.[13]

In the "Mendelejeffian" nomenclature proposed in Arica, using terms beginning with "ego" and containing the first letters of the fixation, the designation "ego-melan" does contain information different from envy, for it addresses itself to the "masochistic" aspect of the character in question, the seeking of love and care through the intensification of pain and helplessness. Yet in point 5, again, the word he proposes, "stinginess," fails to go beyond the scope of avarice. The same is the case in point 6, for "cowardice" does not give much more information than the passion of fear. Though "cowardice" does entail a meaning of "fear in the face of fear," I have preferred to regard accusation, especially self-accusation, as the central cognitive problem of ennea-type VI, as I elaborate in the corresponding chapter.

When I first heard Ichazo teach Protoanalysis in his lectures at the Instituto de Psicologia Aplicada, the word he used for the fixation in point 7 was *charlataneria*, Spanish for charlatanism. Later, addressing himself to an English-speaking audience, he labeled the personality "ego-plan." Planning evokes

---

[12]"The Arica Training" chapter by John C. Lilly and Joseph E. Hart in *Transpersonal Psychologies*, edited by Charles Tart (El Cerrito, CA: Psychological Processes, 1983).

[13]In chapter seven I propose the appropriateness of regarding vanity as belonging to the same sphere as pride (a passion for being in the eyes of the other, rather than a passion for self-inflation) and for regarding deceit and self-deception the cognitive aspect of ennea-type III (in virtue of which the individual identifies with the false self).

the tendency of type VII to live on projects and fantasies and to substitute imagination for action.

In speaking of "ego-venge," again, Ichazo points to a characterological disposition that may be regarded central in the corresponding type, and provides information complementary to that of its "lusty" aspect: ennea-type VIII is not only Dionysian and passionate, but hard and dominant, the bearer of a prejudiced view of life as struggle where the powerful succeed.

In the case of point 9, once more Ichazo's word "ego-in," in reference to indolence, is redundant with "laziness," the word used for the dominant passion. If laziness is understood as psychospiritual inertia—akin to an automatization of life and a loss of inwardness—the implicit conviction underlying the life strategy of ennea-type IX may be regarded as one that over-emphasizes the value of over-adaptation and abnegation.

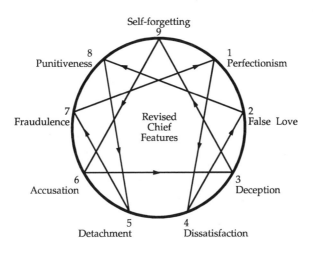

FIGURE 10

A slightly different emphasis comes into play if we choose names for the fixations in view of the identification claimed by Ichazo between these and the "chief feature" of each personality type. The words in Figure 10 fit both definitions of "fixation": they are appropriate to designate the most outstanding feature in the corresponding character structure and they may be understood as inseparable from a cognitive operation.

Thus deception (more appropriate than "deceit" in this context) involves self-deception as well as pretending to others, and a cognitive confusion between what is the case and what is claimed to be true. In the case of punitiveness, too, there is reference to the striking aggression in ennea-type VIII, and also to an implicit view—inseparable from it—that irrationally seeks to make right the past through a retribution of damage or hurt in the present.

In the case of the false generosity and satisfaction of ennea-type II, again this may be regarded as the chief feature and a cognitive mistake on the part of the person akin to deception. The same may be said of the self-frustrating characteristic of ennea-type IV, which involves looking at what is lacking rather than perceiving what is there, and for the detachment of ennea-type V, inseparable from a view to the effect that it is better to "go it alone."

True as it may be that the nine features proposed above are central to the characters and may be considered from a cognitive angle, I feel that more needs to be said about the assumptions, values, and implicit beliefs of each of the characters.

We may say that any of the interpersonal styles into which the passions can crystallize involves a measure of idealization; a hidden view to the effect that such is the way to live. In the psychotherapeutic process sometimes it is possible to recover the memory of a time in life when a decision was made to take revenge, never to love again, to go it alone and never to trust, and so on. When this is possible, we can still make explicit many computations that a person has been taking as truths ever since and which can be questioned; computations of a child in pain and panic that need to be revised, as Ellis proposes in his *Rational-Emotive Therapy*.

Perhaps we may say that each cognitive style is shaped by the characteristic already described in the enneagram of chief features or fixations, yet a number of assumptions exist within the domain of this cognitive style, and each of these assumptions, in turn, is something that we take for granted, and each generates perceptional distortions and false judgments in the course of ordinary life, such as Beck has proposed with his concept of automatic thoughts. Here, for example, is an incomplete list of assumptions typically connected with the ennea-types:

In type I the individual feels that natural impulses are not to be trusted, but controlled, and that duty is more important than pleasure. Pleasure, indeed, tends to be regarded as a negative value in that it interferes with what needs to be done. Also the individual's notions of goodness and correctness are implicitly authoritarian in that they are extrinsic to his experience.

In type II is implicit the idea that everything is permissible in the name of love (as was dramatized by Ibsen in his famous play *The Doll House* where the heroine cannot understand that signing her deceased father's name on a check could bother the bank, since it was done in all good intention). To sustain this perspective, in turn, the person has come to believe that emotion is more important than thinking, and when the two conflict, it is thinking that is to be disregarded. It is congruent to his or her behavior for the individual, also, to feel that it is necessary to be seductive in life, that it is legitimate to manipulate others given the way people are. Not only does he pridefully feel special, he or she feels that, in view of this, she deserves special privileges and attention. An assumption that is not likely to be conscious in the individual's mind, and yet may be of great importance, could be worded as "they could not do it without me." My attention was recently drawn to it through the comments of an acquaintance who, after returning to ordinary life from a spiritual retreat, commented on how shaken he had felt by the insight that the world had continued the same without him. In other words, he was not indispensable and it was not catastrophic that he had removed his extraordinary presence from the world and not been there to assist with his enlightened opinions.

For type III it is common to feel that the world is a theater where everybody is faking. Of course, faking is the only way to success. A corollary of that is that true feelings are not to be expressed. Related to the last is what could be worded as, "I should have no problems"; this may be understood as the result of a combination of the notion that with problems the company would not be so enjoyable plus an over-valuation of pleasing. More basic, I think, is the mistaken assumption that the measure of value is success: what the world values has objective value and is to be valued. Another component of the perspective of type III is a hopelessness that underlies the character's optimism. There is a sense of having to be on top of things, because things would not go well without such watchfulness, and the individual has also a sense that there would be no place for her if she is not useful.

I think that the craziest of assumptions of type IV is the implicit notion that by going over the past and complaining, it may be possible to change it, and there is a need for a deep understanding that there is no point in weeping over spilt milk. There is also the assumption that the greater the need, the greater the entitlement to be loved, and a concomitant idealization of suffering (the more I suffer the more noble I am). The more apparent assumption is the sense of not being as good as others—which is a perspective inseparable from envious comparison. Also, there may be a sense of being owed a compensation by life for the suffering I have experienced.

A typical conviction in ennea-type V might be worded as: "It is better to go it alone." There is a sense that the fewer the commitments, the more that freedom and happiness are possible, and a view of people as moved by self-interest in their seeming love. There is also a sense that it is better to save one's energy or resources for a future possibility that is better than a present involvement, and the fear that through generosity one may end up with nothing. Still another conviction in ennea-type V is that it is better to need little so as not to become dependent on anything or anyone.

Some of the most apparent assumptions in ennea-type VI are bound to a particular subtype as, for instance, the avoidant sense of not being able to cope with his or her own resources, or the counter-phobic's sense of authority as a way out, personal authority as safety. Basic to all, however, is the sense that people are not to be trusted and the sense that one's intuitions and wishes are to be questioned. Authority is over-valued yet is not perceived as necessarily good. It is usually (ambivalently) both good and bad.

In ennea-type VII there is too much a sense of being OK and feeling that others are also OK. The optimistic bias is comparable to the pessimistic bias of type IV. Nothing is seriously forbidden to the self-indulgent, for there is a sense that authority is bad and one who is clever may do what she wishes. There is also a sense of being entitled through talent and a deeper conviction that the best way to succeed is through personal charm.

The world view of ennea-type VIII is that of a struggle where the strong succeed and the weak fail. Also, it is necessary to be fearless to succeed, and to be able to risk. Just as type VIII over-values strength and disparages weakness, it over-values standing on one's own and denigrates neediness. Ennea-type VIII feels that it is OK to cause suffering in the pursuit of his satisfaction for there lingers a vindictiveness concerning a time when it was his turn to suffer for the satisfaction of others. If you want something you go and get it, no matter what stands in the way, he thinks. And he also thinks that "what people call virtue is just hypocrisy." To the lusty VIII person the hindrances of social authority are the enemy and one should act on one's impulses.

The adaptable ennea-type IX not only feels but thinks that the less conflict there is, the better, and it is better not to think too much, to avoid suffering. A corollary of avoiding conflict thus is a tendency to conform and to endorse a conservative ideology. At a deeper and correspondingly less rational level, however, there is a thought in him or her that it is better to deaden oneself than to risk being killed. The taboo on selfishness is not only something that exists at the feeling level but also at the intellectual. The person believes that it is not good to be selfish and that one should defer to the needs of others. A motto of type IX might be: "Do not rock the boat."

However true it may be that every interpersonal style involves a cognitive bias—in the sense of an implicit assumption that such is the best way to be—it is my impression that this does not exhaust an analysis of the cognitive aspect of each personality orientation, and thus, as I have announced in my Foreword, I am examining throughout this book, in addition to fixations and defense mechanisms, what I call "illusions": metaphysical mistakes, implicit misconceptions regarding being.

The view that I articulate throughout the sections entitled "Existential Psychodynamics" I have called the "Nasruddin Theory of Neurosis" in reference to the famous Nasruddin joke about the lost key.

We are told that the Mullah was on all fours looking for something in one of the alleys at the market place. A friend joined him in the search for (as the Mullah explained to him) the key to his own house. Only after a long time had elapsed unsuccessfully did the friend think of asking Nasruddin, "Are you sure that you lost it here?" To which he replied, "No, I'm sure I lost it at home." "Then why are you looking for it here?" inquired his friend. "There is much more light here!" explained the Mullah.

The central idea underlying this book, then, is that we are looking for the "key" in the wrong place. What is this "key" to our liberation and to our ultimate fulfillment? Throughout these pages I call it "Being," though it could be justly said that to give it even that name is too limited and limiting. We may say that we are, but we don't have the experience of being, we don't know that we are. On the contrary, the closer the scrutiny to which we subject our experience, the more we discover at its core a sense of lack, an emptiness and insubstantiality, a lack of selfness or being. It is from the lack of perceived sense of being—it is my contention—that derives "deficiency motivation," the basic oral drive that sustains the whole libido tree.

For neurotic libido is not Eros, as Freud proposed. Eros is abundance, and deficiency is the search for abundance, ordinary motivation. Subsumed under the appellation of libido is "passional," and "passions" which span the spectrum of neurotic motivation are only approximately speaking "instinct derivatives." More exactly, they are the expression of a striving to recover a sense of being that was lost through organismic interference.[14]

It may be said that there is an original psychodynamics at the time of the genesis of the character in childhood and a sustaining psychodynamics in the adult, and I am proposing that these two are not identical. While the original psychodynamics constitutes a response to the crucial issue of being loved or not— or more specifically a response to interpersonal frustration, we may say that it is not principally a love frustration that sustains deficiency motivation in the adult, but an experience of lack that is based upon a self-perpetuated ontic vacuum and the corresponding existential self-interference.

A statement for the systematic analysis of all character structures in light of ontic obscuration and the "search for Being in the wrong place" has been Guntrip's view,[15] where he writes: "Psychoanalytic theory had for a long time the appearance of the exploration of a circle which had no obvious center until ego psychology got on the way. Exploration had to begin with peripheral phenomena—behavior, moods, symptoms, conflicts, 'mental mechanisms,' erotic drives, aggression, fears, guilt, psychotic and psychoneurotic states, instincts and impulses, erotogenic zones, maturational stages and so on. All this is naturally important and must find its place in the total theory, but actually it is all secondary to some absolutely fundamental factor which is the 'core' of the 'person as such.' "

---

[14]Coherently with Kohut's notion of a perturbation of the self underlying narcissistic disorders but more generally, the view spelled out here is one that understands such "perturbation of the self" as the core of every form of psycho-pathology, and the inevitable result of not only fragmentation but the more general perturbation of organismic self-regulation that underlies it.

[15]op. cit.

It is the felt absence of such a core that I am positing as the core of all psychopathology.[16] Such a fundamental factor at the root of all passions (deficiency motivation) is a thirst for being that exists side by side with a dim apprehension of being-loss.

I will only add to this theory at this point the contention that wherever "being" may seem to be, it is not; and that being can only be found in the most unlikely manner: through the acceptance of non-being and a journey through emptiness.

---

[16]Guntrip uses the term *ego* "to denote a state or developmental condition of the psychic whole, the entire self. 'Ego' expresses the psyche's self-realization and every psychic process has 'ego-quality', be it that of a weak ego or a strong one" (p.194, op.cit.). Of ego-weakness, Guntrip writes: "There is a greater or lesser degree of immaturity in the personality structure of all human beings and this immaturity is experienced as a definite weakness and inadequacy of the ego..." Also "The feeling of weakness arises out of a lack of a reliable feeling of one's own reality and identity as an ego." (p.176, op.cit). Of course, I have chosen to speak of "being" or "sense of being" rather than "ego" or "self-identity" for the core of the healthy person, and of "ontic deficiency" or "ontic obscuration" for the core of neurosis—instead of adopting Laing's "ontic insecurity" or Guntrip's "ego weakness," both of which evoke a specific (ennea-type VI) nuance of a more universal experience.

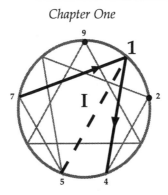

Chapter One

ANGER AND PERFECTIONISM

1. Core Theory, Nomenclature, and Place in the Enneagram

"We may consider wrath in three ways," says Saint Thomas in *Questiones Disputatae*: "Firstly, a wrath which resides in the heart (*Ira Cordis*); also, inasmuch as it flows into words (*Ira Locutionis*), and thirdly, in that it becomes actions (*Ira Actiones*)." The survey scarcely brings to mind the characteristics of the perfectionistic type as we will be portraying it here. Yes, there is anger in the heart, mostly in the form of resentment, yet not so prominently as anger may be experienced by the lusty, the envious, or the cowardly. As for verbal behavior, it is most characteristic of the anger type to be *controlled* in the expression of anger, in any of its explicit forms: we are in the presence of a well-behaved, civilized type, not a spontaneous one. In regard to action, ennea-type I individuals do express anger, yet mostly unconsciously, not only to themselves but to others, for they do so in a way that is typically rationalized; in fact, much of this personality may be understood as a reaction formation against anger: a denial of destructiveness through a deliberate, well-intentioned attitude.

Oscar Ichazo's definition of anger as a "standing against reality" has the merit of addressing a more basic issue than the feeling or expression of emotion. Still, it may be useful to point out at the outset that the label "anger type" is scarcely evocative of the typical psychological characteristics of the personality style in question—which is critical and demanding rather than consciously hateful or rude. Ichazo called the ennea-type "ego-resent," which seems a psychologically more exact portrayal of the emotional disposition involved: one of protest and assertive claims rather than mere irritability. In my own teaching experience, I started out calling the character's fixation "intentional goodness"; later I shifted to labeling it "perfectionism." This seems appropriate to designate a rejection of what is in terms of what is felt and believed should be.

Christian writers who shared an awareness of anger as a capital sin, that is to say, as one of the basic psychological obstacles to true virtue, mostly seem to have failed to realize that it is precisely under the guise of virtue that unconscious anger finds its most characteristic form of expression. An exception is St. John of the Cross, who in his *Dark Night of the Soul* writes with characterological exactitude as he describes the sin of wrath in spiritual beginners:

"There are other of these spiritual persons, again, who fall into another kind of spiritual wrath: this happens when they become irritated at the sins of others, and keep watch on those others with a sort of uneasy zeal. At times the impulse comes to them to reprove them angrily, and occasionally they go so far as to indulge it and set themselves up as masters of virtue. All this is contrary to spiritual meekness." And he adds: "There are others who are vexed with themselves when they observe their own imperfection, and display an impatience that is not humility; so impatient are they about this that they would fain be saints in a day. Many of these persons purport to accomplish a great deal and make grand resolutions; yet, as they are not humble and have no misgivings about themselves, the more resolutions they make, the greater is the fall and the greater their annoyance, since they have not the patience to wait for that which God will give them when it pleases Him."

On the whole, this is a well-intentioned and overly virtuous character arisen as a defense against anger and destructiveness. It would be a mistake, however, to conceive of it as a violent character—for it is on the contrary, an over-controlled and over-civilized interpersonal style. Striking in this style is also an oppositional quality, both in regard to others and to experience in general. While every form of character may be regarded as an interference with instinct, the anti-instinctive orientation of this "puritanical" style is the most striking. A good name for the character (and one applicable beyond the explicitly sick region of the mental health spectrum) is perfectionism—for in spite of the fact that people in some other characterological styles may appropriately refer to themselves as "perfectionistic," this is definitely the orientation in which perfectionism is most prominent. This involves an obsession with improving things that result in making their lives and those of others worse and a narrow-minded concept of perfection in terms of a matching of experience or events with a pre-established code of values, standards, ideas, tastes, rules, and so on.

Perfectionism not only illustrates the fact that the better is the enemy of the best (and the search for the best is the enemy of the better) but may be said to involve a cognitive bias, an imbalance between the allegiances to duty and to pleasure; to gravity and to levity; to work and to play, mature deliberateness and child-like spontaneity.

As a sequel to the word perfectionist—more colloquially —I have caricatured the character as one of "angry virtue," a label that has the advantage of including both the emotional (anger) and the cognitive (perfectionistic) aspects.

Though I personally appreciate Erikson's re-statement of anality as an issue of autonomy that arises at the time of learning sphincter control and walking, I think Abraham and Freud deserve the homage of having for the first time drawn attention to the connection between the prohibition of soiling oneself and obsessive cleanliness.[1]

The position of the anger type in the enneagram is neither at the schizoid nor at the hysteroid corners, but in the group of the upper three characters pervaded by "psychological laziness." It is my experience that, contrary to the fact that many obsessives declare themselves extroverts, this very statement reveals their lack of psychological mindedness, for they are, rather, sensory-motor extroverts with an introverted self-ideal that is part of their refinement and intellectual values. The position of ennea-type I between ennea-types IX and II in the enneagram invites a consideration of how perfectionistic character is not only "anti-intraceptive"[2] but also proud. Indeed the word pride is sometimes used specifically to describe the aristocratic and haughty attitude of the perfectionist rather than the attitude of the type here designated as "proud," whose priding is not so much to be respectable and admirable but to be needed, loved and exalted as very special.

From a survey of many thousands of entries in the literature since 1960, I find that the obsessive-compulsive personality style is the most frequently written about. I imagine that this may be due to its being the most clear cut and recognizable, and yet I also think that a confusion has slipped into the use of the term "anankastic," by which the obsessive-compulsive is frequently designated in Europe. Also, in regard to the "anal personality" syndrome of psychoanalysis I think that sometimes the term has been applied to the obsessive-compulsive proper and at other times to the more controlled and obsessive-like schizoid individuals.[3] In my experience it is the schizoid personality which is more frequently found as the background of ego-dystonic obsessions and compulsions, and

---

[1] Abraham, Karl, Leonard and Virginia Woolf, editors, *Selected Papers on Psychoanalysis* (London: Hogarth Press, 1965).

[2] Henry Murray's word for a motive directed toward the avoidance of inwardness.

[3] The fact that ennea-types I and V have been confused is, I think, an expression of similarity beyond the constructing characteristics. We may also speak of a similarity in the case of those characters mapped at the end of the other two antipodes in the enneagram: IV-VIII and VII-II.

not the obsessive, in which cleanliness and order are ego-syntonic.[4]

2. Antecedents in Scientific Literature on Character

I learned from Kurt Schneider's *Psychopathic Personalities*[5] that it was J. Donath who introduced the concept of anankastic personalities in 1897. Writing in the early twenties Schneider reports that literature on "obsessive state is almost impossible to encompass," yet he doesn't draw a clear distinction between what until recently was called an obsessive neurosis[6] and obsessive personality. Though there is no doubt that he was acquainted with our "perfectionist" and the picture of this character was in his mind as he wrote part of his chapter on the "insecure"[7] the very fact that he did regard the anankastic along with the "sensitive" as varieties of the insecure disposition suggests to me that he fell for the same confusion that became later apparent in the concept of anal personality—a confusion between our perfectionist and the schizoid, which have some common characteristics and yet contrast sharply in other respects.

Reading Von Gebsattel on anankastic personality[8] I have the distinct impression that it is a schizoid form of obsessiveness

---

[4]Psychiatric jargon for psychological characteristics that are welcome or not to the individual's consciousness. In Kurt Schneider we find the "anankastics" described as a form of a broader category of the "insecure" that mostly corresponds to what in the U.S. is being called schizoid. See also my comments on Karl Abraham's and Wilhelm Reich's descriptions of anal and obsessive character below.

[5]Schneider, Kurt, *Las Personalidades Psicopaticas* (Madrid: Ediciones Morata, 1961).

[6]Today in DSM III "obsessive disease."

[7]German term.

[8]Von Gebsattel, V.E., "The World of the Compulsive" in *Existence: A New Dimension in Psychiatry and Psychology*, edited by Rollo May (New York: Basic Books, 1959).

that he has in mind, which inclines me to think that up to this day the confusion survives. Since the ICD-IX,[9] which still has not been superseded by DSM-III in some countries, includes Kurt Schneider's system of classification in regard to personality, it is pertinent to point out that there is no place in this classification for our perfectionist except possibly as a variety of the "insecure." Although theoretically it is admissible that an excessive formality may be a reaction to a deeper insecurity, the terminology leads to a further confusion since it obscures the clear contrast between the assertiveness of our ennea-type I and the withdrawn timidity of ennea-type V at its antipode.

"On the expressive psychology of the anankastic it must be said that, externally they often strike us by their exaggerated meticulousness, pedantry, correctness, and scrupulousness."

In the realm of psychological literature it may be said that the type of person we are discussing was the first of all personality patterns to be observed, when Freud wrote his famous essay on anal character. Karl Abraham picked up and elaborated the idea in the anal character[10] which he begins with a concise summary of Freud's observations:

"Freud has said that certain neurotics present three particularly pronounced character traits, namely, a love for orderliness which often develops into pedantry, a parsimony which easily turns to miserliness, and an obstinacy which may become an angry defiance." Among his original observations is that persons with a pronounced anal character are usually convinced that they can do everything better than other people: "they must do everything themselves."

The next important contribution to the understanding of the ennea-type I syndrome was that of Reich, who writes of it:[11]

"Even if the neurotic compulsive sense of order is not present, a pedantic sense of order is typical of the compulsive character." "In both big and small things, he lives his life according to a preconceived, irrevocable pattern..." In addition,

---

[9]*International Classification of Diseases,* ninth edition (Salt Lake City, UT: Med-Index Publications, 1991).

[10]Abraham, Karl, M.D., op. cit.

[11]Reich, Wilhelm, *Character Analysis* (New York : Simon & Schuster, 1961).

Reich points out the presence of circumstantial, ruminative thinking, indecision, doubt and distrust hidden by an appearance of strong reserve and self-possession. He agrees with Freud's observation of parsimony, especially the form of frugality and also shares the interpretation of the character as deriving from anal eroticism. More importantly, however, he underscores what might be viewed as the other side of self-possession: emotional blockage. "He is just as ill-disposed towards affects as he is acutely inaccessible to them. He is usually even-tempered, lukewarm in his displays of both love and hate. In some cases this can develop into a complete affect-block."

It is not surprising that Freud and others have been more aware of thriftiness than of anger in "anal character," for parsimony and austerity are behavioral traits, while anger is mostly an unconscious motive in the personality under discussion. Yet, true as it may be that the tendency to economize and to amass wealth can be present in ennea-type I, I believe that Freud, Abraham and Reich were inadvertently considering together two different syndromes when they discussed anal character: two syndromes (our anger and avarice ennea-types) mapped at the antipodes of the enneagram, and which yet share the quality of being superego driven, rigid and controlled.[12]

While "anal character" is a rather ambiguous concept, we also find in Wilhelm Reich the description of a personality that corresponds more purely to our perfectionist: his case of "aristocratic character," discussed in *Character Analysis* in support of some general ideas on the function of character. He describes his patient as having "a reserved countenance," and being serious and somewhat arrogant; "his measured, noble stride caught one's attention...it was evident he avoided—or concealed—any hate or excitement...his speech was well phrased and balanced, soft and

---

[12]I find support for this in that some of the traits attributed by Abraham and others to "anal character," such as the conviction that they can do everything better than other people, correspond to ennea-type I, while others—such as procrastination—are typical of ennea-type V. Also relevant is the fact that the expression "compulsive personality," originally equivalent in reference to "anal character," has come to designate ennea-type I in American usage but most commonly ennea-type V in Europe. (See, for instance Von Gebsattel's analysis of an anankastic, included in Rollo May's *Existence*.)

eloquent..." "As he lay on the couch, there was little if any change in his composure and refinement"..."Perhaps it was merely an insignificant ...that one day 'aristocratic' occurred to me for his behaviour," Reich comments, "I told him he was playing the role of an English lord" he proceeds, and goes on to discuss in this patient, who has never masturbated during puberty, being aristocratic served as a defense against sexual excitation: "A noble man doesn't do such things."

The syndrome we have been discussing is today identified in the American DSM III[13] as compulsive personality disorder. The following cues are offered by this manual for the diagnosis of this personality:

    1.   Restrained affectivity (e.g., appears unrelaxed, tense, joyless and grim; emotional expression is kept under tight control).

    2.   Conscientious self-image (e.g., sees self as industrious, dependable and efficient; values self-discipline, prudence and loyalty).

    3.   Interpersonal respectfulness (e.g., exhibits unusual adherence to social conventions and properties; prefers polite, formal and correct personal relationships).

    4.   Cognitive constriction (e.g., constructs world in terms of rules, regulations, hierarchies; is unimaginative, indecisive and upset by unfamiliar or novel ideas or customs).

    5.   Behavioral rigidity (e.g., keeps a well-structured, highly regulated and repetitive life pattern; reports preference for organized, methodical and meticulous work).

Here follows the picture of the behavioral features of compulsive personality in the words of Theodore Millon:[14]

"The grim and cheerless demeanor of compulsives is often quite striking. This is not to say that they are invariably

---

[13]DSM III will be the abbreviation used in this book for *Diagnostic and Statistical Manual of Mental Disorders*, Third Edition, Revised (Washington, D.C.: American Psychiatric Association, 1987).

[14]Millon, Theodore, *Disorders of Personality: DSM-III: Axis II* (New York: John Wiley & Sons, 1981).

glum or downcast but rather to convey their characteristic air of austerity and serious-mindedness. Posture and movement reflect their underlying tightness, a tense control of emotions that are kept well in check....The social behavior of compulsives may be characterized as polite and formal. They relate to others in terms of rank or status; that is, they tend to be authoritarian rather than equalitarian in their outlook."

This is reflected in their contrasting behavior with 'superiors' as opposed to 'inferiors.' Compulsive personalities are deferential, ingratiating, and even obsequious with their superiors, going out of their way to impress them with their efficiency and serious-mindedness. Many seek the reassurance and approval of their position. These behaviors contrast markedly with their attitudes toward subordinates. Here the compulsive is quite autocratic and condemnatory, often appearing pompous and self-righteous. This haughty and deprecatory manner is usually cloaked behind regulations and legalities. Not untypically, compulsives will justify their aggressive intentions by recourse to rules or authorities higher than themselves."

In the final elaboration that Karen Horney left us of her clinical experience, *Neurosis and Human Growth*, she groups together three character types under a general label of "the expansive solutions." These are approaches to life through mastery, in which the individual embraces early in life as a solution to conflicts a strategy of "moving against" others (in contrast to the orientations of those who move seductively "toward" and fearfully "away from" others). One of these three forms of the "solution of mastery" (or "moving against") she calls "perfectionistic" and though she describes it without reference to the earlier "anal" and "compulsive" types in the literature, she contributes substantially to the psychodynamic understanding of the syndrome in question. I quote her: [15]

"This type feels superior because of his high standards, moral and intellectual, and on this basis looks down onto others. His arrogant contempt for others, though is hidden from himself as well—behind polished friendliness, because his very

---

[15]*Neurosis and Human Growth* (New York: W.W. Norton & Co., 1990).

standards prohibit such 'irregular feelings.' His way of beclouding the issue of unfulfilled shoulds are twofold. In contrast to the narcissistic type, he does make strenuous efforts to measure up to his shoulds by fulfilling duties and obligations, by polite and orderly manners, by not telling obvious lies, etc. When speaking of perfectionist people, we often think merely of those who keep meticulous order, are overly punctilious and punctual, have to find just the right word, or must wear just the right necktie or hat. But these are only superficial aspects of their need to attain the highest degree of excellence. What really matters is not those petty details but the flawless excellence of the whole conduct in life. But since all he can achieve is behavioristic perfection, another device is necessary. This is to equate in his mind standards and actualities—knowing about moral values and being a good person....The self-deception involved is all the more hidden from him since, in reference to others, he may insist upon their actually living up to his standards of perfection and despise them for failing to do so. His own self-condemnment is thus externalized.

"As confirmation of his opinion of himself, he needs respect from others rather than glowing admiration (which he bends to scorn). Accordingly his claims are based less on a 'naive' belief in his greatness than on a 'deal' he had secretly made with life. Because he is fair, just, dutiful, he is entitled to fair treatment by others and by life in general. This conviction of an infallible justice operating in life gives him a feeling of mastery. His own perfection therefore is not only a means to superiority but also one to control life. The idea of undeserved fortune, whether good or bad, is alien to him. His own success, prosperity or good health is therefore, less something to be enjoyed than a proof of his virtue."

We may discern the personality under consideration in Jung's extraverted thinking type:[16]

"This type will, by definition, be a man whose constant endeavor—in so far, of course, as he is a pure type—is to make all his activities dependent on intellectual conclusions, which in the last resort are always oriented by objective data, whether these be external facts or generally accepted ideas. This type of

---

[16]*Psychological Types* (New Jersey: Princeton University/Bollingen Books, 1976).

man elevates objective reality, or an objectively oriented intellectual formula, into the ruling principle not only for himself but for his whole environment. By this formula good and evil are measured, and beauty and ugliness determined. Everything that agrees with this formula is right, everything that contradicts it is wrong, and anything that passes by it indifferently is merely incidental. Because this formula seems to embody the entire meaning of life, it is made into a universal law which must be put into effect everywhere all the time, both individual and collectively. Just as the extraverted thinking type subordinates himself to his formula, so, for their own good, everybody round him must obey it too, for whoever refuses to obey it is wrong— he is resisting the universal law, and is therefore unreasonable, immoral, and without a conscience. His moral code forbids him to tolerate exceptions; his ideal must under all circumstances be realized, for in his eyes it is the purest conceivable formulation of objective reality, and therefore must also be a universally valid truth, quite indispensable for the salvation of mankind. This is not from any great love for his neighbor, but from the higher standpoint of justice and truth. Anything in his own nature that appears to invalidate this formula is a mere imperfection, an accidental failure, something to be eliminated on the next occasion, or, in the event of further failure, clearly pathological. If tolerance for the sick, the suffering, or the abnormal should chance to be an ingredient of the formula, special provisions will be made for human societies, hospitals, prisons, missions, and so on, or at least extensive plans will be drawn up.

Generally the motive of justice and truth is not sufficient to ensure the actual execution of such projects; for this, real Christian charity is needed, and this has more to do with feelings than with any intellectual formula. 'Oughts' and 'musts' bulk large in this program. If the formula is broad enough, this type may play a very useful role in social life as a reformer or public prosecutor or purifier of conscience, or as the propagator of important innovations. But the more rigid the formula, the more he develops into a martinet, a quibbler, and a prig, who would like to force himself and others into one world. Here we have the two extremes between which the majority of these types move."

In the domain of testing applications of Jungian typology the best fit is to be found in the "ESTJ" (extraverted, with predominance of sensation over intuition, thinking over feeling, judgment over perception). David Keirsey and Marilyn Bates say of these scorers that the best adjective to describe them would be "responsible."[17]

In the domain of homeopathic medicine the personality picture similar to ennea-type I has been described in connection with individuals who are specifically helped by the use of *Arsenicum*. Thus, in *Portraits of Homoeopathic Medicines* Catherine R. Coulter writes of *Arsenicum* personality as "the *perfectionist* par excellence."[18] She describes in detail the *Arsenicum* child's conscientious and thorough nature.

Corollaries of perfection are to be found in the adult proper compulsively reworking things, never satisfied with results, as in the case of the professor who endlessly rewrites his lectures, and a concomitant anxiety of feeling unprepared, which makes the *Arsenicum* disposition the very antithesis of relaxation. Another corollary is ordinationness, and still another self-criticism. She also describes a strong competitiveness that goes hand-in-hand with the ambition to be the best.

Another word Coulter introduces in the description of *Arsenicum* is fastidiousness—applied to compulsive orderliness, thus: "...In all spheres he is ultra-'picky,' and, in his intolerance of everything slipshod, irritated at any clumsiness—dropping a dish, overturning a glass, spilling food—his own as well as another's." Still another aspect of perfection mentioned in the case of *Arsenicum* is meticulousness—" 'conscientious about trifles': Kent." Says Coulter: "his work manifests that particular 'finishing touch'—that final polish—that reveals a meticulous attention to detail."

Very characteristic of ennea-type I is the anxiety described in connection with *Arsenicum Album*—an anxiety that has to do with the anticipation of troubles and with fussy meticulousness that contributes in making the patient a driven and driving person. Frequent object of concern to *Arsenicum*,

---

[17] Keirsey, David & Marilyn Bates, *Please Understand Me* (Delmar, CA: Prometheus/ Nemesis Book Company, 1984).

[18] Quoted by permission of the author, Catherine R. Coulter, all excerpts in this section are from pp. 235-300, *Portraits of Homoeopathic Medicines*, Vol. 1 (Berkeley, CA: North Atlantic Books, 1986).

according to Coulter, is money. "Whether or not he has any, he thinks and talks about it a great deal, frequently lamenting his poverty or the high cost of living. His liking for money is stronger than that of most constitutional types, and he can even be 'avaricious' (Hering)...."

Also congruent with ennea-type I is the description of *Arsenicum* as a domineering type: "He takes the lead in personal relations, determining their scope and tone, and leaving others no choice but to comply...The domineering *Arsenicum* cannot abide others being in charge and insists on making all decisions himself...."

Further remarks in Coulter's description of the *Arsenicum* type are the over-intellectualizing tendency, a concern with "the meaning of every symptom," and a medical "one-upmanship" that "makes him distrustful even of those from whom he is seeking help." She reports that, while "Many constitutional types dislike any dietary restrictions...*Arsenicum* loves being placed on a diet and will religiously follow the most Spartan regime. He not only delights in nutritional fads, but the necessity of a special diet certifies the seriousness of his condition...."

The correspondence of the *Arsenicum* personality of homeopathy to our ennea-type I is made even more explicit by Coulter's mention of a literary example—Dickens' Miss Betsey in *David Copperfield* "whose snippy, persnickety, and at times fearsome exterior conceals a highly developed moral delicacy and integrity."

I see the reflection of ennea-type I not only in *Arsenicum*, but also in *Carcinosin* (a remedy "made from the scirrhous cancer of the breast"), inasmuch, as Coulter points out, it is related to a "patient where there is a strong history of excessive parental control and pressure...or an excessive sense of duty (Foubister)."[19] Since *Carcinosin* also fits the treatment of an over-responsible, "preoccupied" (Templeton) individual, it particularly seems to relate to a sub-type within ennea-type I characterized precisely by an over-responsible perfectionistic *anxiety*.

---

[19]Catherine Coulter, op.cit., Vol. 2, pp. 242-248

3. Trait Structure

In what follows, I have undertaken to show something of the structure of the perfectionistic character in terms of the underlying traits that may be discerned through a conceptual analysis of some hundred and seventy descriptors.

Anger

More than a trait among others, "anger" may be regarded a generalized emotional background and original root of this character structure. The more specific manifestation of the emotional experience of anger is resentment, and this is most commonly felt in connection with a sense of injustice in face of the responsibilities and efforts the individual undertakes in larger measure than others. It is inseparable from the criticism of others (or significant others) for displaying less zeal, and sometimes it involves the adoption of a martyr role. The most visible expression of anger occurs when it is perceived as justified, and can in such cases take the form of vehement "righteous indignation."

In addition, anger is present in the form of irritation, reproach and hatefulness that remain largely unexpressed, since perceived destructiveness conflicts with the virtuous self-image characteristic of the type. Beyond the perception of anger at an emotional level, however, we may say that the passion of anger permeates the whole of ennea-type I character and is the dynamic root of drives or attitudes such as we discuss in connection with the remaining clusters: criticality, demandingness, dominance and assertiveness, perfectionism, over-control, self-criticism and discipline.

Criticality

If conscious and manifest anger is not always one of the most striking characteristics of this personality, the more common traits in the type may be understood as derivatives of anger, expressions of unconscious anger or anger equivalents.

One of these is criticality, which is not only manifest in explicit fault finding, but sometimes creates a subtle atmosphere that causes others to feel awkward or guilty. Criticality may be described as intellectual anger more or less unconscious of its motive. I say this because, even though it is possible that criticism occurs in the context of felt anger, the most salient quality of this criticality is a sense of constructive intent, a desire to make others or oneself better. Through intellectual criticism, thus, anger is not only expressed but justified and rationalized and, through this, denied.

Moral reproaches are another form of perfectionistic disapproval and not just expressions of anger, but a form of manipulation in the service of unacknowledged demandingness —whereby "I want" is transformed into "You should." Accusation thus entails the hope of affecting somebody's behaviors in the direction of one's wishes.

A specific form of criticality in ennea-type I is that bound to ethnocentrism and other forms of prejudice, in which case there is vilification, invalidation and the wish to "reform" inquisitorially those who constitute an outgroup to one's race, nation, class, church, "Crusader," and so on. [Displaying the mechanism of "authoritarian aggression" (described by Adorno, Sanford, et al.,) anger towards the ingroup's authority is repressed, inhibited, and displaced onto those below in the hierarchical ladder and especially those in the outgroup—who then become scapegoats.]

Demandingness

Demandingness also can be understood as an expression of anger: a vindictive over-assertiveness in regard to one's wishes in response to early frustration. Along with demandingness proper we may group together characteristics such as those which make these individuals the most disciplinarian both in the sense of inhibiting spontaneity and the pursuit of pleasure in others as well as exacting hard work and excellent performance. They tend to sermonize, preach and teach without regard for the appropriateness of such a role, even though this compulsive characteristic of theirs may find its niche in activities such as those of school teacher and preacher.

Together with this corrective orientation is that of being controlling, and this not only in relation to people but to environments or personal appearance: an obsessive is likely to prefer a highly "manicured" garden, for instance, where plants are in clear order and trees pruned into artificial shape, over one that conveys a "Taoistic" organic complexity.

Dominance

Though already implicit in intellectual criticism, which would be without force if not in a context of moral or intellectual authority, and implicit also in the controlling-demanding-disciplinarian characteristic (for how would that be effective without authority), it seems appropriate to regard dominance as a relatively independent trait, comprising such descriptors as an autocratic style, a self-confident and dignified assertiveness, an aristocratic self-concept and a superior, haughty, disdainful and perhaps condescending and patronizing demeanor. Dominance, too, may be regarded as an implicit expression or a transformation of anger, yet this orientation towards a position of power entails subordinate strategies as the above and also a sense of entitlement on the basis of high standards, diligence, cultural and family background, intelligence, and so on.

Perfectionism

Most characteristically, however, the pursuit of mastery in the anger type implies the endorsement of the moral system or human hierarchy in which authority is vested. It may be said that the perfectionist is more obedient to the abstract authority of norms or office than the concrete authority of persons. Also, as Millon remarks, "people with obsessive personality not only do adhere to societal rules and customs, but vigorously espouse and defend them." Such vehement interest in principles, morals and ideals is not only an expression of submission to the demands of a strong superego, but, interpersonally, an instrument of manipulation and dominance, for these enthusiastically endorsed norms are imposed on others and, as was commented above, serve as a cover for personal wishes and demands. Yet ennea-type I individuals are not only oriented to "Law and Order," and themselves obedient to norms, they also subordinate themselves to people in the position of unquestionable authority.

The emphatic endorsement of norms and sanctioned authority usually implies a conservative orientation or, to adopt David Riesman's language, the tendency to be "tradition directed," (a trait shared with ennea-type IX). It is hard to separate, except conceptually, two aspects of perfectionism: the cathexis of ideal standards, i.e., the vehement endorsement of norms and the "perfectionistic intention," i.e., a striving to be better. Both kinds of "good intention" support a sense of personal goodness, kindness, and disinterestedness, and distract the individual from the preconscious perception of self as angry, evil, and selfish. (Among the descriptors grouped in the cluster are included "good boy/girl," "goody-goody," "honest," "fair," "formal," "moral," and so on.)

Not only is compulsive virtue a derivative of anger through the operation of reaction formation, it is also the expression of anger turned inwards, for it amounts to becoming one's own harsh critic, policeman, and disciplinarian. Also, we may conceive a group of traits, ranging from orderliness and cleanliness to a puritanical disposition, as a means to evoke affection through merit and a response to an early emotional frustration.

Particularly important for the therapeutic process, is the understanding of how perfectionism serves anger by preventing its acknowledgment. More specifically, it serves (by supporting felt entitlement), the unconscious expression of anger as dominance, criticality, and demandingness. The image of the crusader may serve as a paradigm for this situation: one who is entitled to break skulls in virtue of the excellence of his cause and his noble aspirations. When the strategy maneuver is visible enough, we find it appropriate to speak not only of "compulsive" virtue but of "hypocritical" virtue—for even though (as Horney points out) a certain level of honesty is characteristic of the perfectionist, his obsessive preoccupation with right and wrong, or good and bad, entails an unconscious dishonesty in its intent.

From the preceding analysis it is clear that the psychodynamic relation between anger and perfectionism is reciprocal: just as we may surmise that the strategy of striving to do better has been preceded by anger in the course of early development and continues to be fueled by unconscious anger, it is easy to understand how anger itself continually arises from self-frustration and from interpersonal consequences of the irritating activity and rigidity of the perfectionist.

While I have grouped together under the single label of "perfectionism" those traits ranging from "love of order," "law abidingness," and "an orientation to rules," to "do-goodism" and "dutiful nurturance," such as make people adopt fathering or mothering roles toward others, I have grouped the three traits of "over-control," "self-criticism," and "discipline" separately below. These traits stand in the same relationship to perfectionism as "criticality," "demandingness," and "dominance" stand in relation to perfectionistic anger directed toward others. Just as criticality, demandingness, and dominance are hard to separate, over-control, self-criticism, and discipline—three attitudes toward oneself that constitute, we may say, the underside of perfectionism—are closely related as facets of a single underlying disposition. Perfectionism may be singled out, along with anger, as a pervasive dynamic factor in the character and as its root strategy.

Over-Control

What dominance—a transformation of anger—is to others, self-control is to perfectionism. Excessive control over one's behaviors goes hand-in-hand with a characteristic rigidity, a sense of awkwardness, a lack of spontaneity with the consequent difficulty to function in non-structured situations and whenever improvisation is required. To others the over-control may result in boringness. Excessive control over one's self extends, beyond outer behaviors to psychological functioning in general, so that thinking becomes excessively rule bound, i.e. logical and methodical, with loss of creativity and leaps of intuition. Control over feeling, on the other hand, leads not only to the blocking of emotional expression but even to alienation from emotional experience.

Self-Criticism

What the criticism of others is to anger, self-criticism is to perfectionism. Though self-disparagement may not be apparent to the outside observer and tends to be hidden behind a virtuous and self-dignified image, the inability to accept oneself and the process of self-vilification not only are the source of chronic emotional frustration (and unconscious anger) but an ever present psychodynamic background for the perfectionistic need to try harder in the pursuit of worthiness.

Discipline

What angry demandingness is to anger, an implicitly hateful and exploitative demanding from oneself is to perfectionism. Beyond do-goodism proper, i.e., an orientation toward correction and moral ideas, self-demanding involves a willingness to strive at the expense of pleasure, which makes ennea-type I individuals hard-working and disciplined as well as over-serious. And just as a vindictive element may be discerned in interpersonal demands, a masochistic element may be discerned in the postponement of pleasure and natural impulses, for beyond a mere subordination of pleasure to duty the individual develops, to a greater or lesser extent, a "puritanical" disposition of being opposed to pleasure and the play of instinct.

4. Defense Mechanisms

There is wide spread agreement as to the close association between the mechanisms of reaction formation, reparation and undoing with obsessiveness. These three constitute variations of a single pattern of doing something good to over-compensate for something felt to be bad, and I will concentrate on reaction formation, for reparation and undoing are more specifically connected to the symptoms of obsessive-compulsive neurosis, while reaction formation may be regarded as the more universal of the three and the most intimately connected with obsessive personality or perfectionistic character.

The notion of reaction formation was proposed by Freud as early as 1905 in his three essays on A Sexual Theory, where he observed that "opposing psiquic forces" arise in the service of suppressing uncomfortable sensations through the mobilization of "disgust, modesty, and morality." As is well known, his interpretation posits that a drive toward soiling during the child's anal sadistic stage of development is defended against through disgust and will result in an excessive concern with cleanliness. I think a consideration of obsessive personality suggests that reaction formation is not only a matter of covering up something through the opposite, but a distracting oneself from the awareness of certain *impulses* through opposite *activities*. Even when it is not exactly the case that morally approved action serves to distract the person from the awareness of sexuality and angry rebellion, we can say that it is intention—i.e., a disposition to action that serves the function of remaining unconscious of emotions.

We may say that reaction formation underlies and is also the mental operation through which the psychological energy of anger is transformed into that of obsessive "drivenness." Moreover reaction formation may be regarded as the process indicating the transformation of gluttony into anger. For the self-indulgence of gluttony constitutes a most avoided attitude of the perfectionist—whose character is the least self-indulgent of all, the most highly endowed with a "virtuous austerity."

It is not only the case of a *repression* of oral passive needs in view of the active and self-reliant attitude of anger, but a *transformation*: for we may consider anger as an alternative way of getting a selfsame underlying love-need satisfied—not through a hedonistic regression, but through an anhedonic progression to a premature self-control and increased tolerance of frustration. Rather than being a mere issue of relinquishing oral expectations, as it might superficially seem, the case of anger is one in which expectations are assertively endorsed, yet at the same time rationalized as legitimate demands. According to this analysis, then, reaction formation both generates anger and constitutes a defense against its recognition, in addition to constituting the underlying mechanism for perfectionism, moralism, conscious benevolence, "well-intended" criticality, anhedonic ethic of hard work, and so on.

5. Etiological and Further Psychodynamic Remarks[20]

I find that generally speaking ennea-type I individuals are pyknics and most commonly ectopenic mesoendomorphs.[21] There are exceptions, however, mostly among those of the social subtype who tend to be athletic but slender and wiry. It is possible to think that the aggressiveness of ennea-type I is supported by somatotonia in their inborn temperament.

Freud, who was the first to observe the character disposition that we are here labeling as ennea-type I, was also the first to formulate a theory concerning its etiology: the toilet training theory, according to which an excessive concern with cleanliness and orderliness, as well as the retentiveness in individuals with an "anal personality" is explained as a result of premature or exaggerated demands of cleanliness at the toilet training period, and also understood in terms of the attempt to

---

[20]According to Oldham and Frosch, writing on compulsive personality in Cooper et al.'s *Psychiatry,* some studies suggest that "a genetic fact may be a predisposition to the development of obsessional traits." Also many clinicians, from Freud onwards, have proposed that constitutional factors play a role in the development of the disorder. The authors quote Rado suggesting that "compulsive patients had constitutionally excessive amounts of rage inducing power struggles with others from an early age." We also quote Erikson suggesting that "the future compulsive patient, as a child, was either inherently excessively autonomous, or that the parents doled out inordinate reproof and control." And conclude that "variations of the latter formulation seem to be the most frequently proposed psychodynamics of this disorder in the current clinical literature." They also quote Ingram suggesting that "the compulsive patient's need to control represents identification with authoritarian parents." And Millon thought that "they need to keep impulses, mainly hostile ones, at bay due to overcontrolling parents." And Lidz stated "one might surmise, for example, that the parents of obsessional patients tend to be obsessional themselves, unable to tolerate expressions of instinctual drives and autonomy in themselves or in the children..." Cooper, Arnold M., M.D., Allen J. Frances, M.D., and Michael H. Sacks, M.D., *Psychiatry*, Vol. 1: *The Personality Disorder and Neurosis* (New York: Basic Books, 1990).

[21]That is muscular but with rounded features and not delicate or fragile.

deny through over-compensation an angry desire to soil and let go of control. Later psychoanalytic observation also recognized that the "retentive" individual harbors an ("oral aggressive") desire to soil and let go of control and defends against the forbidden wish with an over-compensatory, over-formal goody-goodyness.

Since Freud's time this theory has been mostly revised by Erikson, who proposes that it is not only the issue of sphincter-control that we should see as being the focus of parental over-control and rebellion, but that of locomotion, mastered during the same stage. Underlying both, Erikson claims, is the issue of an autonomy that asserts or over-asserts itself. I think that we can even go further and say with Fromm that this, like every other personality orientation, is a way of coping with life in general; that has arisen in response to a broader situation than sphincter control—a generalized situation of excessive demands and frustration in regard to recognition. I quote from a group reporting on the origin of their shared character:

"Almost all of us agreed that we all took responsibility early. It wasn't given to us, but we took it. From the age of three all the way up, you know people remembered early in childhood up to the age of nine and then of course continued it through our adolescent and adult life. Often it was around, being, taking care of the children, I mean being that person that saw that the kids got fed and clothed and sent where they were supposed to be sent. Kind of assuming almost in a sense the mother's role a little bit and a lot of, and then wanting to be recognized almost all of us felt that no matter how hard we tried what we did and tried harder and harder to be good and to do those things because we wanted to get some kind of recognition or acknowledgment from our parents, and we *never* felt it."

Even so, we may continue to speak of the toilet training situation as paradigmatic and symbolic of the personality disposition, for the perfectionist has not only developed under stringent demands of striving harder for some desired behavior and exerting utmost control over his own organism, but is one who inwardly rebels angrily in face of both external and internalized control, and who has learned to alienate from his awareness and inhibit the manifestations of this anger through the mechanism of reaction formation.

It is easy to trace back the motivation to strive hard in the perfectionist to an early experience of affective dissatisfaction so that seeking to be a better person represents a hope of gaining more approval or closeness from one of the parents. Later in life, however, such striving also takes on a competitive implication, as if saying to father or mother: "I will be better than you and rise beyond your capacity to evaluate me: I will show you!": a vindictive turn in which there is not only in success a hope but also a claim and a vindictive denigration.

I find ennea-type I somewhat more frequent among women. And among them I find that the parent for whose love the little girl has striven and who has been perceived as cold is more often the father. Besides an atmosphere of love scarcity, however, there is also in perfectionistic striving an element of modeling, a taking on by the subject of the hard-working, perfectionistic personality of one or another parent. Frequently there is a perfectionistic father or mother in the family of the perfectionist, and when not, there is commonly an ennea-type VI father of an over-dutiful disposition (which has much in common with the demanding perfectionist).

The over all situation is one of excessive demands coupled with scant acknowledgment, so the child has felt the need to push on and on in an atmosphere of sustained frustration.

It is my impression that an over-accommodating mother (ennea-types IX or VI) may contribute to the unmitigated power of an over-demanding and distant father. It would seem that in these cases an excessively symbiotic or an excessively timid mother betrays the child out of a comparatively greater need to accommodate her excessively demanding mate.

The individual's response to the situation thus far described involves not only an attitude of "See how good I am, will you now love me?", but also one of claiming a recognition or affection through an appeal to moral justice, a protest: "See how good I am—you *owe me* respect and recognition." Towards earning this recognition and respect that are felt to be missing (at first from parents, later in people in general) the child learns to become a little attorney for himself or herself, as well as a moralist who specializes in making others play by the rules.

As an outcome of this process, the search for love that kindled perfectionistic development becomes the search for right and respectability—which characterizes this hard and distant personality style and interferes with the satisfaction of a still latent—though repressed—need for tenderness.

6. Existential Psychodynamics

Before considering the existential psychodynamics of ennea-type I, it may be well to reiterate the postulate that is to be articulated through the contemplation of the nine characters in the book: that passions arise out of a background of ontic obscuration; that the loss of a sense of I-am-ness sustains a craving-for-being that is manifested in the differentiated form of the ego's nine basic emotions.

In the case of ennea-type I, the proximity of the character to that of psychospiritual laziness (indeed the fact of being a hybrid between it and pride) makes the issue of ontic obscuration something that lies near the foreground of their psychological style. This is to say that there is in the life-attitude of ennea-type I a loss of the sense of being which, as is the case in the three characters at the upper region of the enneagram, manifests as an "unconsciousness of unconsciousness" that gives them a particular self-satisfaction, opposite to felt deficiency or to "poverty in spirit" of those at the bottom of the enneagram. Unconscious dissatisfaction, however, is converted into the hottest of the passions, which, however ignored by active unconsciousness, underlies the quality of interpersonal relationships.

While ontic obscuration involves a sort of psychological coarsening in the case of type VIII and type IX psychology as will be seen, in type I it is covered up by an excessive refinement; it could be said that reactive formation also takes place at the ontic level: perceived ontic deficiency becomes stimulus for compensation through activities purporting to sustain false abundance. The main activity that promises abundance to the ennea-type I mind is the enactment of perfection. We might say that precisely in virtue of this obscuration, the search for being can turn into a search for the substitute being of the good life, in which behavior fits an extrinsic criterion of value. The wrathful are in special need, however, of understanding Lao-Tse's statement:

> *"Virtue (Te) does not seek to be virtuous;*
> *precisely because of this it is virtue."*

In other words: Virtue, by not being "virtuous," is virtue.

It would be too narrow, however, to say that the substitute for being in type I is virtue, for sometimes the quality of life is not so much a moralistic one but one with the quality of "correction," a goodness of fit between behavior and a world of principles; or a goodness of fit between ongoing life and some implicit or explicit code.

On the whole, it may be said that the preconscious perception of being-scarcity and the imagination of destructiveness and evil in ennea-type I is compensated for with an impulse to being a "person of character": one endowed with a certain over-stability, a certain strength to resist temptations and stand by what is right. Also, loss of being and value supports activity designed to sustain the impression of somebody worthy which, as we have seen, is sought through a sort of worship of goodness and worthiness.

In the Nasruddin corpus of jokes, ennea-type I may be recognized in the grammarian whom Nasruddin, as boatman, carries to "the other shore." After Nasruddin's answers some inquiry from the grammarian with incorrect speech, the grammarian asks "Haven't you studied grammar?" At Nasruddin's answering to the effect that this was not the case, he proffers out of his righteousness and well informed self-satisfaction, "You have lost half of your life." Later, Nasruddin asks the grammarian "Do you know how to swim?" And since our worthy grammarian responds that this is not the case, Nasruddin remarks, "Then you have lost your *whole* life, for we're sinking."

The joke poignantly alludes to the dissociation between the "grammarian mentality" and life. A process of rigidification and loss of meaning through excessive concern for form and detail has taken place. Even when the pursuit of goodness rather than that of formal correction, such as in school matters, there is beyond consciously cultivated kindness a coldness that entails both lovelessness and insubstantiality, or being-loss.

Chapter Two

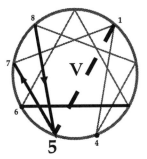

AVARICE AND PATHOLOGICAL DETACHMENT

ENNEA-TYPE V

1. Core Theory, Nomenclature, and Place in the Enneagram

As a spiritual "missing of the mark" or spiritual hindrance, avarice must have naturally been understood by the church fathers in more than its literal sense, and so we see confirmed in Chaucer's "Parson's Tale" from *The Canterbury Tales*, a reflection of the spirit of his time: "Avarice consists not only of greed for lands and chattles, but sometimes for learning and for glory."[1]

---

[1]p. 595, *The Canterbury Tales*, modern English version by J.U. Nicholson (New York: Garden City Books, 1934).

If the gesture of anger is to run over, that of avarice is one of holding back and holding in. While anger expresses greed in an assertive (even though unacknowledged) way, greed in avarice manifests only through retentiveness. This is a fearful grasping, implying a fantasy that letting go would result in catastrophic depletion. Behind the hoarding impulse there is, we may say, an experience of impending impoverishment.

Yet, holding on is only half of ennea-type V psychology; the other half is giving up too easily. Because of an excessive resignation in regard to love and people, precisely, there is a compensatory clutching at oneself—which may or not manifest in a grasping onto possessions, but involves a much more generalized hold over one's inner life as well as an economy of effort and resources. The holding back and self-control of avarice is not unlike that of the anger type, yet it is accompanied by a getting stuck through clutching at the present without openness to the emerging future.[2]

Just as it can be said of the wrathful that they are mostly unconscious of their anger and that anger is their main taboo—it may be said of the avaricious that their avarice is mostly unconscious, while consciously they may feel every gesture of possession and drawing up of boundaries as forbidden. It might be said that the avaricious is internally perfectionistic rather than critical of the outer world, but most importantly the difference between the two ennea-types lies in the contrast between the active extroversion of the former and the introversion of the latter, (the introversion of a thinking type that avoids action).

Also ennea-type I is demanding while ennea-type V seeks to minimize his own needs and claims, and is prone to be pushed around in virtue of a compulsive obedience. Though both types are characterized by a strong super-ego, they are like cops and robbers respectively, for the former identifies more with its idealized superego-congruent self, while ennea-type V

---

[2]See von Gebsattel's analysis below.

identifies with the overwhelmed and guilty sub-personality that is the object of super-egoic demands.[3]

The polarity between pathological detachment and the attachment of holding-on echoes the polarity in ennea-type I between anger and an over-civilized compulsive virtue. Neediness in ennea-type V is deeply hidden in the psyche, behind the veil of indifference, resignation, stoic renunciation. And just as perfectionism nurtures the anger that sustains it, we may also say here that the prohibition of needs (not simply from their satisfaction but even from their recognition within the psyche) must contribute to the impoverishment of life that underlies the urge to hold on.

Ichazo's word for the fixation corresponding to ennea-type V is "stinginess," which stands, I think, too close to "avarice" — the ruling passion or emotion. "Meanness" with its connotation of an unknowing failure to give would come closer to capturing the dominant aspect of the ennea-type V strategy in face of the world: self-distancing and the giving up of relationships. Still better, however, is to speak of being detached, withdrawn, autistic, and schizoid.

2. Antecedents in the Scientific Literature on Character

Just as the image of the anankastics that we find in Schneider smacks of a certain contamination with the schizoid (in that Schneider emphasizes formality as an expression of insecurity) there is in Kurt Schneider's concept of the "sensitive" —the personality disposition that most resembles our schizoid —

---

[3] As I have pointed out in the discussion of ennea-type I, I think that what they have in common have caused them to be confused at times—notably in the observations of Freud, Abraham and Reich on anal and compulsive characters. While the ennea-type I individual is frugal, a consciously generous intent makes it quite different in regard to economic behavior from ennea-type V, where the main motive in stinginess is the fear of remaining without resources and the avoidance of effort and the loss of freedom or autonomy involved in work commitment.

some emphasis on the obsessive element, for he tells us that the more esthenic (i.e. assertive) among these have excessive "moral scruples." There is no doubt, however, that Kurt Schneider has in mind our schizoid when he describes the sensitives as those "subjects that have an increased capacity for impressions with regard to all kinds of experiences without the ability of expressing them." He speaks of a "retentive elaboration of all experiences that is turned against the self." And adds that "the sensitive individual seeks firstly the blame for every event or failure in himself."[4]

The syndrome of aloof retentiveness has not only been observed but also received much attention in contemporary psychology.

Aside from the possibility that the schizoid form of retentiveness probably contributed to Freud's abstraction of an anal character, it corresponds to the syndrome described by Ernst Kretschmer, pioneer of systematic characterology. When in his study of schizophrenic patients at his clinic he described the syndrome that he proposed to call schizoid, the following were the main group of traits he observed to be the most frequent:

1. Unsociable, quiet, reserved, serious (humorless)
2. Timid, shy, with fine feelings, sensitive,
    nervous, excitable, fond of nature and books
3. Pliable, kindly, honest, indifferent, silent

Groups two and three stand in certain opposition to one another, forming a contrast similar to that he described between depression and elation in his cyclothymic type.[5] "If we want to give a short account of the basis of the schizoid temperament," he says, "we must say: the schizoid temperament lies between the extremes of excitability and dullness, in the same way that a cycloid temperament lies between the extremes of cheerfulness and sadness."

Both among his patients as among the bearers of what he proposed to call "schizothymic" temperament (among his "normal" acquaintances), Kretschmer had the merit of pointing

---

[4]op. cit.

[5]Kretschmer, E, *Korpebau und Charakter* (Berlin: Springer Verlag, 1925).

out the polarity between hypersensitivity and insensitivity in this personality: sometimes it is one or the other that is the chief characteristic, while in others an alternation or a transition from early "hyperaesthesia" to late apathy. More generally, I think, we may say the individual is characterized by an exaggerated vulnerability and by a self-protective distancing from his excessively fine and vulnerable feelings. I quote Kretschmer again:

"He alone, however, has the key to the schizoid temperament who has clearly recognized that the majority of schizoids are not either over-sensitive or cold, but they are over-sensitive and cold at the same time, and, indeed, in quite different relational mixtures." "Out of our schizoid material we can form a continuous series, beginning with what I call the 'Hölderlin type,' those extremely sensitive, abnormally tender, constantly wounded, mimosa-like natures, who are "all nerves"- and winding up to those cold, numbed, almost lifeless ruins left by the ravages of a severe attack of dementia praecox, who glimmer dimly in the corner of the asylum, dull-witted as cows."

This polarity, Kretschmer emphasizes, is not to be found in the middle of the range. He finds individuals like Strindberg, who said of himself: "I am hard as ice, and yet so full of feeling that I am almost sentimental." "But even in that half of our material, which is primarily cold, and poor in affective response, as soon as we come into close personal contact with such schizoids, we find, very frequently, behind the affectless, numbed exterior, in the innermost sanctuary, a tender personality-nucleus with the most vulnerable nervous sensitivity, which has withdrawn into itself and lies there contorted."

The unsociable (or "autistic") characteristic of his schizoid is something that could be understood either in relation to hypersensitivity or to insensitivity toward others, as in the case of those sensitive natures that "seek as far as possible to avoid and deaden all stimulation from the outside; they close the shutters of their houses, in order to lead a dream-life, fantastic, poor in deeds and rich in thought (Hölderlin) in the soft muffled gloom of the interior. They seek loneliness, as Strindberg so beautifully said of himself, in order to " 'spin themselves into the silk of their own souls'." Kretschmer's view on schizothymia was further elaborated by Sheldon who endorsed Kretschmer's threefold conception of human constitution, interpreted the "aesthenic" body-build as "ectomorphia" (originating in the predominance of the embryonic ectoderm), and viewed the schizoid disposition as a variable in temperament that he called "cerebrotonia."[6]

Related to ectomorphy, "cerebrotonia" appears to express the function of exteroception, which necessitates or involves cerebrally-mediated inhibition of both the other two primary functions, somatotonia and viscerotonia. It also involves or leads to conscious attentionality and thereby to substitution of symbolic ideation for immediate overt response to stimulation. Attendant upon this latter phenomenon are the "cerebral tragedies" or hesitation, disorientation and confusion. These appear to be the by-products of over-stimulation, which is doubtless one consequence of an over-balanced investment in "exteroception." Though Sheldon is more concerned with variables than with types, it is clearly in ennea-type V that we see the highest expression of both ectomorphic constitution and cerebrotonic traits, among which Sheldon lists the following twenty as most distinctive:

1. Restraint in Posture and Movement, Tightness
2. Physiological Over-Response
3. Overly Fast Reactions
4. Love of Privacy
5. Mental Over-intensity, Hyper-attentionality, Apprehensiveness
6. Secretiveness of Feeling, Emotional Restraint
7. Self-conscious Motility of the Eyes and Face
8. Sociophobia
9. Inhibited Social Address
10. Resistance to Habit and Poor Routinizing
11. Agoraphobia
12. Unpredictability of Attitude
13. Vocal Restraint and General Restraint of Noise
14. Hypersensitivity to Pain
15. Poor Sleep Habits, Chronic Fatigue

---

[6]Sheldon, William, op. cit.

16. Youthful Intentness of Manner and Appearance
17. Vertical Mental Cleavage, Introversion
18. Resistance to Alcohol and to other Depressant Drugs
19. Need of Solitude when Troubled
20. Orientation Toward the Later Periods of Life.

Many of these traits express the over sensitive aspect of the temperament (Physiological Over-response, Hyper-attentionality, Apprehensiveness, Resistance to Habits and Unpredictability of Attitude), while others have to do with inhibition and with moving away from others, such as Restraint in Movement, Secretiveness, Sociophobia, Inhibited Social Address.

Introversion, the gist of the variable, seems to constitute a convergence of both: a movement away from the outer to the inner, and sensitivity to inner experiences.

Moving from the realm of temperamental dispositions to character proper, we observe that "compulsive" or "anankastic" character in the European usage corresponds to ennea-type V and not ennea-type I as the syndrome called "compulsive personality disorder" in the DSM III. This is immediately apparent from the opening lines of V.E. von Gebsattel in his pioneering essay on the existential analysis of the anankastic disposition:[7] "What always fascinates us in encountering the compulsive person is the unpenetrated, perhaps impenetrable, quality of his being different. Seventy years of clinical work and scientific research have not altered this reaction. Kept alive by the contradiction between the intimate closeness of the presence of a fellow man and the strange remoteness of a mode of being completely different from our own, the affect of psychiatric amazement never ceases."

Addressing himself to the anankastic psychopaths of Schneider and others through the study of a case, von Gebsattel observes a mode of being in the world that I have already

---

[7]Von Gebsattel, V.E., "The World of the Compulsive" in *Existence: A New Dimension in Psychiatry and Psychology*, edited by Rollo May (New York: Basic Books, 1959).

alluded to in the description of avarice at the beginning of this chapter: a getting stuck, a blocking of the life process.[8]

While Sheldon, more than Kretschmer even, undertakes to study a temperamental disposition—which may be the soil of a character but not a character itself—Karen Horney, speaking out of her psychotherapeutic experience, was to describe the crystallization of an interpersonal strategy: the neurotic disposition to move away from people and conflicts, the "solution of detachment." Like Sheldon—who, in spite of the arbitrariness of his rating the components of temperaments from one to seven, may appear to be correct in stating that these may be found in different degrees and combinations—Horney might well have come to distinguish degrees and forms of expression of the tendency to move away from people. Yet it is at the same time clear that just as cerebrotonia does, sociophobia (in the sense of compulsive avoidance of sociability and relation) clearly culminates in the schizoid disposition, and it is the picture of ennea-type V that we gather from her discussion of the "solution of detachment."

I quote from *Neurosis and Human Growth*[9]: "The third major solution of the intrapsychic conflict consists essentially in the neurotic's withdrawing from the inner battlefield and declaring himself uninterested. If he can muster and maintain an attitude of 'don't care,' he feels less bothered by his inner conflicts and can attain a semblance of inner peace. Since he can do this only by resigning from active living, 'resignation' seems a proper name for this solution". "Resignation" she clarifies, "may have a constructive meaning. We can think of many older people who have recognized the intrinsic futility of ambition and success, who have mellowed by expecting and demanding less, and who through renunciation of nonessentials have become wiser. In many forms of religion or philosophy renunciation of nonessentials is advocated as one of the conditions for greater spiritual growth and fulfillment: give up the expression of personal will, sexual desires and cravings for worldly goods for

---

[8]Von Gebsattel, V.E., op. cit.

[9]Horney, Karen, *Neurosis and Human Growth* (New York: W.W. Norton & Co., 1990).

the sake of being closer to God. Give up personal strivings and satisfactions for the sake of attaining the spiritual power which exists potentially in human beings. For the neurotic solution we are discussing here, however, resignation implies settling for a peace which is merely the absence of conflicts...His resignation therefore is a process of shrinking, of restricting, of curtailing life and growth."

The distinction she draws here is similar to a parallel one which we drew between genuine virtue and the false virtue of moralism. It is the case of an introversive, rather than an extraversive, form of religiosity, where neurotic renunciation stands in place of a healthy capacity to forgo gratification. Horney tells as that the basic characteristic of neurotic resignation is distinguished by an aura of restriction, of something that is avoided, that is not wanted or not done. "There is some resignation in every neurotic. What I shall describe here is a cross section of those for whom it has become the major solution."

She begins her description by telling us that "the direct expression of the neurotic having removed himself from the inner battlefield is his being an outlooker at himself and his life...Since detachment is a ubiquitous and prominent attitude of his, he is also an outlooker upon others. He lives as if he were sitting in the orchestra and observing a drama acted on the stage, and a drama which is most of the time not too exciting at that. Though he is not necessarily a good observer, he may be most astute. Even in the very first consultation he may, with the help of some pertinent questions, develop a picture of himself replete with a wealth of candid observation. But he usually adds that all this knowledge has not changed anything. Of course it has not— for none of his findings has been an experience for him. Being an outlooker at himself means just that: not actively participating in living and unconsciously refusing to do so.

In analysis he tries to maintain the same attitude. He may be immensely interested, yet that interest may stay for quite a while at the level of a fascinating entertainment—and nothing changes." Horney's next observation is that "intimately connected with nonparticipation, is the absence of any serious striving for achievement and the aversion of effort...he may compose beautiful music, paint pictures, write books—in his imagination.

This is an alternative means of doing away with both aspiration and effort. He may actually have good and original ideas on some subject, but the writing of a paper would require initiative and the arduous work of thinking the ideas through and organizing them. So the paper remains unwritten. He may have a vague desire to write a novel or a play, but wait for the inspiration to come. Then the plot would be clear and everything would flow from his pen. Also he is most ingenious at finding reasons for not doing things. How much good would be a book that had to be seated out in hard labor! And are not too many books written anyhow? Would not the concentration on one pursuit curtail other interests and thus narrow his horizon? Does not going into politics, or into any competitive field, spoil the character?" "This aversion to effort may extend to all activities. It then brings about a complete inertia to which we shall return later. He may procrastinate over doing such simple things as writing a letter, reading a book, shopping. Or he may do them against inner resistance, slowly, listlessly, ineffectively. The mere prospect of unavoidable larger activities, such as moving or handling accumulated tasks in his job, may make him tired before he begins"....."In analysis it appears that his goals are limited and again negative.

"Analysis, he feels, should rid him of disturbing symptoms, such as awkwardness with strangers, fear of blushing or fainting in the street. Or perhaps analysis should remove one or another aspect of his inertia, such as his difficulty in reading. He may also have a broader vision of a goal which, in characteristically vague terms, he may call 'serenity.' This, however, means for him simply the absence of all troubles, irritations and upsets. And naturally whatever he hopes for should come easily, without pain or strain. The analyst should do the work. After all, is he not the expert? Analysis should be like going to a dentist who pulls out the tooth, or to a doctor who gives an injection: he is willing to wait patiently for the analyst to present the clue that will solve everything. It would be better though if the patient didn't have to talk so much. The analyst should have some sort of X ray which would reveal the patient's thoughts." And she continues: "A step deeper and we come to the very essence of resignation: the restriction of wishes." Though we may also speak of resignation in the cyclothymic ennea-type IX—where we find extraverted resignation, resignation in relationship manifesting as abnegation—in the schizoid personality we find a resignation without participation, a resignation that goes as far as giving up contact.

Says Horney: "He is particularly anxious not to get attached to anything to the extent of really needing it. Nothing should be so important for him that he could not do without it. It is all right to like a woman, a place in the country, or certain drinks, but one should not become dependent upon them. As soon as he becomes aware that a place, a person or a group of people means so much to him that its loss would be painful he tends to retract his feelings. No other person should ever have the feeling of being necessary to him or take the relationship for granted. If he suspects the existence of either attitude he tends to withdraw."

The most extreme expression of the pathology may be recognized in the catatonic syndrome in schizophrenia, for even though the latter constitutes an extreme complication of the schizoid way of being in the world, precisely because of this it allows us to see a caricature of some of its traits: unrelatedness, laconism, a seeming flight from the world in which personal world is relinquished, and a passivity in which the individual seems to surrender his life and body to others, and the characteristic symptom of *flexibilitas cerea* in which the person adopts whatever position others manipulate the body into—a caricature of automatic obedience.

Next in the gradient from psychosis to mental health is Kernberg's "Narcissistic Personality Organization," in which the negative self-image coexists not only with an idealized self-image, but with an orientation to seek recognition through intellectual or creative excellence.

Better known today than Horney's description of the "solution of detachment" are Fairbairn's observations and reflections on schizoid character—all of them pertinent to our ennea-type V. In addition to being best known among those who have contemplated the schizoid syndrome, Fairbairn is known for his claim to the effect that the schizoid phenomenon is the root of all psychopathology. This statement reflects, I think, his understanding of the existential issue of what I am calling "Being Scarcity"—or to use his vocabulary, "ego weakness" as the root of all psychopathology, and I think that it would have been more exact to leave it as that, for the schizoid personality is only the one in which this pervasive issue of the human condition makes itself most apparent. Just as the resigned ennea-type IX is blind to its blindness, ennea-type V is, in regard to the perception of ontic deficiency, what might be called a hypersensitive: structurally an introvert and usually an intuitive, he is most attuned to his internal experiences, and his avarice is interdependent with a sense of impoverishment at the spiritual level as well as at the psychological and the material.

One of Fairbairn's findings in his psychoanalysis of schizoid personalities was that beyond the analysis of superego pathology, schizoid patients were in need of understanding that, their process of detachment (in transference and in life) constitutes a defense "against a dreaded activation of a basic relationship in the transference characterized by a libidinal investment of the analyst experienced as a preoedipal, particularly oral, mother."[10] I have taken the statement above from Otto Kernberg's summary, as also the following: "This libidinal investment seemed a major threat to these patients, a threat derived from the fear that their love of the object would be devastatingly destructive to the object." Yet the schizoid's fear is not only the fear of destroying the object, it is also one of losing oneself through an excessive love thirst, being engulfed through the intensity of dependency needs—as R.D. Laing has pointed out in *The Divided Self.*

All in all, Fairbairn's contention of the sense of negative expectation concerning mother love has contributed a cornerstone to our understanding of this personality, to which he contributed various other observations, such as noting "the chronic subjective experience of artificiality and of emotional detachment of schizoid personalities .... these patients' attitude of omnipotence, objective isolation and detachment, and marked preoccupation with inner reality."[11]

---

[10]Fairbairn, W.R.D., quoted in Otto Kernberg, *An Object-Relations Theory of the Personality,* (New York: Basic Books, 1952).

[11]Fairbairn, W.R.D., *Borderline Conditions and Pathological Narcissism* (New York: Jason Aronson, Inc., 1985).

Let me end by remarking that without mentioning the word avarice, Fairbairn's understanding of the schizoid clearly involves the recognition that it involves an unwillingness of the person to invest herself in relationships and an avoidance of giving.

In DSM III we find our type in the "schizoid personality disorder."

I quote the correspondent description:

A. Emotional coldness and aloofness, and absence of warm, tender feelings for others.
B. Indifference to praise or criticism and to the feelings of others.
C. Close friendships with no more than one or two persons, including family members.
D. No eccentricities of speech, behavior, or thought characteristic of Schizo-typal Personality Disorder.
E. Not due to a psychotic disorder such as Schizophrenia or Paranoid Disorder.
F. If under 18, does not meet the criteria for Schizoid Disorder of Childhood or Adolescence.

There is a personality type in DSM III that is defined on the basis of a single trait, and which, because of this, may be a diagnosis ascribed to more than one of the characters in this book: the passive-aggressive personality. It's resistance to external demands is most typical of ennea-type V, yet is also a trait that may be found in ennea-types IV, VI, and IX. Theodore Millon, who was on the committee that originated DSM III, has proposed both a change in name of passive-aggressive, and a description of the syndrome that takes into account other characteristics, such as "frequently irritable and erratically moody, a tendency to report being easily frustrated and angry, discontented self-image...disgruntled and disillusioned with life; interpersonal ambivalence," as evidence in a struggle between being independently acquiescent and assertively independent; and the use of unpredictable and sulking behaviors to provoke discomfort in others.

On the whole, I get the impression passive-aggressive is one more complication of ennea-type V, and find corroboration for this impression in the resemblance that Millon[12] points out between this passive-aggressive personality and compulsive personality, beyond their obvious contrast (a similarity within contrasts that I have already commented upon), "both share an intense and deeply rooted ambivalence about themselves and others. Compulsives deal with this ambivalence by vigorously suppressing the conflicts it engenders, and they appear as a consequence, to be well controlled and single-minded in purpose; their behavior is perfectionistic, scrupulous, orderly, and quite predictable. In contrast, the passive-aggressive, referred to in Millon's theory as the 'active-ambivalent,' fails either to submerge or to otherwise resolve these very same conflicts; as a consequence, the ambivalence of the passive-aggressives intrudes constantly into their everyday life, resulting in indecisiveness, fluctuating attitudes, oppositional behaviors and emotions, and a general erraticism and unpredictability. They cannot decide whether to adhere to the desires of others as a means of gaining comfort and security or to turn to themselves for these gains, whether to be obediently dependent on others or defiantly resistant and independent of them, whether to take the initiative in mastering their world or to sit idly by, passively awaiting the leadership of others."

Unlike the case of most of our character types I find that the shadow of ennea-type V appears in more than one of Jung's descriptions of introverted types.[13] Speaking of the introverted thinking type, for instance, which as we shall see corresponds mostly to our ennea-type VI,[14] it is possible to find some schizoid characteristics, such as "his amazing unpracticalness and horror of publicity" or the observation that "he lets himself be brutalized and exploited in the most ignominious way if only he can be left in peace to pursue his ideas." Also it is most typical of ennea-type V that "he is a poor teacher, because all the time he is teaching, his thought is occupied with the material itself and not with its presentation." Also in the description of the introverted

---

[12]op.cit.

[13]Jung, C. G., op. cit.

[14]A correspondence confirmed by the illustrative reference to Kant and Nietzsche.

feeling type, which will be quoted in reference to our ennea-type IX, traces of ennea-type V overlap, such as "expressions of feeling therefore remain niggardly, and the other person has a permanent sense of being undervalued..."

In spite of these traces of ennea-type V character in the above-mentioned psychological types of Jung, it is definitely in the introverted sensation type that we find the best match for our character. We read, for instance, that:

"He may be conspicuous for his calmness and passivity, or for his rational self-control. This peculiarity, which often leads a superficial judgment astray, is really due to his unrelatedness to objects."

Or:

"Such a type can easily make one question: why one should exist at all, or why objects in general should have any justification for their existence since everything essential still goes on happening without them."

Scanning the descriptions given by Keirsey and Bates[15] of the sixteen profiles obtained through a test derived from the Myers-Briggs, I find ennea-type V psychology reflected in that of the "INTP"—i.e., the introvert who has a predominance of intuition over sensation, thinking over feeling, and perception over judgment. I quote some of their statements:

"The world exists primarily to be understood. Reality is trivial, a mere arena for proving ideas....

"The INTP's should not....be asked to work out the implementation or application of their models to the real world. The INTP is the architect of a system and leaves it to others to be the builder and the applicator...

"They are not good at clinical tasks and are impatient with routine details. They prefer to work quietly, without interruption, and often alone.

"They are not likely to welcome constant social activity or disorganization in the home...INTP's are, however, willing, complaint and easy to live with, although somewhat forgetful of appointments, anniversaries, and the rituals of daily living - unless reminded. They may have difficulties expressing their

---

[15]op cit.

emotions verbally, and the mate of an INTP may believe that
he/she is somewhat taken for granted..."

In the homeopathic tradition the characteristics of ennea-
type V may be found in people with personalities associated
with *Sepia*, which is the remedy claimed to benefit them.[16] The
homeopathic is made from the fresh ink of the cuttlefish—a
creature who lives alone rather than in a group, lives in the
crevices of rocks, and ejects ink for camouflage when seeking
escape or stalking its prey. *Sepia* is associated with women, either
withdrawn, dissatisfied, or contented in a career. One instance is
that of women worn out with the cares of home and children,
and not seeming to have the energy for it. Coulter remarks:

"All manifestations of love—marital, parental, filial, and
even close friendship—are a drain on her reserves of energy and
an obstacle to her need for a certain amount of privacy and independence." She quotes Kent as remarking of them "love does not
go forth into affection." And comments "love is not absent, but
the manifestation of love is benumbed and cannot be expressed."
She further quotes Hering as finding *Sepia* people "averse to
company" and elaborates: "she does not want to go out, largely
because of the physical effort which sociability demands." The
dominant feeling is one of indifference—the wish of wanting to
"crawl into her lair and be left alone, not touched, approached or
bothered." Thus there is not only an emotional unresponsiveness
but a seeking to escape from close emotional ties and obligations.
The wish to emancipate herself from the "burden of love" may
be expressed in personality or a profession.

Coulter observes that the type can be "spirited, creative and
attractive, but even when socially outgoing she may still lack
warm sympathy"..."she may appear deficient in feminine
receptivity and the finer shades of emotional responsiveness."
Sepia feels too stressful an impingement of life on its independent
and private meanings, shown characteristically in a straightforward negativity "whether due to an inability to conceal her
nature, a need to feel rejected, excessive candor, or simply a
complete lack of interest in producing a good impression."

---

[16]Quoted by permission of the author, Catherine R. Coulter, all excerpts on *Sepia*
are from pp. 125-139, *Portraits of Homoeopathic Medicines*, Vol. 1 (Berkeley, CA:
North Atlantic Books, 1986).

Also evocative of ennea-type V is the personality picture associated in homeopathic medicine with *Silica*. I quote from Coulter:[17]

"The *inflexibility* of flint is manifested on the mental plane in *Silica*'s 'obstinacy' (Boenninghausen) ... He is not aggressive or argumentative, will smile, remain pleasant, and appear mild enough—but still proceeds as he deems best...."

She describes a child who dislikes boarding school but will only use "passive persuasion" methods with his parents. She also describes the picture of a young adolescent girl or young woman, to whom it is impossible to give advice or even give a present. "...This is not from an overall negativeness but from rigidity of views. The girl (or boy) can be just as rigid and selective in her judgment of people and thus has particular difficulty finding friends, and later, an acceptable partner in life. Persons who remain single, not from aversion to the marital state but from being too exacting—no one is ever quite suitable—will often exhibit *Silica* characteristics."

Coulter compares a *Silica* individual with the "stalk of wheat," which is delicate and yielding and yet provided with a stiff outer covering. In personality this relative firmness corresponds to an intellectual stability and a power of concentration, while the individual lacks vitality and "he may expend so much energy coping with his physical environment that little is left over for enjoyable living."

Also fitting the picture of ennea-type V is the observation of forgetfulness and abstraction in *Silica* personalities, their faint-heartedness, lack of courage, and the refusal to shoulder responsibility. Coulter quotes Whitmont's likening of the *Silica* individual to "a timid delicate white mouse which still fiercely maintains the integrity of its own small territory."

---

[17]Reprinted with permission, op. cit., Vol. 2, pp. 67-106.

3. Trait Structure

Retentiveness

As usual, it is possible to find in this character a cluster of descriptors corresponding to the dominant passion. In it, along with avarice, belong such characteristics as lack of generosity in matters of money, energy and time, and also meanness—with its implication of an insensitivity to the needs of others. Among the characteristics of retentiveness it is important to take note of a holding on to the ongoing content of the mind, as if wanting to elaborate or extract the last drop of significance —a characteristic that results in a typical jerkiness of mental function, a subtle form of rigidity that militates against the individual's openness to environmental stimulation and to what is emerging, the transition of the present mental state to the next. This is the characteristic which von Gebsattel has pointed out in "ananchastics" as a "getting stuck."[18]

We may say that the implicit interpersonal strategy of holding on implies a preference for self-sufficiency in regard to resources instead of approaching others. This, in turn, involves a pessimistic outlook in regard to the prospect of either receiving care and protection or having the power to demand or take what is needed.

Not Giving

Also the avoidance of commitment can be considered as an expression of not giving since it amounts to an avoidance of giving in the future. In this avoidance of commitment, however, there is also another aspect: the need of type V individuals to be completely free, unbound, unobstructed, in possession of the fullness of themselves—a trait representing a composite of avarice and an over-sensitivity to engulfment (to be discussed

---

[18]op.cit.

later). It may be pointed out that hoarding implies not just avarice, but a projection of avarice into the future—a protection against being left without. Here, again, the trait represents a derivation not only from avarice, but also from the intense need of autonomy of the character (see below).

Pathological Detachment

Given the reciprocity of giving and taking in human relationships, a compulsion to not give (surely the echo of perceiving in early life that it goes against survival to give more than is received) can hardly be sustained except at the expense of relationship itself—as if the individual considered: "If the only way to hold on to the little I have is to distance myself from others and their needs or wants, that is what I will do."

An aspect of pathological detachment is the characteristic aloofness of ennea-type V; another, the quality of being a "loner," i.e., one accustomed to being solitary and who, out of resignation in regard to relating, does not feel particularly lonely. Seclusiveness is, of course, part of the broader trait of detachment, since it requires emotional detachment and repression of the need to relate, to be in isolation. The difficulty that type V individuals have in making friends may be considered also here, for an important aspect of this difficulty is the lack of motivation to relate.

Though it is easy to see how detachment can arise as a complication of retentiveness, the giving up of relationship is interdependent with the inhibition of needs—for it could hardly be compatible to give up relationships and to be needy, and thus giving up relationship already implies a relinquishment or minimization of needs. While resignation in regard to one's own needs is practically a corollary of detachment, the inhibition of the expression of anger in this character involves not only resignation in regard to love needs, but also the fear that is present in the schizoid personality in virtue of its position next to the left corner of the enneagram.

Fear of engulfment

The fear and avoidance of being "swallowed up by others" might be a corollary of the avoidance of relationships, yet not only this, for it is also the expression of a half-conscious perception of one's own suppressed need to relate, and (as Fairbairn has emphasized) a fear of potential dependency. The great sensitivity to interference and interruption of ennea-type V individuals is not only the expression of a detached attitude, but also a function of the person's proneness to interrupt herself in the face of external demands and perceived needs of others. In other words, a great sensitivity to interference goes hand-in-hand with an over-docility, in virtue of which the individual interferes all too easily with her own spontaneity, with her preferences, and with acting in a way coherent with her needs in the presence of others. Also, in light of this over- docility (understandable as a by-product of a strong repressed love need) we can understand the particular emphasis in aloneness in ennea-type V. To the extent that the relationship entails alienation from one's own preferences and authentic expression there arises an implicit stress and the need to recover from it: a need to find oneself again in aloneness.

Autonomy

The great need for autonomy is an understandable corollary of giving up relationships. Together with developing the "distance machinery" (to use H.S. Sullivan's expression), the individual needs to be able to do without external supplies. One who cannot get to others to satisfy his desires needs to build up his resources, stocking them up, so to speak, inside his ivory tower. Closely related to autonomy and yet a trait on its own is the idealization of autonomy which reinforces the repression of desires and underlies a life philosophy much like that which Hesse puts in Siddhartha's mouth: "I can think, I can wait, I can fast."[19]

---

[19]Hesse, Herman, *Siddhartha* (New York: New Directions, 1951).

Feelinglessness

Though I have already alluded to a repression of needs, and mentioned the suppression of anger of ennea-type V, it seems desirable to group these descriptors along with others in a more generalized trait of feelinglessness. It has to do with the loss of awareness of feelings and even an interference with the generation of feeling, which results from the avoidance of expression and action. This characteristic makes some individuals indifferent, cold, unempathic, and apathetic. Also anhedonia might be placed here, though the greater or lesser incapacity to enjoy pleasure is a more complex phenomenon: while ennea-type I is aversive to pleasure, ennea-type V simply appears as having a diminished capacity to experience it. In this is implicit, however, the fact that pleasure does not rank high in the scale of values of this character for it is postponed to more "urgent" drives, such as the drive to keep a safe distance from others and the drive for autonomy.

Postponement of Action

We may say that to act is to invest oneself, to put one's energies into use, which goes against the grain of retentive orientation of type V. Yet, more generally, action can not be considered as separate from interaction, so when the drive to relate is low the drive to do is concomitantly lessened. On the other hand, action requires an enthusiasm for something, a presence of feelings—which is not the case in the apathetic individual. To do is also something like showing one's self to the world, for one's actions manifest one's intentions. One who wants to keep his intentions hidden (as the avaricious typically does) will also inhibit his activity on these grounds and develop, instead of a spontaneous movement and initiative, an excessive restraint. The characteristic trait of procrastination may be regarded as a hybrid between negativism and the avoidance of action.

Cognitive Orientation

Ennea-type V is not only introversive (as is implied in moving away from relationships) but also typically intellectual (as introverts generally tend to be). Through a predominantly cognitive orientation the individual may seek substitute satisfaction—as in the replacement of living through reading. Yet the symbolic replacement of life is not the only form of expression of intense thinking activity: another aspect is the preparation for life—a preparation that is intense to the extent that the individual never feels ready enough. In the elaboration of perceptions as preparation for (inhibited) action, the activity of abstraction is particularly striking, type V individuals lean towards the activity of classification and organization, and not only display a strong attraction towards the process of ordering experience, but tend to dwell in abstractions while at the same time avoiding concreteness. This avoidance of concreteness, in turn, is linked to the type's hiddenness: only the results of one's perceptions are offered to the world, not its raw material.

Related to abstraction and the organization of experience is an interest in science and a curiosity in regard to knowledge. Also the inhibition of feelings and of action, along with the emphasis of cognition gives rise to the characteristic of being a mere witness of life, a non-attached yet keen observer of it, who in this very keenness seems to be seeking to replace life through its understanding.

Sense of emptiness

Naturally, the suppression of feelings and the avoidance of life (in the interest of avoiding feelings) constitutes the avoidance of action along with an objective impoverishment of experience. We may understand the sense of sterility, depletion, and meaninglessness that are typical of type V as the result of an objective impoverishment in the life of relatedness, feeling, and doing. The prevalence of such a sense of inner vacuum in modern times (when other symptomatic neuroses have been relatively eclipsed by the "existential ones") reflects the proportion of ennea-type V individuals in the consulting rooms of psychotherapists today. One psychodynamic consequence of this existential pain of feeling faintly existing is the attempt to compensate for the impoverishment of feeling and active life through the intellectual life (for which the individual is usually well endowed constitutionally) and through being a curious and/or critical "outsider." Another more fundamental consequence, however, is the fact of "ontic insufficiency" in stimulating the dominant passion itself—as is the case in each one of the character structures.

Guilt

Ennea-type V (along with type IV, at the bottom of the enneagram) is characterized by guilt proneness—even though in type IV, it is more intensely felt—"buffered" by a generalized distancing from feelings.

Guilt manifests in a vague sense of inferiority, however, in a vulnerability to intimidation, in a sense of awkwardness and self-consciousness, and, most typically, in the very characteristic hiddenness of the person. Though guilt can be understood in light of the strong superego of type V, I believe that it is also a consequence of the early implicit decision of the person to withdraw love (as a response to the lovelessness of the outer world). The cold detachment of type V may thus be regarded as an equivalent to the anger of the vindictive type VIII, who sets out to go it alone and fights for his needs in a hostile world. His moving away from people is an equivalent to moving against, as if, in the impossibility to express anger, he annihilated the other in his inner world. In embracing an attitude of loveless disregard, he thus feels a guilt that is not only comparable to that of the tough-minded bully, but more "visible" since in the bully it is defensively denied, while here it manifests as a pervasive and Kafkaesque guilt proneness.

High Super-ego

The trait of high super-ego may be regarded as interdependent with guilt: the superego's demanding results in guilt and is a compensatory response to it (not unlike the reaction formation involved in the high super-ego of ennea-type

I). Like the type I individual, type V feels driven, and demands much out of himself as well as of others. It may be said that ennea-type I is more externally perfectionistic, ennea-type V internally so. Also, the former holds on to a relative identification with his super-ego, while the latter identifies with his inner "underdog."

Negativism

A source trait related to the perception of the needs of others as binding, and also a form of rebellion against one's own (superegoic) demands, is that which involves, beyond an avoidance of interference or influence, a wish to *subvert* the perceived demands of others and of oneself. Here we can see again a factor underlying the characteristic postponement of action, for sometimes this involves a wish *not* to do that which is perceived as a should, a wish not to "give" something requested or expected, even when the source of the request is internal rather than societal. A manifestation of such negativism is that anything that the individual chooses to do on the basis of true desire is likely to become, once an explicit project, a "should" that evokes a loss of motivation through internal rebellion.

Hypersensitivity

Though we have surveyed the insensitive aspect of type V, we also need to include its characteristic hypersensitivity, manifest in traits ranging from a low tolerance of pain to fear of rejection.

It is my impression that this trait is more basic (in the sense of being psychodynamically fundamental) than that of feelinglessness and that, as Kretschmer[20] has proposed, emotional dullness sets in precisely as a defense against the hypersensitive characteristic. The hypersensitive characteristic of ennea-type V involves a sense of weakness, a vulnerability and also a sensitivity in dealing with the world of objects and even

---

[20]Kretschmer, Ernst, *Physique and Character: An Investigation of the Nature of Constitution and the Theory of Temperament* (New York: Cooper Square, 1936).

persons. To the extent that the individual is not autistically disconnected from the perception of others, he is gentle, soft and harmless. Even in his dealing with the inanimate environment this is true: he does not want to disturb the way things are; he would like, so to speak, to walk without harming the grass on which he treads. Though this hypersensitive characteristic may be ascribed, together with the cognitive orientation and introversive moving away from people, to the cerebrotonic background of the type, we can also understand it as partly derived from the experience of half-conscious psychological pain: the pain of guilt, the pain of unacknowledged loneliness, the pain of emptiness. It seems to me that an individual who feels full and substantial can stand more pain than one who feels empty.

Lack of pleasure and of the feeling of insignificance, thus, would seem to influence the limit of pain that can be accepted, and hypersensitivity itself, no doubt, stands as a factor behind the individual's decision to avoid the pain of frustrating relationships through the choice of isolation and autonomy.

4. Defense Mechanisms

Though it is possible to speak of reaction formation in connection with the super-egoic aspect of type V (i.e., the good boyish or good girlish, not greedy and not angry characteristics) it is not reaction formation that predominates in type V character —but isolation.

Of course, what is meant by isolation in this technical sense of the word is not the behavioral isolation of a schizoid in the social world—and yet there seem to be some relation between interpersonal isolation and the defense mechanism called isolation in Psychoanalysis, i.e., between the interruption of the relationship with others and an interruption of the relationship with oneself or with the representation of others in one's inner world.

Anna Freud describes isolation as a condition in which the instinctive drives are separated from their context, while at the same time persist in awareness. Matte-Blanco,[21] speaking of painful traumatic experiences, says that it can be observed in cases when the intellectual content of what has occurred is isolated from the intense emotion that was experienced, "which is coolly recollected by the patient as if it referred to something that happened to somebody else, and does not matter to him". In these cases, he adds, "it is not only the emotional content that is isolated, but the connection bearing within the intellectual content itself, which results in the loss of the true and deep meaning of the traumatic experience and of the instinctive impulses that have been at play in relation to it. The result of this is, then, the same as in repression through amnesia."

The concept of isolation has been applied to the process of separating an experience from the contextual horizon of experience through the interpolation of a mental vacuum immediately after. The symptom of blocking in schizophrenia may be said to correspond to an extreme form of self-interruption through a sort of stopping of mental activity. This process was called by Freud motor isolation and interpreted as a derivative of normal concentration (in which also the irruption of thoughts or mental states is prevented). Matte-Blanco comments further: "In the normal process of directing the stream of thoughts the ego may be said to engage much isolation work."

The mechanism of ego splitting is closely related to that of isolation and just as prominent in type V. While splitting in the psyche is a general characteristic in neurosis (and is implicit in the separation of super-ego, ego and id), ego-splitting proper —in which contradictory thoughts, roles, or attitudes coexist in the conscious psyche without awareness of contradiction—is more prominent in type V than in any other, and explains not only the simultaneity of grandiosity and inferiority but also the simultaneity of positive and negative perceptions of others. We may say that isolation is a core of type V character in that the characteristic detachment not only from people but more generally from the world (including one's own body) depends on the inactivation of feelings and also corresponds to an avoidance

---

[21]Matte-Blanco, Ignacio, *Psicologia Dinamica* (Santiago: Estudios de Ed. de le Universidad de Chile, 1955).

of the situation in which feelings normally arise: an interruption of the life process in the service of feeling-avoidance.

The incongruence of aloofness with the ordinary human need for contact is maintained through a dulling of the emotional life; at other times in the more hypersensitive variety of individual, it exists side by side with intense feelings, which appear in greater association with the aesthetic and the abstract than with the interpersonal world. Also the avoidance of action in type V may be seen in light of an avoidance of feeling and of the isolation mechanism, and would deserve the name of motoric isolation better than the interruption of thoughts and the disturbance of gestalt perception through mental blocking.

Where there is remoteness not only from others but also from the world, action is unnecessary, and conversely, the avoidance of action supports the avoidance of relationship.

As in other characters here too we may ask ourselves whether the mechanism of isolation has arisen in connection with a particularly avoided realm of experience, so that its typical operation matches a typical repressed content. The answer seems to be given by the enneagram structure itself, for once more we may understand that the attitude of type V is most opposite to that of type VIII, and it would seem that its over-control, diminished vitality, and disposition not to invest itself in any particular course of action or relationship entails a corresponding taboo on intensity and fear of potential destructiveness. Type V is the very negation of lusty super-abundance, and thus we are invited to think about the mechanism of splitting as arisen from an individual's way of protecting himself against a primitive and impulsive response to the environment. His skill in separating himself conceptually and analytically considering the aspects of a situation allows him to see such situations as something unrelated to personal needs—and thus leads to the restriction of personal needs that goes hand-in-hand with avarice in self-spending.

5. Etiological and Further Psychodynamic Remarks[22]

As a group ennea-type V individuals constitute the most ectomorphic in the enneagram, and it is reasonable to think that a cerebrotonic disposition has contributed to the "choice" of a moving away as a solution to the problems of life. Occasionally the individual has memories of fear related to a sense of physical fragility.

What is most striking in regard to the form of love deprivation in the story of ennea-type V is early onset, so that the child never had an occasion to establish a deep bond with its mother. Unlike ennea-type IV whose emotional reaction is that of mourning a loss, ennea-type V feels an emptiness and does not know what he is missing. The syndrome of hospitalism described by Spitz—in which children provided with nourishment but not with maternal care may languish to the point of death—seems emblematic of what happens more subtly in the aloof adult who suffers from apathy and a depression without sadness.

The situation of mother deprivation (literal or psychological) may be complicated by a lack of alternative relationships when the child is the only one in the family and the father is either distant or the mother jealously interferes with the child's relationship to him. Unrelatedness to others in such instances stems from the lack of a deep relationship experience at home.

Another element often encountered in the childhood of ennea-type V is that of a "devouring," invasive, or excessively

---

[22]In Siever's and Kendler's chapter on dealing with the schizoid personality in Cooper et al.'s *Psychiatry* the authors say: "Genetic studies suggest that genetic isolation in childhood and adulthood may be observed in the life of schizophrenics, although results are not uniform in this regard." He quotes the study claiming that there is "a constitutionally determined antagonia and a lack of pleasure derived from interpersonal relationship." Also they quote evidence of there being "inadequate or unreliable mothering, leading to a sense of isolation and a feeling of being overwhelmed by others."

manipulative mother.[23] Before such a mother the child protects his inner life by withdrawing and learns to be secretive.

These and other experiences contribute in the story of the ennea-type V individual to a sense that it is better to go it alone in life, that people are not loving or that it is "bad business" to relate to others for what love they offer is manipulative and entails the expectation of receiving too much in exchange. Thus life is organized around not needing others and saving one's resources.

As is well known in connection with schizophrenia research, schizoid persons often have a schizoid parent. I know somebody in whom both parents were schizoid: "They formed a couple that was like a capsule, a world apart." She says, "I lacked nothing but I never knew what was happening at home. When I was little my mother jokingly answered when I called her, after not responding for a while:'I?, I am not your mother!' "

No less common, however, is the antecedent of a type VI parent. A young man with an ennea-type VI father and an ennea-type IV mother reports: "I felt a little caged in, the best was outside, my greatest interest has been to run away, to be far from my parents. I had a difficult time with my parents because they constrained me too much, and my solution was to escape inwardly. Even when I was able to move away outwardly I continued to do so.

"If I had learned to disappear or not be there or the idea of abandonment, I sometimes wonder if it started when the doctor abandoned me when I was to be born. The nurses said, he just left for lunch and they tied my mother's legs together. Another abandonment, maybe I learned from was, as a baby in the crib, my parents left the phone off the hook and they worked in a restaurant and they said, 'We listened sometimes to see if you were crying or not and then we'd come'."

As in the case of ennea-type VIII, ennea-type V seems to have given up in the search for love. To the extent that his dependency needs are only under control, however, he longs for a love that is expressed through the willingness to leave him alone, without demands, deception, or manipulation. The

---

[23]What used to be called a schizophrenogenic mother.

vehemence of the ideal militates—as in other instances—against its earthly realization.

6. Existential Psychodynamics

While it makes much sense to view the schizoid disposition as a withdrawal in the face of assumed lovelessness, and it is useful to take into account the fact that the sense of lovelessness continues to exist not only as a "phantom pain" but also as a result of the fact that his basic distrust leads him to invalidate the positive feelings of others towards him as manipulative—I think that a whole new therapeutic vista opens up when we take into account the repercussions of an emptiness which the individual inadvertently creates precisely through the attempt to fill it up. Thus we may say that it is not just mother love that the adult type V is needing right now, but true aliveness, the sense of existing, a plenitude that he sabotages moment after moment through the compulsive avoidance of life and relationship.

Thus it is not in receiving love that lies his greatest hope (particularly since he cannot trust other people's feelings) but in his own ability to love and relate.

Just as inwardness is animated by a thirst for enrichment and ends up in impoverishment, so also a misplaced search for being perpetuates ontic obscuration. The self-absorbed schizoid would remove himself away from the interfering world; yet in the act of thus removing himself, he also removes himself from himself.

An implicit assumption in ennea-type V is that being is to be found only beyond the realm of becoming: away from the body, away from the feelings, away from thinking itself. (And so it is—yet with a "but"; for it can only be perceived by one who is *not avoiding* the body, the feelings, and the mind).

While it is easy to understand grasping as a complication of ontic thirst, it may be well to dwell on how grasping is also—together with avoidance—at its source. The process is conveyed by the story of Midas, who in his wish for riches, wished that whatever he touched turned into gold. The unanticipated tragic consequences of his wish—the turning into gold of his daughter

—symbolizes, better than conceptual thinking alone can convey, the process by which reaching for the most valuable can entail a dehumanization—and reaching for the extraordinary, an impoverishment in the capacity to value the ordinary.

Chapter Three

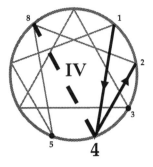

ENVY AND DEPRESSIVE MASOCHISTIC CHARACTER

ENNEA-TYPE IV

1. Core Theory, Nomenclature, and Place in the Enneagram

The emotional state of envy involves a painful sense of lack and a craving toward that which is felt lacking; the situation involves a sense of goodness as something outside oneself which needs to be incorporated.

Though an understandable reaction to early frustration and deprivation, envy constitutes a self-frustrating factor in the psyche, for the excessive craving for love that it entails never answers the chronic sense of inner scarcity and badness, but on the contrary, stimulates further frustration and pain.

Frustration is a natural consequence of envy. In addition, over-desiring can lead to painful situations as portrayed by Quevedo in his dream of hell, when he tells us that when the envious arrive there and see the different souls subjected to the various tortures of the hell realms, they are frustrated and suffer by seeing that there is no place reserved for them.[1]

The position of envy in the enneagram is that of a satellite to vanity and a neighbor to point 5, avarice, which entails a comparable sense of deprivation to envy, though it involves a different attitude in face of the experience of scarcity. While point 4 represents a forceful reaching out, an intense demand for that which is missed, point 5 is characterized by a psychic attitude of giving up the expectation of anything receiving from the outside and, rather, a concern about holding in one's energy, caring, and attention.

The connection with vanity is even more important than the one with avarice, since point 4 constitutes a member of the triad in the right corner of the enneagram, which, as a whole, gravitates around an excessive concern with the image of the self. While an ennea-type III person identifies with that part of the self that coincides with the idealized image, the ennea-type IV individual identifies with that part of the psyche that *fails* to fit the idealized image, and is always striving to achieve the unattainable. Here is a person animated by a vanity that fails to reach its goal because of the admixture of the sense of scarcity and worthlessness (of point 5).

Even though the ennea-types mapped at the positions 4 and 5 (envy and avarice) have in common the sense of worthlessness, guilt, and lack, and both may be described as depressed, they are in marked contrast in various regards. While guilt in envy is conscious torture, in avarice it is partially veiled over by a seeming moral indifference (that it shares with ennea-type VIII and constitutes a rebellion against its own excessive demands and accusations); while depression in envy manifests as overt grief, the avaricious often have trouble in crying or

---

[1]De Quevedo, Francisco,"Sueño del Infierno" in *Sueños y Discursos,* English translation in *Dreams and Discourses* (U.K.: Aris & Philips, 1989).

contacting their pain, so that their depression manifests, rather, as apathy and a sense of emptiness. It may be said that ennea-type V is a "dry" depression contrary to the "wet" depression of ennea-type IV: just as avarice is resigned, envy is passionate. In this is reflected a sharply differentiated feature: dry avarice is apathetic, wet envy, most intense; if the one is a desert, the other is a marsh. (The French use of *envie* to mean "desire" underscores the implicit observation that envy is the most passionate of passions.) While ennea-type V involves an internal atmosphere of quietness, ennea-type IV involves an atmosphere of turmoil and turbulence. The most characteristic aspect of ennea-type IV character besides envious motivation may be seen in the tendency to self-victimization and frustration.

Kernberg and others have rightly criticized DSM III for not taking account of the depressive, self-defeating, masochistic personality style. I am pleased to see that it has been brought in, at least tentatively, to the DSM III revision, for it surely constitutes one of the most common sources of interpersonal problems. Grumbling, lamenting, and the tendency to discontent on the other hand, have been observed since antiquity, while the masochistic pattern which was already described by Kurt Schneider, was rediscovered by Abraham in his observation of the oral-aggressive character and has been elaborated upon at length by Horney.

2. Antecedents in the Scientific Literature on Character

Though the masochistic and self-defeating personality syndrome was not acknowledged in DSM-III, this was the result of having included the tendency to depression that is so characteristic of such character among the mood disturbances. The recognition of a definite personality style surrounding depression is very old, however, and Schneider quotes

Kraepelin[2] as speaking of personalities in which there is a "constant emotional emphasis in the somber emotions involved in all the experiences of life." Schneider depicts a kind of person who is "pessimistic and skeptical and who, at bottom, denies life," and "yet surrounds it with a sort of unrequited love." "This is an over serious kind of person who is embittered and for whom everything is somewhat rotten.... All this is not necessarily obvious, however, for the melancholic individual is hidden...they may manifest joy and a hypomanic activity as a way of escaping sadness." Schneider quotes in this regard a poem of Hölderlin concerning jokers, in which he says "you are always playing and joking, you cannot help it friends, I am deeply touched because only the desperate are forced to do so." Also Schneider notices a tendency to vanity among the melancholic.

"Comparing themselves with those who live happily and knowing the simplicity characteristic of such people leads them to consider suffering something noble and to regard themselves rather in an aristocratic manner. Others see suffering as a merit, which together with their tendency to reflect and ponder bitterness of earthly life and the deep need for help, leads them to seek a philosophical or religious refuge." He notes too "an esthetic preoccupation among the melancholic which may be manifest in their way of dressing and living and can even lead to presumptuousness." Finally he draws a distinction between those depressive individuals that are properly melancholic (such as those that Kretschmer aligned among the cyclothymic and labeled as having "heavy blood") and others that are predominantly "ill-humoured": "they are cold and selfish, grumbling and hateful, irritable and critical, even mean and ill-intentioned. Their pessimism in face of all things and also in regard of their own fate has something fanatical about it. They almost rejoice at new failures, and neither do they desire anything good for others."

The ennea-type IV syndrome has been recognized since early in the history of psychiatry, as we can observe reading Kurt

---

[2]Kraepelin, E., *Die Psychopathischen Personlichkeiten* (Vienna: Franz Deuticke, 1950) quoted in K. Schneider, *Las Personalidades Psicopaticas* (Madrid: Ed. Morete, 1962).

Schneider's   volume   on   psychopathic   personalities.[3]
Summarizing German publications of before his time, he quotes,
for instance, the following observation on the "depressive
psychopath":

"At bottom he refuses life and still surrounds it by a sort
of unrequited love. Frequently, too, we see him develop a
tendency toward vanity, a comparison with those who are
contented and happy, the awareness of simplicity, even of the
excessive simplicity that often characterize these brings the
sufferers to deem suffering as something noble and themselves
as aristocratic...Others see in suffering a merit which is no
different from their tendency to reflect and to brood...Not rarely
one finds that in the environment and way of living there is an
aesthetic   preoccupation   that   can   convey   arrogance   and
dissimulates an inner despondency.   Other depressives are
rather in a bad mood, are cold and selfish, grumbling and
embittered, irritable and critical, cruel and ill intentioned. They
are pessimists in the face of everything and also in the face of
their own they almost cheer up when they meet new failures.
Neither do they desire anything good for others." Such character
has been designated by Kraepelin as "irritable predisposition"
and by Bleuler under "irritable dysthymia," designations that
also correspond to the eternally discontented and the resentful of
Aschaffenburg.[4]

In the history of psychoanalysis it was Karl Abraham
who first drew attention to the ennea-type IV syndrome in his
description of "oral aggressive character," as he sought to relate
character structure to vicissitudes in the unfoldment of the libido
corresponding to Freudian theory. Here is how Goldman-Eisler
describes the oral aggressive or oral pessimistic character in their
classical   investigation   of   "Breast   Feeding   and   Character
Formation":[5]

---

[3]op. cit.

[4]The syndrome described by Butler in his "Litigious Man" (i.e., a pathological
wish to punish others through justice) has also been known in European
psychiatry—where it has gone by the name of "querulous."

[5]Goldman-Eisler, Frieda, "Breastfeeding and Character Formation" in *Personality
in Nature, Society & Culture*, 1st ed., Clyde Kluckhohn & Henry A. Murray,
editors (New York: A.A.Knopf, 1948).

"This type is characterized by a profoundly pessimistic outlook on life, sometimes accompanied by moods of depression and attitudes of withdrawal, passive-receptive attitude, a feeling of insecurity, a need of assurance of getting one's livelihood guaranteed, an ambition which combines an intense desire to climb with a feeling of unattainability, a grudging feeling of injustice, sensitiveness to competition, a dislike of sharing and an impatient importunity." Edmund Bergler describes a similar syndrome which he calls "oral pessimism." He emphasizes its narcissistic aspect and interprets it as a compulsion to repeat the experience of the original frustration supposedly caused by the loss of mother's breast. In seeking to interpret this orientation of personality in line with Freud's idea of fixation, he believes that by being fixated to frustration the oral pessimist would derive pleasure from anticipating calamity and disappointment and this must give him satisfaction from being the victim.

It is curious to note that the concept of "masochistic character," introduced by Reich through a paper in the *International Journal for Psychoanalysis* (1932/33), makes no reference to the oral aggressive or oral-pessimistic syndrome—which suggests that Reich believed he was describing an independent character structure. The distinguishing mark of masochistic character is for him "a chronic subjective feeling of suffering which is manifested objectively and specially stands out as a tendency to complain. The most important additional trait is the 'chronic tendency' to inflict pain upon and to debase oneself."

The main thrust of Reich's paper was his controversy with Freud in regard to the existence of a death instinct—a controversy which motivated the publication of this paper together with a reply entitled "The Communist Discussion of Psychoanalysis." Though descriptively accurate, I think most of us today would disagree with both Freud and Reich's alternative to Freud's theory of masochistic behavior: "the specific masochistic inhibition of the orgasm function, which became manifest as a fear of dying or fear of bursting."

Among the theoreticians of psychology none has emphasized envy more than Melanie Klein, however. She tells us in *Envy and Gratitude*[6]:

"I arrived at the conclusion that envy is the most potent factor in undermining feelings of love and gratitude at their root, since it affects the earliest relation of all, that of the mother. The fundamental importance of this relation for the individual's whole emotional life has been substantiated in a number of psycho-analytic writings, and I think that by exploring further a particular factor that can be very disturbing at this early stage, I have added something of significance to my findings concerning infantile development and personality formation."

Essentially she shows how envy contributes to the infant's difficulties in building up his good object, for his frustration leads him to the perception of his mother as evil. Ms. Klein draws a distinction between envy and greed, that we may read as a differentiation of "lust" and "envy":

"Greed is an impetuous and insatiable craving, exceeding what the subject needs and what the object is able and willing to give. At the unconscious level, greed aims primarily at completely scooping out, sucking dry, and devouring the breast: that is to say, its aim is destructive introjection; whereas envy not only seeks to rob in this way, but also put a badness, primarily bad excrements and bad part of the self, into the mother, and first of all into her breast, in order to spoil and destroy her. In the deepest sense this means destroying her creativeness."

Whether we are willing to believe as Kleinians do that the child indeed fantasizes putting excrements into her mother or whether we perceive such a fantasy as one that the adult projects back onto the screen of childhood, we may regard her statements in the same way that we read a surrealist caricature, i.e., symbolically and phenomenologically.

Something similar may be said to the standard psychoanalytic statements concerning the oedipal situation: whether we take the sexual symbols literally or not, they contain an appropriate description of the relationship of the child with the parents:

---

[6]Klein, Melanie, *Envy and Gratitude* (London: Tavistock, 1957).

"Throughout this section I am speaking of the primary envy of the mother's breast, and this should be differentiated from its later forms (inherent in the girl's desire to take her mother's place and in the boy's feminine position) in which envy is no longer focused on the breast but on the mother receiving the father's penis, having babies inside her, giving birth to them, and being able to feed them."[7]

Penis envy is certainly a reality, if we take it to mean, metaphorically, an envy of masculine prerogatives, and occasionally, also literally—as part of a desire to identify with the privileged sex, even physically and also in view of a concomitant disidentification with a hated mother. Yet I am sure the basic issue is love, and only secondarily sex. Klein's more original contribution on the emphasis of the primitive nature of envy is her stress of envy as "a spoiling of the object."

While the masochistic pattern is widely recognized today among psychologically sophisticated laymen, this is not to be attributed so much to the influence of Melanie Klein (who failed to point out an envy-centered personality type) nor to Reich (for the word masochistic in bioenergetics has shifted in its original meaning and has come to designate our cyclothymic ennea-type IX) but, rather, to Eric Berne's *Games People Play* where it is echoed in the games labeled "Ain't it Awful," "Blamish," "Kick Me," and "Broken Skin." "Ain't it Awful," according to Berne, finds its most dramatic expression in "polysurgery addicts"[8]: "They are Doctor Shoppers, people who actively seek surgery even in the face of some medical opposition." Concerning this type of person he makes the same observation that Schneider records concerning his "depressive" psychopaths: "Overtly expresses distress but is covertly gratified at the prospect of the satisfaction he can bring from his misfortune."

Of "Kick Me" he says that " this is played by men whose social manner is equivalent to wearing a sign that reads 'Please don't kick me' up to 'My misfortunes are better than yours'."

---

[7]Klein, Melanie, op.cit.

[8]Berne, Eric,*Games People Play* (New York: Ballantine Books, 1985).

In Steiner's *Scripts People Play* I find a life pattern labeled "Poor Little Me," characterized by the role of a victim looking for a rescuer.[9] I quote some of the more original observations:

"She experiences some intimacy from her child ego state in relation to the Parent ego state of others, but rarely experienced intimacy as an equal. Because she has permission to be childlike she can be spontaneous in a childlike and helpless way and be inventive about acting 'crazy.' She learns she can get things more easily if she tells people about her troubles and thus she becomes invested in not giving up that self-image. She spends a lot of time complaining about how awful things are and trying to get others to do something about it. She keeps proving that she's a Victim by setting up situations in which she first manipulates people into doing things for her that they really don't want to do, then getting persecuted by them when they feel resentful towards her."

Otto Kernberg,[10] as I have already pointed out, draws attention to how depressive-masochistic personality is ignored by DSM III.[11] Here is his description:

"The person places himself or herself in situations that are self-defeating and have painful consequences even when better options are clearly available...Reasonable offers of assistance from others are rejected...The person's reaction to positive personal events may be depression or feelings of guilt...Characteristically, people with this disorder act in such a way as to cause others to be angry or to reject them... Opportunities for pleasure may be repeatedly avoided... The person frequently attempts to do things for others that require excessive self-sacrifice that engenders a sense of pride and enhances the subject's self-esteem."

Since people with a masochistic character typically perceive themselves as problem-ridden and seek help, one may wonder how they have been diagnosed thus far by DSM III users. I conjecture that many have been assigned to the

---

[9]Steiner, Claude H., *Scripts People Play* (New York: Bantam Books, 1985).

[10]Kernberg, Otto, in *Severe Personality Disorders: Psychotherapeutic Strategies* (New Haven: Yale University Press, 1984).

[11]In the revised version of DSM III a syndrome of "self-defeating personality disorder" is proposed among the categories needing further study.

"borderline personality disorder" category, for, in spite of the more general sense in which Kernberg proposes that we use the expression "borderline" (in reference to a level of psychopathology rather than a specific interpersonal style) the "borderline" diagnosis in practice is made in terms of ennea-type IV traits such as these: variability of mood, self-condemnation, impulsivity, rage, excessive dependency and tempestuous transference.[12]

Grinker's cluster analysis based on the borderline population sample further confirms the association of this diagnostic category with ennea-type IV for I can recognize in three of the resulting clusters the three subtypes of ennea-type IV in protoanalysis: the angry hateful, the shameful guilty, and the depressed.[13]

Describing borderlines, Millon[14] writes:

"Not only do they need protection and reassurance to maintain their equanimity, but they become inordinately vulnerable to separation from these external sources of support. Isolation or aloneness may be terrifying not only because borderlines lack an inherent sense of self but because they lack the wherewithal, the know-how, and equipment for taking mature, self-determined and independent action. Unable to fend adequately for themselves, they not only dread potential loss but often anticipate it, 'seeing it' happening, when, in fact, it is not. Moreover, since most borderlines devalue their self-worth, it is difficult for them to believe that those upon whom they depend could think well of them.

"Consequently, they are exceedingly fearful that others will depreciate them and cast them off. With so unstable a foundation of self-esteem, and lacking the means for an autonomous existence, borderlines remain constantly on edge, prone to the anxiety of separation and ripe for anticipating

---

[12]According to Perry and Klerman "the borderline term neither connotes nor communicates a behavioural pattern that portrays distinctive stylistic features." in "The Borderline Patient" in *Archives of General Psychiatry*, 35, pp. 141-150, 1978.

[13]Grinker, R.R., *The Borderline Syndrome* (New York: Basic Books, 1968). A fourth cluster clearly belongs to the squizoid and maybe attributable to the presence of ennea-type V individuals in the sample.

[14]op.cit.

inevitable desertion. Events that stir up these fears may precipitate extreme efforts at restitution such as idealization, self-abnegation, and attention-gaining acts of self-destruction or, conversely, self-assertion and impulsive anger."

The masochistic aspect of ennea-type IV is clearly portrayed in Millon's observation that by "sacrificing" themselves, borderlines "not only assure continued contact with others but serve as implicit models for others to be gentle and considerate in return. Virtuous martyrdom, rather than sacrifice, is a ploy of submissive devotion that strengthens the attachment borderlines need."

Of depression itself, he remarks that "...the pleading anguish, despair, and resignation voiced by borderlines serve to release tensions and to externalize the torment they feel within themselves. For some, however, depressive lethargy and sulking behavior are a means primarily of expressing anger. Depression serves as an instrument for them to frustrate and retaliate against those who have 'failed' them or 'demanded too much.' Angered by the 'inconsiderateness' of others, these borderlines employ their somber and melancholy sadness as a vehicle to 'get back' at them or 'teach them a lesson.' Moreover, by exaggerating their plight and by moping about helplessly, they effectively avoid responsibilities, place added burdens upon others, and thereby cause their families not only to take care of them but to suffer and feel guilty while doing so."

I think that the most insightful and articulate discussion of masochistic character in the literature thus far is that by Karen Horney—who, however, sometimes discusses the syndrome in terms of the over-generalization of "self-effacement." Here is what Horney's disciple Harold Kelman says of masochism in Wolman's *International Encyclopedia of Psychology*[15] :

"According to Horney masochism is neither a love for suffering for its own sake nor a biologically predetermined self negating process. It is a form of relating and its essence is the weakening or extinction of the individual self and merging with

---

[15]Mitchell, Arnold, and Harold Kelman, "Masochism: Horney's View" in *International Encyclopedia of Psychiatry, Psychology, Psychoanalysis, and Neurology*, Vol. 7, pp. 34-35, edited by Benjamin B. Wolman (New York: Van Nostrand / Reinhold, 1977).

a person or power believed to be greater than oneself." This observation corresponds with the self-shrinking aspect of envy, and an intense craving to absorb into oneself the values perceived in others, but also a willingness to suffer for this "love" or, more exactly said, love-need. The entry continues:

"Masochism is a way of coping with life through dependency and self minimizing. Though it is most obvious in the sexual area, it encompasses the total range of human relations. As part of a neurotic character development, masochism has its own special purposes and value system. The neurotic suffering may serve the defensive purposes of avoiding recriminations, competitions, and responsibility. It is a way of expressing accusations and vindictiveness in a disguised form. By exaggerating and inviting suffering, it justifies demands for affection, control and reparations. In the distorted value system of the masochism, suffering is raised to a virtue and serves as the basis for claims to love, acceptance and rewards. Since the masochist takes pride in and identifies with the self-effacing suffering, subdued self, an awareness of conflicting drives towards expansiveness and self-glorification as well as a healthy striving for growth would be destructive to his self-image. By abandoning himself to uncompromised hatred for the intolerable side of himself, the masochistic attempts to eliminate the conflict of contradictory impulses, thus a masochist has engulfed himself in self-hate and suffering."

In *Neurosis and Human Growth*, Karen Horney devotes a chapter to "Morbid Dependency," in which she begins by commenting upon the fact that among the three possible "solutions" to the basic conflict between approaching others, asserting oneself in a movement against them and withdrawing, the "self-effacing" one is the one that entails the greater subjective feelings of unhappiness than the others: "The genuine suffering of the self-effacing type may not be greater than in other kinds of neurosis, but subjectively he feels miserable more often and more intensely than others because of the many functions suffering has assumed for him. Besides his needs and expectations of others make for a too great dependency upon them. And, while every enforced dependency is painful, this one is particularly unfortunate because his relation to people cannot but be divided. Nevertheless love (still in its broad meaning) is the only thing that gives a positive content to his life.

"Erotic love lures this type as the supreme fulfillment. Love must and does appear as the ticket to paradise, where all woe ends: no more loneliness, no more feeling lost, guilty or unworthy; no more responsibility for self; no more struggle with a harsh world for which he feels hopelessly unequipped. Instead love seems to promise protection, support, affection, encouragement, sympathy, understanding. It will give him a feeling of worth, it will give meaning to his life, it will be salvation and redemption. No wonder then that for him people often are divided into haves and have-nots, not in terms of money and social status but of being (or not being) married or having an equivalent relationship."

Together with pointing out this "envy of love" she goes on to explain the significance given to love in terms of all that is expected from being loved and also remarks how psychiatric writers describing the love of dependent persons have put a one-sided emphasis on this aspect which they have called parasitic, sponging, or "oral erotic." "And this aspect may indeed be in the foreground. But for the typical self-effacing person (a person with prevailing self-effacing trends) the appeal is as much in loving as in being loved. To love for him, means to lose, to submerge himself in more or less ecstatic feelings, to merge with another being, to become one heart and one flesh, and in this merge to find a unity which he cannot find in himself."

Just as it was a surprise not to find a description of ennea-type IV in DSM III (before revision) it was surprising not to find it clearly echoed in Jung's psychological types. I would have assumed its characteristics to be found under the label of "the introverted feeling type," for a feeling type it certainly is, and the most introverted among them—as the proximity to ennea-type V indicates in the enneagram. Yet what Jung says of the introverted feeling type fits only very fragmentarily. It fits in that he states that "it is principally among women that I have found the predominance of introverted feeling," for the masochistic-depressive type is indeed most predominant among women. What also fits is Jung's important statement that "their temperament is inclined to melancholy." Yet most of Jung's statements are more appropriate to ennea-types V and IX rather than to ennea-type IV.[16]

Turning to Keirsey and Bates'[17] portraits of individuals according to testing results I find characteristics of ennea-type IV including in the two intuitive subtypes of introverted feeling, the INFJ and the INFP. INFJ's (in whom judgment predominates over perception) are described as having strong empathic abilities, particularly in regard to distresses or illness of others; as being vulnerable and prone to introjection; imaginative and able to create works of art, being "the most poetic of all the types." INFP people (with a predominance of perception over judgment) are described as having "capacity for caring" which is not always found in other types, as being idealistic and living a paradox: "drawn to purity and unity but looking over the shoulder toward the sullied and discreated."

The personality corresponding to our ennea-type IV in the homeopathic tradition is one said to have an affinity with *Natrum muriaticum*, common salt. I quote Catherine R. Coulter:[18]

"Even as an adult, he may forever harp on his parents' inadequacies or offenses...Yet, it is part of the nature's complexity and perversity to suffer inordinately from deprival of parental affection even when rejecting it. He thereby creates a 'no win' situation for his parents and himself... At times *Natrum muriaticum*'s pathology stems from early sibling rivalry....

"Thereafter, projecting his childhood experience onto the world at large, he will be quick to sense others' repressions, rejections, thwarted longings, and victimizations...The remedy is probably indicated if the physician is tempted to tell a 'forever remembering' patient belaboring past slights and offenses, 'Put that sorrow behind you....'

The practitioner may suspect *Natrum muriaticum* "of *seeking injury,* even if unconsciously, or at least of placing himself in a situation where injury can occur....

---

[16]"Their true motives remain hidden" fits the schizoid and also that they may be suspected of indifference or coldness. "The impression of pleasing response, or of sympathetic response" suggest ennea-type IX.

[17]op.cit.

[18]Coulter, Catherine R. , op.cit., Vol. 1, excerpts quoted by permission of the author from pp. 349-361.

"On the other hand, *Natrum muriaticum* can be his own worst enemy by allowing some specific emotional injury, or the cloud of depression constantly hanging over him, to be the lens through which he views reality. An apposite term for this distorting lens is 'bleakness,' implying, as it does, not only isolation, barrenness, and desolation, but also cheerlessness and discouragement ('sad and dejected': Hahnemann)...."

The *Natrum muriaticum* person may appreciate artistic beauty for its melancholy associations: "...at times he will turn to affecting music to indulge his bittersweet sorrow or voluptuously to reinforce some ancient (or recent) hurt... "Over and above everything else, there is *romantic love*! With its enormous potential for pain, disappointment, and sorrow, it is fated to catch *Natrum muriaticum* at his most vulnerable... Even if the love is requited, he may put himself into insoluble difficulties, courting relationships that will inevitably lead to grief."

Though the forceful *Lachesis* personality evokes the counter-phobic type VI, I think that its perfect match is the sexual type IV: "he is highly emotional—far more so than *Sulphur*, whose intellect clearly predominates. In fact, the intensity of feeling which *Phosphorus* tries to sustain is already present in *Lachesis*—who is often incapable of relinquishing it (the feeling possesses *him*, rather than he the feeling). Finally, the type is strongly given to sensual gratification... Without the calming effect of a normal sex life, deep depression may set in. The patient may exhibit manic behavior with sexual passion." Since it is easy to recognize Voltaire as an ennea-type IV, I find it of interest that Coulter gives him as an exemplar of a *Lachesis* personality.

3. Trait Structure

Envy

If we understand the essence of envy as an excessively intense desire for incorporation of the "good mother," the concept coincides with the psychoanalytic notion of a "cannibalistic impulse" which may manifest not only as a love hunger, but as a more generalized voraciousness or greediness.

Though a guilty and controlled greed is part of type IV psychology, it is no greater than the exploitative and uninhibited greed of type VIII, and not so peculiar to envious characters as is envy in Melanie Klein's conception:[19]

"Greed is an impetuous and insatiable craving, exceeding what the subject needs and what the object is able and willing to give. At the unconscious level, greed aims primarily at completely scooping out, sucking dry, and devouring the breast: that is to say, its aim is destructive introjection; whereas envy not only seeks to rob in this way, but also put a badness, primarily bad excrements and bad part of the self, into the mother, and first of all into her breast, in order to spoil and destroy her. In the deepest sense this means destroying her creativeness."

Whether we agree or not with Klein in regard to the envious fantasies that she attributes to the infant at the breast, I think that it is reasonable to take them as a symbolic expression of experiences in the adult—and, more particularly, the characteristic process of self-frustration that seems inseparable from envy, as the ongoing basis of its over-desiring characteristic. Whatever the truth about the beginnings of envy during breastfeeding, too, in the experience of many envy is not consciously experienced in connection with the mother but toward a preferred sibling, so that the individual has sought to be her or him rather than himself in the pursuit of parental love. Often there is an element of sexual envy that Freud observed in women and—from the point of view of his sexual and biological interpretation—branded as "penis envy." Since envy of women is also experienced by some men in distinctly erotic terms we might also speak of "vagina envy"—though I am of the opinion that sexual fantasies are derivative from a more basic phenomenon of gender-envy involving a sense of the superiority of the other sex. Given the patriarchal bias of our civilization it is no wonder that envy of the male is more common (and, indeed, ennea-type IV women loom large in the liberation movement) but both forms of sexual envy are striking in the case of the counter-sexual identification underlying homosexuality and

---

[19]*Envy and Gratitude* (London: Tavistock, 1957).

lesbianism (both of them more frequent in type IV than in any other character).

Another realm of expression of envy is social, and can manifest both as an idealization of the upper classes and a strong social climbing drive, as Proust has portrayed so masterfully throughout the first volumes of *Remembrance of Things Past*. Still more subtly, envy can manifest as an ever present pursuit of the extraordinary and the intense, along with the corresponding dissatisfaction with the ordinary and non dramatic.

A primitive pathological manifestation of the same disposition is the symptom of bulimia, which I have observed to exist in the context of type IV character; many people experience a subtle echo of that condition: occasional feelings of painful emptiness at the pit of the stomach.

Whereas avarice and, most characteristically, anger are hidden traits in the personality syndromes of which they are part (since they have been compensated by pathological detachment and reactive traits of benignity and dignity, respectively) in the case of envy the passion itself is apparent, and the person thus suffers from the contradiction between an extreme neediness and the taboo against it. Also in light of this clash between the perception of intense envy and the corresponding sense of shamefulness and vileness in being envious we can understand the "bad image" trait discussed below.

Poor Self-image

The most striking of traits from the point of view of the number of descriptors in it is that which conveys a poor self-concept. Included among the specific characteristics are not only "poor self-image" itself, but others such as "feeling inadequate," "prone to shame," "sense of ridicule," "feeling unintelligent," "ugly," "repulsive," "rotten," "poisonous" and so on. Even though I have chosen to speak of "bad self-image" as a separately (thus echoing the appearance of an independent conceptual cluster of descriptors) it is impossible to dissociate the phenomenon of envy from this bad self-image, which object relations theorists interpret as the consequence of the introjection of a "bad object."

It is such self-denigration that creates the "hole" out of which arises the voracity of envy proper in its clinging, demanding, biting, dependent, overattached manifestations.

Focus on suffering

I still have not commented upon the cluster of traits usually designated by the label "masochistic." In the understanding of these we should invoke, beyond the suffering that arises through a bad self-image, and the frustration of exaggerated neediness, the use of pain as vindictiveness and an unconscious hope of obtaining love through suffering. Ennea-type IV individuals, as a result of these dynamic factors and also of a basic emotional disposition are not only sensitive, intense, passionate, and romantic, but tend to suffer from loneliness and may harbor a tragic sense of their life or life in general.

Possessed of a deep longing, dominated by nostalgia, intimately forlorn and sometimes visibly liquid-eyed and languorous, they are usually pessimistic, often bitter and sometimes cynical. Associated traits are lamenting, complaining, despondent, and self-pitying . Of particular prominence in the painful landscape of type IV psychology is what has to do with the feeling of loss, usually the echo of real experiences of loss and deprivation, sometimes present as a fear of future loss and particularly manifest as a proneness to suffering intensely from the separations and frustrations of life. Particularly striking is the propensity of type IV to the mourning response, not only in relation to persons but also pets. It is in this cluster, I think, that we are closest to the core of the character type, and particularly in the maneuver that it entails of focusing upon and expressing suffering to obtain love.

Just as it is a functional aspect of crying, in the human infant, to attract mother's protective care, I think the experience of crying contains that of seeking attention. Just as ennea-type III children learn to shine to get attention (and those who will develop the type V or type VIII character, hopeless about ever getting it, prefer the way of withdrawal or the way of power), here the individual learns to get "negative" attention through the intensification of need—which operates not only in a histrionic manner (through the imaginative amplification of suffering and the amplification of the expression of suffering), but also through walking into painful situations—i.e., through a painful life course. Crying may be, indeed, not only a pain, but a satisfaction for a type IV individual. It remains to say that (as the word "masochistic" brings to mind), there can be a sad sweetness in suffering. It feels real, though it is also the opposite—for the main self-deception in ennea-type IV is exaggerating a position of victimization, which goes hand-in-hand with their "claiming," demanding disposition.[20]

"Moving Toward"

More than those of any other character, ennea-type IV individuals can be called "love addicted," and their craving for love is in turn supported by a need of the acknowledgment that they are unable to give themselves. "Dependency"—its corollary —can manifest not only as a clinging to relationships that are frustrating, but as an adhesiveness—a subtle imposition of contact which seems the outcome of not only a contact need, but an anticipated defense or postponement of separation. Related to the craving for care is also the commonly observed "helplessness" of type IV individuals, which, as in type V, manifests as a motivational inability to care properly for themselves and may be interpreted as an unconscious maneuver to attract protection. The need for financial protection, specifically, may be supported by the desire to feel cared for.

Nurturance

Ennea-type IV people are usually considered thoughtful, understanding, apologetic, soft, gentle, cordial, self-sacrificing, humble, sometimes obsequious. Their nurturant quality not only appears to constitute a form of "giving to get," i.e., dependent on

---

[20]Arietti, Sylvano, "Affective Disorders" in *American Handbook of Psychiatry*, Volume III, S. Arietti, Editor-in-Chief (New York: Basic Books, 1974). Arietti has proposed precisely this expression "claiming" for the most common personality background of neurotic depression (in contrast to that of psychotic depression,which we will discuss in connection to ennea-type IX).

the love need alone, but on an empathic identification with the needs of others that causes them to be concerned parents, empathetic social workers, attentive psychotherapists, and fighters for the underdog. The nurturant characteristic of type IV can be dynamically understood as a form of seduction in the service of the intense need of the other and its painful frustration. Caring for others may be masochistically exaggerated to a point of self-enslavement, and contributes thus to the self-frustration and pain that in turn activates the demanding and litigious aspects of the character.

Emotionality

The word "emotional," though implicit in a high level of suffering, deserves to be placed by itself in view of the determining contribution of feeling-dominance to the structure of ennea-type IV character. We are in the presence of an "emotional type," just as in the case of ennea-type II, only here with a greater admixture of intellectual interests and introversion. (Indeed, these are the two kinds of character most properly regarded as emotional, for the word applies to them more exactly than in the case of the cheerful and helpful seductiveness of gluttons, and the defensive warmth of the more outwardly fearful and dependent cowards.) The quality of intense emotionality applies not only to the romantic feelings, the dramatization of suffering, and to the love-addicted and nurturant characteristics, but also to the expression of anger. Envious people feel hate intensely, and their screams are the most impressive. Also found in ennea-types II and III, at the right corner of the enneagram, is that quality that psychiatry has called "plasticity" in reference to a capacity to role-play (related to the capacity to modulate the expression of feelings).

Competitive Arrogance

Connected to a hateful emotionality, an attitude of superiority sometimes exists along with—and in compensation for—a bad self-image. Though the individual may seethe in self-deprecation and self-hate, the attitude to the outer world is in this case that of a "prima-donna" or at least a very special person. When this claim of specialness is frustrated it may be complicated by a victimized role of "misunderstood genius." In line with this development, individuals also develop traits of wit, interesting conversation, and others in which a natural disposition towards imaginativeness, analysis, or emotional depth (for instance) are secondarily put to the service of the contact need and the desire to summon admiration.

Refinement

An inclination to refinement (and the corresponding aversion to grossness) is manifest in descriptors such as "stylish," "delicate," "elegant," "tasteful," "artistic," "sensitive," and sometimes "arty" and "affected," "mannered" and "posturing." They may be understood as efforts on the part of the person to compensate for a poor self-image (so that an ugly self-image and the refined self-ideal may be seen as reciprocally supporting each other); also, they convey the attempt on the part of the person to be something different from what he or she is, perhaps connected to class envy. The lack of originality entailed by such imitativeness in turn perpetuates an envy of originality—just as the attempt to imitate original individuals and the wish to emulate spontaneity are doomed to fail.

Artistic Interests

The characteristic inclination of ennea-type IV towards the arts is over-determined: at least one of its roots lies in the refined characteristic of envious character. It is supported too, by the feeling-centered disposition of the type. Other components are the possibility of idealizing pain through art and even transmuting it—to the extent that it becomes an element in the configuration of beauty.

Strong Superego

Refinement is perhaps the most characteristic of ways in which ennea-type IV seeks to be better than he or she is, and in doing so exercises discipline. More generally there is a typically strong superego that the type IV character shares with type I, but on the whole, type IV is more keenly aware of his or her standards and his or her ego ideal is more aesthetic than ethical. Along with discipline (which may reach a masochistic degree) the superego characteristic of ennea-type IV involves descriptors of tenacity and of being rule-oriented. Love of ceremony reflects both the aesthetic-refined and the rule-oriented characteristics. A strong super ego is, of course, involved in the guilt propensity of ennea-type IV, in its shame, self-hate, and self-denigration.

4. Defense Mechanisms

In my experience the dominant defense mechanism in ennea-type IV is distinctly introjection, the operation of which becomes apparent through a consideration of the character structure itself. We may say that the bad self-image of type IV is the direct expression of an introjected self-rejecting parent and that an envious neediness results from the chronic self-hate entailed by such introject—the need of external approval and love being in the nature of a need to compensate for the inability to love oneself.

The concept of introjection was introduced by Ferenczi in "Introjection and Transference."[21] The concept was taken up by Freud in his analysis of the mourning process (in "Mourning and Melancholia") where he observes that the individual reacts to the loss of love by becoming like the loved one (as if saying to the dead loved one: I don't need you, I now have you inside myself).

While in Ferenczi and Freud the emphasis lies in the idea of bringing into oneself a "good object," it was Melanie Klein who stressed the importance of bad introjects. In these cases it is as if the person—driven by an excessive love need—wanted to

---

[21]Ferenczi, S., *First Contributions to Psycho-Analysis* (London: Hogarth Press, 1952). Where he writes "whereas the paranoid expels from his ego the impulse that has become unpleasant, the neurotic helps himself by taking into the ego as large as possible a part of the outside world..."

bring a parental figure into the self at all costs (i.e. "masochistically").

In connection with the subject of introjection it may be useful to point out that Freud frequently used the terms "introjection" and "incorporation" without differentiating their meanings. In present usage "incorporation" retains the meaning of a fantasy of bringing a person into one's body while in "introjection" the notion is more abstract, so that in speaking of "introjection into the ego," for instance, there is no particular reference to body boundaries. The word "internalization" is also used in the same sense as "introjection" sometimes, though it may be more proper to retain it to indicate the transposing of a relationship from the outer world to the inner.

Even in this case, however, its operation goes hand in hand with introjection. As Laplanche and Pontalis[22] observe, "we may say that ... with the decline of the oedipal complex the subject introjects the parental image while internalizing the conflict of authority with the father." In similar fashion and more specifically (in connection with our topic) we may say that ennea-type IV internalizes parental rejection or introjects an unloving parent, and thus brings into his psyche a constellation of traits ranging from a bad self-concept to the pursuit of special distinction and involving chronic suffering and a (compensatory) dependency on external acknowledgment.

Though Melanie Klein gives much importance to projection in the mechanism of envy (as in the paradigmatic fantasy of putting excrements in mother's breast), I think that the process through which in type IV "familiarity breeds contempt" (and through which the available is never as desirable as the unavailable) is more like an "infection" in virtue of which self-denigration extends to those, who, through intimacy, have come to partake to some extent of a "self-quality." Unlike the situation of projection, in which something is "spit out" of the psyche as a means of not acknowledging its presence, in this situation there is no disavowal of personal characteristics, but the manifestation of the fact that the sense of self—which is never fixed (but, as Perls proposed, an "identity function")—seems in the more

---

[22]Leplanche, J., and J.-B. Pontalis, *The Language of Psychoanalysis* (New York: W.W. Norton & Co.,1973).

dependent personalities to extend furthest into the world of intimate relationships.

Also striking in type IV psychology (particularly as it is manifested in the therapeutic process) is the mechanism that Psychoanalysis calls "turning against the self" (roughly the same mechanism that Perls calls "retroflection"). While self-hating or self-rejection is implicit in the notion of an introjected "bad-object," the idea of retroflection invites the thought that anger generated in consequence of frustration is aimed not only at the outer source of frustration (and to the original frustrator in one's life) but also—in consequence of its introjection—at oneself.

It remains to consider aside from a dominant defense mechanism the existence of a dominant content of repression in type IV, a content to the repression of which introjection may be most specifically suitable. I think that it may be said that the most avoided attitude for type IV is that of demanding superiority which is so natural in type I. In light of this, introjection is a mechanism that makes it possible for the person to transform superiority into inferiority as he adopts the masochistic strategy in interpersonal relationships. It is as if the introject were a stone tied to the person's feet to make sure that he sinks—at the same time maintaining a position of neediness and avoiding a superiority that might have been dysfunctional through early childhood adaptation.

Demandingness will survive the transition from ennea-type I to ennea-type IV, yet the sense of justice in demanding at the time of shift will turn into an association of claiming with guilt (which perpetuates the position of inferiority). As in other cases, the dynamic represented by the enneagram structure signifies not only the repression of one emotion (anger), but its transformation into the next (envy)—for in envy, through the intensification of oral strivings, the individual seeks to satisfy the same needs that in the type I approach are satisfied through assertive demanding.

5. Etiological and Further Psychodynamic Remarks[23]

Constitutionally ennea-type IV is most often ectomesomorphic in body build—neither as high in ectomorphia as type V nor as mesomorphic as type III—though occasionally they may be of more rounded contours in body build, particularly with aging and among men. The over-sensitivity and the measure of withdrawnness characteristic of type IV is thus consistent with the cerebrotonia that is the counterpart of ectomorphia. The plasticity or dramatic ability of type IV (which it shares with the other characters in the hysteroid corner of the enneagram) may also correspond to a constitutional endowment. Though congenital defects may support a sense of inferiority (just as it is said that the limp are envious) more commonly stature or the lack of physical beauty have a part. Of course, however, some type IV women are outstandingly beautiful and the source of envy is found in environmental sources of deprivation and injury to self-esteem.

It is pertinent to quote here the famous Frieda Goldman-Eisler[24] study, showing a correlation between oral-aggressive tendencies and problematic breast feeding. This correlation has been usually understood as a confirmation of the idea that insufficient breast feeding lingers as adult pain, yet it is possible to think that it may also reflect the fact that a child constitutionally endowed with a greater oral aggressiveness, (i.e. a tendency to bite the nipple) displeases its mother, which may contribute to the interruption of breast feeding. Beyond what it

---

[23]Stuart S.Asch writing on the masochistic personality in Cooper, Arnold M., Allen J. Frances, and Michael Sacks' *Psychiatry, Vol. I, The Personality Disorder and Neurosis* (New York: Basic Books, 1990), begins by stating that "despite the multiplicity of explanations that have been suggested the etiology of masochistic personalities is basically unknown." Among the suggestive data that he quotes, it is of interest to draw attention to some work with imprinting in chicks that had shown that "painful stimuli presented during the critical first 18 hours of life establish a more rapid and more firmly entrenched attachment to the parent object than occurs in controls." He quotes Berliner stating that "the masochist insists on being loved by the punishing person because it may be the only kind of intimacy he has known." Yet adds that "it is uncommon to find a history of severely punitive parents in the childhood of the moral masochist."

[24]Goldman-Eisler, Frieda, op. cit.

literally proves, it may be viewed as paradigmatic of a more general relationship between childhood frustration and adult discontent. Indeed, later psychoanalysis has emphasized a frustration in maternal affection at a later stage, after the "rapprochement" stage of establishing an early bonding with her. This accounts for a "paradise lost" quality to the experience of type IV individuals. Unlike the apathetic type V individual, who does not know what he has missed, the type IV person remembers it very well at an emotional level—if not necessarily through reminiscences.

Occasionally an intense experience of abandonment was not matched by an obvious external fact, but has been subtle enough not to be perceived by others and may be forgotten until it is recovered in the course of psychotherapy. More than abandonment, we see in these cases events in which the child was disillusioned in regard to a parent, moments of discovery that the parent has never been there for him or her. As for instance in the following passage from an interview: "I wanted to be a tap dancer, I was seven, eight years old and that was the rage. And I can remember we had very little money. We had just come to New York and we had lost everything in the depression and my mother had saved up, and saved up, and saved up. And anyhow I was going to get this one day the dancing shoes, the tap dancing shoes and the leotard and my father was going to lower side New York, East side, to get an inexpensive one and I can remember all that day, I was just, Oh! talk about being on the heights of the world, the top of the world and that evening coming up the stairs, I remember my mother went toward the door and I was with her and the door opened and he had nothing with him. He had nothing with him. He did not have a package with him. And so mom, I mean this was all I was talking about for ages, and mom went to him and said well where is, you know where is Monica's shoes. And he looked at her and at that moment he didn't remember. I don't know if he didn't remember or what, but he said, 'Oh,' he said, 'I fell asleep and I left it on the subway.' And it was just awful. I think with that it was always like, you know, you're worthless."

The typical life history of type IV is painful, and it is often apparent that the causes for pain were unusually striking, so it is clear that painful memories are not only a consequence of claiming attitude or tendency to dramatize pain. Beyond the cases of rejection, I have encountered some instances where there was a loss of a parent or other family members. I have noticed how frequent the experience of being ridiculed or scorned by parents or siblings has been. Sometimes poverty contributed to the painful situation of all, and other times a cultural or national difference between the family of origin and its environment contributed to a generalized sense of shame.

In the following illustration various sources of pain converge: "I grew up on an ethnic street. My mom and dad were Slovak, and everybody on the street spoke Slovak, and we had our own little variety store, and the kids played together. So it was very strange for me to go to school, to an English School and then come home and be in an altogether different environment, in a different culture. And my sister-in-law who married my brother, she's English, and she says that she was told never to go down to Water Street, because that's where all "those kids" were, you know, that you don't associate with and always kind of had that sense when I was growing up that I was very different. What I'd like to comment on is the abandonment by mom, and that was in a couple, three other cases. When dad was in a rage, mother would back down. When some change was needed, like when we needed to move our home. Or to get him to find a job, she was the dominant one, but when he became very violent and abusive—and he was violent—then she would back down and would sort of stand in the background and say don't do it, but even not that,.... Once when there was a great deal of violence, I don't even remember her taking care of me afterwards. I didn't feel abandoned by my mother physically. She was there and I felt used by her to king of maybe fill her needs. My dad went off to war, and she would dress me up and pretty me up and carry me around, and I was the first child and the first girl and the first grandchild on my dad's side, and grandmother took care of me a lot when mom was busy later in the store after we moved from my grandmother's house, but my mom took me to her mother's house when I was two months old, we were already traveling on the train back and forth. And I've done a lot of traveling and movement back and forth all my life. Maybe I, has a connection with my inner movement, I'm always going, I don't know. The other thing I wanted to, well, the being used, used in all the roles

—victim and scapegoat and every family member practically and then feeling used in my relationships after a time whenever I would go through feeling very pleasured and filled and fulfilled, there would come a point where all of a sudden I felt used. And I would just kind of like drop off and stop everything and a lot of fear in that too. I don't know why the feeling used and the fear would come in there together.

Besides ethnic background, the presence of alcoholism or other social disgraces may have inspired a feeling of not having a normal family and become a source of envy. A daughter of poor parents says, for instance: "I felt envy towards a girl who attended school in a uniform."

The experience of siblings is, of course, a common factor in that of early envy. Thus a young man says: "I was the fifth among seven, I was neither with the older ones nor with the little ones. I felt alone without a place."

Another man says: "I was a boy among four girls. My mother didn't touch me very much, so as to avoid making me 'soft', so that I wouldn't be like the girls, but at the same time there was a message of 'don't be like your father'. I strongly felt a lack of warmth and shame." Still another says: "I have been the eldest among my brothers and all went well until others appeared and then I entered in a dynamic of incessant competition with much complaining." Still another says: "I wept a lot, I felt the competition of my brother who studies much and was an athlete. I sought refuge in books and identified with those I read."

Particularly striking in the early history of ennea-type IV women is the frequent occurrence of a more or less incestuous relationship with the father, or sexual abuse by another male relative.[25] For some this experience has not been problematic ("I miss the physical contact I used to have with my father."). For others it caused difficulty with the parent of the same sex. Still others remember it with disgust or guilt. The following situation is surely not unique: "I loved my father, he made me feel a happy woman, but he ridiculed me and rejected me later."

---

[25] I became aware of this reflecting on the personality of women raped by their father in my past psychotherapeutic experience.

Most ennea-type IV individuals answer "yes" to the question whether did they receive more attention and care through suffering and needing. "Pleasure was forbidden" says one, "a reasonable cause was the best incentive." Another observes: "They didn't pay any attention if my whipping was unfounded," another pointed out that she has always played the victim to get attention, but she usually did not succeed and was rejected instead.

It is clear that occasionally a type IV child was not conscious of suffering until puberty or suffered secretly. So one answered to the question above "yes and no—no because it was a silent suffering and few people saw it; yes because my body and my face expressed it and that attracted attention." Of course it is not uncommon for the parents to react differently to the child's need: "My mother had compassion and received suffering well, even though not always she paid attention to me when I wept. My brother ridiculed crying." Occasionally it is possible to discern an element of seduction in being sick, in that the mother liked the role of nurse: "My mother liked to take care of me when I was sick, and in that way she dominated me."

It is quite common for "self-defeating" women to have had a mother of the same character along with a weak father. Also I have noticed more sadistic fathers (ennea-type VIII) in the histories of type IV's than any other except for type VIII itself. In such instances, of course, the sado-masochistic relation with the parent of the opposite sex contributed to the crystallization of the overall personality style.

On the whole we may say that the suffering individual inwardly cultivates his pain, as those beggars in Oriental countries who cultivate their wounds. While type I seeks to be good and claims his due in the name of justice, type IV only claims in the name of pain and unfulfilled need. If the pursuit of love in type I becomes a pursuit of respect, in the self-defeating type it becomes to some extent an implicitly dependent pursuit of care and empathy.[26]

---

[26] The sexual sub-type of an ennea-type IV character introduces a complexity into discussion, since it develops a striking need to be special, which can in turn manifest as a measure of arrogant vindictiveness.

6. Existential Psychodynamics

While we have good reason to believe that the pattern of envy originates in frustration of the child's early attachment needs and we may understand the chronic pain in this character as a residue of the pain of the past, it is useful to consider that it may also be a trap for ennea-type IV individuals to get stuck in lamenting over the past. Also, while it is very true that it was love that the child needed urgently and sought, the exaggerated and compulsive search for love *in the present* may be regarded as a disfunction and only a mirage or approximate interpretation of what the adult is in dire need of. This, rather than outer support, acknowledgment, and care, is the ability to acknowledge, support, and love him- or herself; and also the development of a sense of self as center that might counteract the "ex-centric" expectation of goodness from the outside.

We may envision type IV psychology precisely from the point of view of an impoverishment of being or selfhood that envy seeks to "fill up" and which is, in turn, perpetuated through self-denigration, though the search for being through love and through the emulation of others. ("I am like Einstein, therefore I exist"). The type IV psyche functions as if it had concluded early in life "I am loved therefore I am not worthless" and now pursues worthiness through the love that was once missing (love me so I know I am all right) ,and through a process of self-refining distortion—through the pursuit of something different and presumably better and nobler than what he or she is.

These processes are self-frustrating, for love, once obtained, is likely to be invalidated ("he cannot be worthwhile if he loves me") or, having stimulated neurotic claims, leads to frustration and also invalidation on that basis; yet, more basically, the pursuit of being through the emulation of the self-ideal stands on a basis of self-rejection and of blindness to the value of one's true self (just as the pursuit of the extraordinary involves denigration of the ordinary). Because of this, type IV needs, in addition to insight into these traps, and more than any other character, the development of self-support: the self-support that comes, ultimately, from appreciative awareness and the sense of dignity of self and of life in all of its forms.

There is a pathology of values entailed in envy that may be explained in light of the metaphor (which I find in the Arcipreste de Hita's *Book Of Good Love*)[27] of a dog who carries a bone and who, believing his reflection upon a pool to be another dog with a more desirable bone, opens his jaws as he lunges for it, losing in the process the bone he has. We may say: the reflection of a bone has no "being," just as there is no being in either idealized or deprecated self-images.

---

[27] *Libro de Buen Amor*, ed. by Maria Brey Mariño (Madrid: Editorial Castalia, 1982).

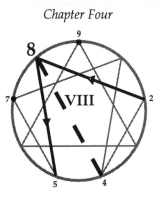

Chapter Four

SADISTIC CHARACTER AND LUST

ENNEA-TYPE VIII

1. Core Theory, Nomenclature, and Place in the Enneagram

The Spanish dictionary from the Spanish Royal Academy—where I dictate this chapter—says concerning lust that it is a "vice consisting in the illicit use or disordered appetite for carnal pleasures," and gives the additional meaning of "excess in certain things."

It is the latter definition which coincides with the meaning given to the term by Ichazo in his exposition of Protoanalysis, and we may view the former., i.e. the more common sense of the term., as its derivative or corollary. I will therefore use the word "lust" to denote a passion for excess, a passion that seeks intensity, not only through sex, but in all manner of stimulation: activity, anxiety, spices, high speed, the pleasure of loud music, and so on.

Lust is mapped in the enneagram next to the upper vertex of the inner triangle, which indicates a kinship to indolence, to a sensory-motor disposition, and the predominance of cognitive obscuration or "ignorance" over "aversion" and "craving" (at the left and right corners respectively). The indolent aspect of the lusty may be under-stood not only as a feeling of not-alive-enough-except-through-over-stimulation but also in a concomitant avoidance of inwardness. We may say that the greed for ever more aliveness, characteristic of the lusty personality, is but an attempt to compensate for a hidden lack of aliveness.

Opposite to envy on the enneagram, lust may be said to constitute the upper pole of a sado-masochistic axis. The two personalities, VIII and IV, are in some ways opposites (as these terms suggest), though also similar in some regards, such as in the thirst for intensity. Also, just as a masochistic character is in some ways sadistic, there is a masochistic aspect in the character of lust; and while a sadistic character is active, a masochistic disposition is emotional: the former reaches out without guilt towards the satisfaction of its need; the latter yearns and feels guilty about its neediness.

Just as the envy-centered character is the most sensitive in the enneagram, ennea-type VIII is the most *in*sensitive. We may envision the passion for intensity of ennea-type VIII as an attempt to seek through action the intensity that ennea-type IV achieves through emotional sensitivity, which here is not only veiled over by the basic indolence that this ennea-type shares with the upper triad of the enneagram but also by a desensiti-zation in the service of counter-dependent self-sufficiency.

The characterological syndrome of lust is related to that of gluttony in that both are characterized by impulsiveness and hedonism. In the case of gluttony, however, impulsiveness and hedonism exist in the context of a weak, soft and tender-minded characterological context, while in lust the context is that of a strong and tough-minded character.[1] As usual, the character

---

[1] The connection between gluttony and lust has been observed long ago, it seems, for we may read in Chaucer's, "The Parson's Tale" (op.cit.): "After gluttony, then comes lechery; for these two sins are such close cousins that oftentimes they will not be separated."

stands in polar opposition to each of those connected with it by the inner flow of the enneagram: just as ennea-type II is over-feminine and sensitive, ennea-type VIII is over-masculine and insensitive; and just as ennea-type V is intra-punitive and shy, ennea-type VIII is extra-punitive and bold. In each case the transition from one to the other can be understoood at the same time as a defense and a transformation of psychic energy.

The anti-social personality disorder described in DSM-III may be regarded as a pathological extreme and a special instance of ennea-type VIII. The broader syndrome may be better evoked through Reich's label of "phallic narcissistic"[2] character or Horney's description of the vindictive personality. The word "sadistic" seems particularly appropriate in view of its position opposite the masochistic character of ennea-type IV.

2. Antecedents in the Scientific Literature on Character

As we turn from literature to the observation of character in Psychiatry and Psychology, we find that the personality we are considering corresponds to that designated by Kurt Schneider[3] as "explosive" (preferring this term to Kraepelin's earlier expression "excitable"). Of these "explosive psychopaths" he tells us that they are disobedient and defiant and that they are very well known in life and in clinical experience, those who "at the least provocation become enraged or even violent without any consideration; a reaction that has been appropriately called a short-cut reaction."

In a similar vein, Scholtz[4] describes a "moral anesthesia" of people "who know the moral laws perfectly well, but don't feel them and because of this, do not subordinate their behavior to them."

---

[2]Quoted in Erich Fromm, *Man for Himself: An Inquiry Into the Psychology of Ethics* (New York: Holt, Rinehart and Winston, 1964).

[3]op. cit.

[4]Scholtz, F., *Die Morelische Anästhesie* (Leipzig: 1904).

In tracing the history of "the aggressive pattern" of personality, Millon[5] points out that "toward the end of the XIXth century, German psychiatrists turned their attention away from the value-laden theories of the English alienists and toward what they judged to be observational research." And at this time Koch proposed replacing the label "moral insanity" by "psychopathic inferiority." Still this label reflected the belief of a physical basis for the syndrome. It had been already Kraepelin's opinion in the second edition of his major work,[6] that "the 'morally insane' suffer congenital defects in their ability   to restrain the gratification of their immediate desires." By the fifth edition he changed the name to "psychopathic states" and by the eighth described psychopaths as deficient in either affect or volition. Among the personality peculiarities of these he listed subtypes: the excitable, the unstable, the impulsive, the eccentric, the liars and swindlers, the anti-social and the quarrelsome.

Millon also reports that it was Birnbaum, who (in 1914), writing in Germany at the time of Kraepelin's final edition, was the first to suggest that "sociopathic" might be a more appropriate term for the majority of these cases. One of the most insightful pictures of the "psychopaths" or "sociopaths" has been from Cleckley,[7] who counts among the main traits in this syndrome guiltlessness, incapacity for object love, impulsivity, emotional shallowness, superficial social charm, and inability to profit from experience.

As Millon points out, Cleckley's contribution was significant in drawing attention to the fact that antisocial personalities are found not only in prisons, but in mainstream society "where tough hard-headed 'realism' is admired as an attribute necessary for survival." In spite of this observation, I don't see that anybody has pointed out the identity of the syndrome in question with Reich's "phallic narcissistic" personality to which I turn now.

Reich's description was first presented at the Vienna Psychoanalytic society in 1926 and was later included in his

---

[5]op. cit.

[6]Kraepelin, E., *Psychiatrie: Ein Lehrbuch* , 2nd.ed. (Leipzig: Barth, 1887).

[7]Cleckley, H., *The Mask of Sanity* (St.Louis: Mosby, 1941).

Character Analysis. He observes that in terms of physique this character is predominantly athletic, "hardly ever an aesthenic type," while his behavior is never cringing, but usually arrogant, either coldly reserved or contemptuously aggressive. The "narcissistic element, stands out in the attitude towards the object, including the love object, and is always infused with more or less concealed sadistic characteristics."

"In everyday life, the phallic narcissistic character will usually anticipate any impending attack with an attack of his own. The aggression in his character is expressed less in what he does and says than in the way he acts. Particularly he is felt to be totally aggressive and provocative by those who are not in control of their own aggression. The most pronounced types tend to achieve leading positions in life and are ill suited to subordinate positions among the rank and file...Their narcissism, as opposed to that of other character types, is expressed not in an infantile but in a blatantly self-confident way, with a flagrant display of superiority and dignity, in spite of the fact that the basis of their nature is not less infantile than that of the other types." He observes too that "relationships with women are disturbed by the typical derogatory attitude toward the female sex."

In Fromm's characterology[8] we find our ennea-type VIII under the label of the "exploitative orientation," concerning which he observes that here the person "does not expect to receive things from others as gifts, but to take them away from others by force or cunning," that "their attitude is colored by a mixture of hostility and manipulation" and that "one finds here suspicion and cynicism, envy and jealousy." In the DSM III the more delinquent extreme of ennea-type VIII is found under the label of anti-social personality, for which the following diagnostic criteria are given:

1. Inability to sustain consistent work behavior
2. Lack of ability to function as a responsible parent

---

[8]Fromm, Eric, *Man for Himself: An Inquiry into the Psychology of Ethics* (New York: Holt, Rinehart and Winston, 1964).

3. Failure to accept social norms with regard to lawful behavior
4. Inability to maintain enduring attachment to a sexual partner and promiscuity
5. Irritability and aggressiveness
6. Failure to honor financial obligations
7. Failure to plan ahead
8. Disregard for the truth as indicated by "conning" for personal profit, etc.
9. Recklessness

In his discussion of antisocial personality Millon recommends that "we progress beyond moral and social judgment as a basis for clinical concepts," and in line with this he quotes in *Disorders of Personality* the following descriptions of criteria proposed in his formulation of the "Active Independent Personality"—which served as the initial working draft for what was ultimately labeled as "antisocial personality" by the DSM III task force.

1. Hostile affectivity (e.g., pugnacious, an irascible temper flares readily into arguments and attack; exhibits frequent verbally abusive and physically cruel behaviors).
2. Assertive self-image (e.g., proudly characterizes self as self-reliant, vigorously energetic and hard headed; values tough, competitive and power oriented life style).
3. Interpersonal vindictiveness (e.g., reveals satisfaction in derogating and humiliating others; contemptuous of sentimentality, social compassion and humanistic values).
4. Hyperthymic fearlessness (e.g., high activation level evident in impulsive, accelerated and forceful responding; attracted to and undaunted by danger and punishment).
5. Malevolent projection (e.g., claims that most persons are devious, controlling and punitive; justifies own mistrustful, hostile and vengeful attitudes by ascribing them to others).

In a paper read before the Association For The Advancement Of Psychoanalysis and which appeared in the *American Journal of Psychoanalysis* in 1948, Horney proposed to change the expression "sadistic" in reference to character and proposed a psychodynamic interpretation of "openly aggressive vindictiveness,"[9] in contrast to self-effacing vindictiveness (ennea-type IV) and "detached vindictiveness" (ennea-type V) deviating from Freud's sexual theory. Again we find descriptions of this character in *Our Inner Conflicts* and in *Neurosis and Human Growth*, where vindictive character is regarded an expression of the more general "solution of mastery" or expansive solution (to which I have made reference in connection with ennea-type I). This is a way of being where the individual identifies more with his glorified self than with his despised self.

Also "the appeal of life lies in its mastery. It chiefly entails his determination, conscious or unconscious, to overcome every obstacle—in or outside himself—and the belief that he should be able, and in fact is able, to do so. He should be able to master the adversities of fate, the difficulties of a situation, the intricacies of intellectual problems, the resistances of other people, conflicts in himself. The reverse side of the necessity for mastery is his dread of anything connoting helplessness; this is the most poignant dread he has."[10]

In the specific form of the "expansive solution" that concerns us, Horney describes the main motivating force in life: "the need for vindictive triumph is a regular ingredient in any search for glory. Our interest therefore is not so much concerned with the existence of this need but with its overwhelming intensity. How can the idea of triumph get such a hold on an individual that he spends all his life chasing after it? Surely it must be fed by a multitude of powerful sources. But the knowledge of these sources alone does not sufficiently elucidate its formidable power. In order to arrive at a fuller understanding we must approach the problem from still another vantage point. Even though in others the impact of the need for

---

[9]Our ennea-type VIII.

[10]Horney, Karen, *Our Inner Conflicts: A Constructive Theory of Neurosis* (New York: W.W. Norton & Co., 1992).

vengeance and triumph can be poignant, it usually is kept within limits by three factors: love, fear, and self-preservation. Only if these checks are temporarily or permanently malfunctioning can the vindictiveness involve the total personality—thereby becoming a kind of integrative force as in Medea—and sway it altogether in the one direction of vengeance and triumph...it is the combination of these two processes—powerful impulse and insufficient checks—that accounts for the magnitude of vindictiveness." As we see in the description thus far, Horney cannot omit from her interpretation the psychopathic aspect of this character: insufficient checks. It is as if the person thought that, just as he suffered in the past humiliation and limitation at the hands of tyrannical or neglectful parents, it is now for him to turn the tables and have his pleasure, even at the expense of the pain of others.

It seems that Horney, through allegiance to the concept of vindictiveness, here over-generalizes to include ennea-type IV as in her reference to Medea (an envy type) as an example. While the envious person may commit a crime of passion, the lusty one can be criminal not out of recklessness so much as out of generalized hostility, insensitivity, and as an anti-social orientation. Other than this, however, the portrait continues to fit the lust type. "He is convinced that everybody at bottom is malevolent and crooked, that friendly gestures are hypocritical, that it is only wisdom to regard everyone with distrust, unless he has been proved honest. But even such proof will readily make room for suspicion at the slightest provocation.

"In his behavior towards others he is openly arrogant, often rude and offensive, although sometime this is covered with a thin veneer of civil politeness. In subtle and gross ways, with or without realizing it, he humiliates others and exploits them. He may use women for the satisfaction of his sexual needs with utter disregard for their feelings. With a seemingly naive egocentricity, he will use people as a means to an end. He frequently makes and maintains contacts exclusively on the basis of their serving his needs for triumph: people he can use as stepping stones in his career, influential women he can conquer and subdue, followers who give him blind recognition and augment his power. He is a past master in frustrating others— frustrating their small and big hopes, their needs for attention, reassurance, time, company, enjoyment. When others demonstrate against such treatment it is their neurotic sensitivity that makes them react this way." Another expression of his vindictiveness, according to Horney, is that "he feels entitled both to having his neurotic needs implicitly respected and to being permitted his utter disregard of others' needs or wishes. He feels entitled for instance to the unabridged expression of his unfavorable observations and criticisms but feels equally entitled never to be criticized himself."

She goes on to comment that "whatever accounts for the inner necessity of such claims, they certainly express a contemptuous disregard for others." When these claims are not fulfilled, they assume a punitive vindictiveness "which may run the whole gamut from irritability to sulking, to making others feel guilty, to open rages...the undiluted expression of these feelings also serves as a measure to assert his claims by intimidating others into a subdued appeasement." Horney's vindictive arrogant person becomes furious at himself and scolds himself for "getting soft." The need to deny positive feelings is intimately related to the need for triumph, for "the hardening of feelings, originally a necessity for survival, allows for an unhampered growth of the drive for a triumphant mastery of life." She does not fail to point out this personality's characteristic self-reliance: "For a person as isolated and as hostile as he, it is of course important not to need others. Hence he develops a pronounced pride in godlike self-sufficiency."

She elaborates on the pride in the honesty, fairness, and justice of the vindictive person. "Needless to say, he is neither honest, fair nor just and cannot possibly be so. On the contrary, if anybody is determined—unconsciously—to bluff his way through life with a disregard for truth, it is he... But we can understand his belief that he possesses these attributes to a high degree if we consider his premises. To hit back or—preferably— to hit first appears to him (logically!) as an indispensable weapon against the crooked and hostile world around him. It is nothing but intelligent, legitimate self-interest. Also, not questioning the validity of his claims, his anger, and the expression of it must appear to him as entirely warranted and 'frank.'

"There is still another factor which greatly contributes to his conviction that he is a particularly honest person and which is important to mention. He sees around him many compliant people who pretend to be more loving, more sympathetic, more generous than they actually are. And in this regard he is indeed more honest. He does not pretend to be a friendly person; in fact he disdains doing so."

Finally, I quote Horney's observations on the little sympathy this kind of person has for others. "This absence of sympathy has many causes, lying in his hostility towards others and in his lacking sympathy for himself. But what perhaps contributes most to his callousness toward others is the envy of them. It is a bitter envy—not for this or that particular asset, but pervasive—and stems from his feeling excluded from life in general. And it is true that, with his entanglements, he actually is excluded from all that makes life worth living—from joy, happiness, love, creativeness, growth. If tempted to think along too neat lines, we would say here: has not he himself turned his back on life? Is he not proud of his ascetic not-wanting and not-needing anything? Does he not keep warding off positive feelings of all sorts? So why should he envy others? But the fact is, he does. Naturally, without analysis his arrogance would not permit him to admit it in plain words. But as his analysis proceeds he may say something to the effect that of course everybody else is better off than he is." Which brings us back to an earlier comment, that just as the gist of envy can be seen as repressed lust, lust may be seen as repressed envy.

Though intended to be a description of temperament rather than character, Sheldon's Somatotonia[11] should not be left out of this discussion, for just as cerebrotonia reaches its maximal expression in ennea-type V, somatotonia clearly finds its maximum in ennea-type VIII. "Constitutionally related to mesomorphic development (skeleton, muscles and connective tissue) somatotonia expresses the function of movement and predation," says Sheldon.

I list below the twenty main somatotonic traits that were used by Sheldon in his research.

1.   Assertiveness of Posture and Movement

---

[11]Sheldon, W.H., *The Varieties of Temperament* (New York: Harper & Brothers, 1942).

2. Love of Physical Adventure
3. The Energetic Characteristic
4. Need and Enjoyment of Exercise
5. Love of Dominating, Lust for Power
6. Love of Risk and Chance
7. Bold Directness of Manner
8. Physical Courage for Combat
9. Competitive Aggressiveness
10. Psychological Callousness
11. Claustrophobia
12. Ruthlessness,
13. Freedom from Squeamishness
14. General Noisiness
15. Overmaturity of Appearance
16. Horizontal Mental Cleavage,
17. Extraversion of Somatotonia
18. Assertiveness and Aggression under Alcohol
19. Need of Action When Troubled
20. Orientation Toward Goals and Activities of Youth

The connection between somatotonia and the lust type reaffirms the original idea of a constitutional factor behind psychopathic personality—though not necessarily that of the constitutional "defect." It is easy to conjecture that the strategy of vindictive self-assertion, that is to say, sadistic character, would be implicitly preferred by one who comes into life with a constitutionally determined orientation to action and a disposition to fight.

In Jung we can recognize our ennea-type VIII under the label of the Extraverted Sensation Type[12], though only in its aspects of realism and lusty orientation and not in that of dominance, for Jung curiously tells us that (at least "on the lower levels") this type who "is the lover of tangible reality, with little inclination for reflection" has "no desire to dominate." In spite of this discrepancy, Jung's reference to Wulfen's description of *der Genussmensch*; his commentary to the effect that the type "is by no means unlovable," on the contrary "his lively capacity for

---

[12]Jung, C.G., op.cit.

enjoyment makes him very good company"; plus his observation to the effect that conjectures beyond the concrete are of no interest to him and that the main pursuit is the intensification of sensations, leave little doubt as to the character's identity, which is confirmed through the observation of his or her exploitativeness:

"Although the object has become quite indispensable to him, yet, as something existing in its own right, it is none the less devalued. It is ruthlessly exploited and squeezed dry, since now its sole use is to stimulate sensation."

The anti-social inclination of the extraverted sensation type is also insinuated by Jung who remarks that his easy-going attitude accepts indiscriminately everything that happens and that "although this does not by any means imply an absolute lawlessness and lack of restraint, it nevertheless deprives him of the essential restraining power of judgment."

In the domain of homeopathic medicine the remedy best fitting ennea-type VIII is *Nux Vomica*, made from the seed of *Strychnos nux vomica*, that is the natural source of strychnine. Because is has been typically prescribed for physical states of excitation and overstimulation, it has been called "temper medicine" (Tyler).[13] Hahnemann wrote: "*Nux* is chiefly successful with persons of an ardent character, of an irritable, impatient temperament, disposed to anger, spite, or deception."

Catherine R. Coulter describes the personality for which *Nux Vomica* is most remedial as irritable, power-driven, and prone to addiction. "Turning to the bottle in times of depression, this type can become abusive and even violent; he is the alcoholic wife-beater or child-abuser." She reports, quoting Hahnemann, that he is "fiery and hot-tempered" and "a human powder-keg that is set off by the least spark." He can also be "tight, testy, and agitated in manner." She remarks that "these are the outward signs of a psychic restlessness and inability to let events move along at their own natural pace. If things are going too smoothly at home or work, he proceeds to stir them up. He constantly raises contentious issues or voices contradictory opinions."

---

[13]Coulter, Catherine R., op. cit., Volume 2, all excerpts on *Nux Vomica* quoted by permission of the author from pp. 3-46.

Particularly confirmatory of the ennea-type VIII disposition is Coulter's observation of the type's refusal "to even try curbing his temper.... Even the shrewd and successful businessman can forget himself completely in a petty temper outburst, defying all civilized rules of behavior and acting heedless or unaware of the impression he may be making on others."

Similarly fitting is the observation that "*Nux Vomica* may resort to 'invective mixed with indelicate expressions' (Hahnemann), or 'profanity' (Boenninghausen)."

Also the non intellectual disposition of ennea-type VIII (shared with ennea-type IX) is echoed in the description of the *Nux* personality's reluctance to concentrate, impatience, and unsuitability to intellectual work.

In regard to authority and power Coulter comments on the type's "authoritarian nature" both in the home and in the workplace, and she adds: "But when *Nux* is too ambitiously pursuing his interests and trying to reach the top, he not only 'uses' others to raise himself up but, to gain his ends, is occasionally willing to trample underfoot those of unlike mind, or who are merely in his way."

This discussion of *Nux Vomica* would not be complete, however, without remarking that the description of its associated personality also includes traits contradictory to those of ennea-type VIII. While Coulter claims that the above described traits can coexist with over-sensitivity and perfectionism, I believe that it is not the same individuals who show such traits, but that in the description of "*Nux* personality" these traits are observations of not only ennea-type VIII persons but also some of the angrier varieties of ennea-types I and IV. It definitely does not apply to ennea-type VIII to say that "the type's pain threshold is extremely low" (an ennea-type IV trait) or that "his fussy, precise nature, he is never contented or satisfied and is [constantly] disturbed by his surroundings."[14]

Particularly characteristic of ennea-type I is the following: "*Nux Vomica* is more likely to criticize from virtue (he is everything he accuses others of not being—organized,

[14]op. cit., pp 12-13.

efficient, clear-thinking) and to be 'reproachful' (Hahnemann) of faults or defects that differ from his own, while being reasonably tolerant of those that are similar to his."

3. Trait Structure

Lust

Just as anger may be regarded the most hidden of passions, lust is probably the most visible, seeming an exception to a general rule that wherever there is passion, there is also taboo or injunction in the psyche against it. I say "seemingly" because even though the lusty type is passionately in favor of his lust and of lust in general as a way of life, the very passionateness with which he embraces this outlook betrays a defensiveness—as if he needed to prove to himself and the rest of the world that what everybody calls bad is not such. Some of the specific traits that convey lust, such as "intensity," "gusto," "contactfulness," "love of eating," and so on, are intimately bound to the constitutional stratum of personality. A sensory-motor disposition (the somatotonic background of lust) may be regarded as the natural soil in which lust proper is supported. Other traits, such as hedonism, the propensity to boredom when not sufficiently stimulated, the craving for excitement, impatience, and impulsiveness, are in domain of lust proper.

We must consider that lust is more than hedonism. There is in lust not only pleasure, but pleasure in asserting the satisfaction of impulses, pleasure in the forbidden and, particularly, pleasure in *fighting for pleasure*. In addition to pleasure proper there is here an admixture of some pain that has been transformed into pleasure: either the pain of others who are "preyed upon" for one's satisfaction or the pain entailed by the effort to conquer the obstacles in the way to satisfaction. It is this that makes lust a passion for intensity and not for pleasure alone. The extra intensity, the extra excitement, the "spice," comes not from instinctual satisfaction, but from a struggle and an implicit *triumph*.

Punitiveness

Another group of traits intimately connected to lust is that which could be labeled punitive, sadistic, exploitative, hostile. Among such traits we can find "bluntness," "sarcasm," "irony," and those of being intimidating, humiliating, and frustrating. Of all characters, this is the most angry and the one least intimidated by anger.

It is the angry and punitive characteristic of ennea-type VIII Ichazo addresses in his calling the fixation of the lusty "revenge." The word, however, has the drawback of being associated with the most overtly vindictive of the characters, ennea-type IV, whose hatefulness sometimes manifests in explicit *vendettas*. In this overt sense type VIII is not strikingly vindictive; on the contrary, the character retaliates angrily at the moment and gets quickly over his irritation. The revenge which is most present in ennea-type VIII is (aside from "getting even" in the immediate response) a long-term one, in which the individual takes justice in his own hands in response to the pain, humiliation, and impotence felt in early childhood. It is as if he wanted to turn the tables on the world and, after having suffered frustration or humiliation for the pleasure of others, has determined that it is now his turn to have pleasure even if it involves the pain of others. Or *especially* then—for in this, too, may lie revenge.

The sadistic phenomenon of enjoying the frustration or humiliation of others may be regarded as a transformation of having to live with one's own (as a byproduct of vindictive triumph), just as the *excitement* of anxiety, strong tastes, and tough experiences represents a transformation of pain in the process of hardening oneself against life.

The anti-social characteristic of ennea-type VIII, like rebellion itself (in which it is embedded), may be regarded as a reaction of anger and thus a manifestation of vindictive punitiveness. The same may be said of dominance, insensitivity, and cynicism along with their derivatives. Punitiveness can be regarded as the fixation in sadistic or exploitative character—and we may credit Horney and Fromm for being ahead of their times in stressing these last-mentioned characteristics.

Rebelliousness

Though lust itself implies an element of rebellion in its assertive opposition to the inhibition of pleasure, rebellion stands out as a trait on it own, more prominent in ennea-type VIII than in any other character. Even though type VII is unconventional, the emphasis of this rebellion is intellectual. He is a person with "advanced ideas," perhaps a revolutionary outlook, while type VIII is the prototype of the revolutionary activist. Beyond specific ideologies, however, there is in the character not only a strong opposition to authority, but also a scorn for the values enjoined by traditional education. It is in virtue of such blunt invalidation of authority that "badness" automatically becomes the way to be. Generalized rebellion against authority can usually be traced back to a rebellion in the face of the father, who is the carrier of authority in the family. Vindictive characters frequently learn not to expect anything good from their fathers and implicitly come to regard parental power as illegitimate.

Dominance

Closely related to the characteristic hostility of the ennea-type, is dominance. Hostility may be said to be in the service of dominance, and dominance, in turn, regarded as an expression of hostility. Yet, dominance also serves the function of protecting the individual from a position of vulnerability and dependency. Related to dominance are such traits as "arrogance," "power seeking," "need for triumph," "putting others down," "competitiveness," "acting superior," and so on. Also related to these traits of superiority and dominance are the corresponding traits of disdain and scorn for others. It is easy to see how dominance and aggressiveness are in the service of lust; particularly in a world that expects individual restraint, only power and the ability to fight for one's wishes can allow the individual to indulge in his passion for impulse expression. Dominance and hostility stand in service of vindictiveness, as if the individual had early in life decided that it doesn't pay to be weak, accommodating, or seductive, and has oriented himself toward power in an attempt to take justice into his hands.

Insensitivity

Also closely related to the hostile characteristic of enneatype VIII are traits of toughness, manifest through such descriptors as "confrontativeness," "intimidation," "ruthlessness," "callousness." Such characteristics are clearly a consequence of an aggressive style of life, not compatible with fear or weakness, sentimentality or pity. Related to this unsentimental, realistic, direct, brusque, blunt quality, there is a corresponding disdain for the opposite qualities of weakness, sensitivity and, particularly, fear. We may say that a specific instance of the toughening of the psyche is an exaggerated risk-taking characteristic, through which the individual denies his own fears and indulges the feeling of power generated by his internal conquest. Risk-taking, in turn, feeds lust, for the type VII individual has learned to thrive on anxiety as a source of excitement, and rather than *suffering*, he has—through an implicit masochistic phenomenon—learned to wallow in its sheer intensity. Just as his palate has learned to interpret the painful sensations of a hot spice as pleasure, anxiety—and/or, rather the process of hardening oneself against it—has become, more than a pleasure, a psychological addiction, something without which life seems tasteless and boring.

Conning and Cynicism

The next two traits can be considered intimately connected. The cynical attitude to life of the exploitative personality is underscored by Fromm's traits of skepticism, the tendency to look upon virtue as always hypocritical, distrust in the motives of others, and so on. In these traits, as in toughness, we see the expression of a way and a vision of life "red in tooth and claw."[15] In regard to conning and cunning, it should be said that ennea-type VIII is more blatantly deceptive than type VII, and is easily seen as a cheat, the typical "used car salesman" who knows how to bargain assertively.

Exhibitionism (Narcissism)

Ennea-type VIII people are entertaining, witty, and often charming, yet not vain in the sense of being concerned with how they appear. Their seductiveness, bragging, and arrogant claims are consciously manipulative; they are geared to gaining influence and elevation in the power and dominance hierarchy. They also constitute a compensation for exploita-tiveness and insensitivity, a way of buying out others or making themselves acceptable despite traits of unaccountability, violence, invasiveness, and so on.

Autonomy

As Horney has remarked, we could not expect anything other than self-reliance in one who approaches others as potential competitors or targets of exploitation. Along with the characteristic autonomy of ennea-type VIII is the *idealization* of autonomy, a corresponding rejection of dependency and passive oral strivings. The rejection of these passive traits is so striking that Reich postulated that phallic-narcissistic character constitutes precisely a defense against them.[16]

Sensory-motor dominance

Beyond the concepts of lust and hedonism, rebellion, punitiveness, dominance, and power-seeking, toughness, risk taking, narcissism, astuteness, is in ennea-type VII the predominance of action over intellect and feeling, for this is the most sensory-motor of characters. The characteristic orientation

---

[15]Fromm, Erich, op.cit.

[16]Reich, Wilhelm, *Character Analysis*, translated by Vincent Carfagno (New York: Simon and Schuster, 1972).

of ennea-type VIII to a graspable and concrete "here and now"—
the sphere of the senses and the body-sense in particular—is a
lusty clutching at the present and an excited impatience toward
memory, abstractions, anticipations, as well as a desensitization
to the subtlety of aesthetic and spiritual experience.
Concentration on the present is not simply as a manifestation of
mental health as it could be in other character dispositions, but
the consequence of not deeming anything real that is not tangible
and an immediate stimulus to the senses.

4. Defense Mechanisms

When we consider what mechanism may be most
characteristic of lusty-vindictive character, we are at first struck
by how this personality disposition gravitates in a direction
opposite to the repression of instinctual life that Freud
emphasized in the neurosis in general. Indeed, while the
inhibition of sexuality is apparent in most characters (except in
ennea-types II and to some extent VII) and the inhibition of
aggression is even more generalized, it is the non-inhibition of
these that characterize lusty impulsiveness. Yet in his
interpretation of phallic-narcissistic character, Reich expressed
the view that this whole orientation to life may be understood as
being of a defensive nature: a defense against dependency and
passivity. We will say that the over "masculine" type VIII strives
through an excessive assertiveness and aggression to avoid a
position of "feminine" powerlessness—a powerlessness that
would involve submission to societal constraints and resignation
in regards to his own impulses.

Also, in order to compensate for feelings of guilt, shame
and worthlessness evoked by his disregard of others the
individual has engaged in a process of guilt denial and in a
repression (in the broad sense of the term) of the super-ego
rather than of the id. This rebellious turning against inhibitions
in an attitude of solidarity with the intrapsychic under-dog
doesn't seem to have received a specific name in psychoanalysis,
though it may be regarded as akin to denial to the extent that
there is a disavowal of internalized authority and its values.

Since Freud used the expression "denial" (*verleugnung*) mostly in connection with the disavowal of external reality, I prefer not to bring it to this discussion except metaphorically, and simply point out the need for a more specific term that denotes repression that is not of the instinctual side of conflict but of the counter-instinctual. An expression like "counter-repression" or "counter-identification" might serve the purpose—the latter particularly since rebellious traits are understandable as inverse identifications with behaviors and attitudes expected by society and the parents. The opposition of type VIII to type IV in the enneagram suggests, however, that "counter-introjection" may be even more specific for, unlike type IV, who all too regularly brings bad objects into his psyche as foreign bodies, ennea-type VIII is the opposite of one willing to swallow and is most ready to spit out what doesn't agree with his wishes.

Equally characteristic of the ennea-type VIII manner of repressing is the specially developed capacity to keep pain out of awareness—a condition in which the person may be unaware of a high fever or of an infection in the middle ear, for instance. At the psychological level, the insensitivity to psychological discomfort of tough-minded, sadistic individuals involves a relative insensitivity to shame and explains a seeming absence of guilt. I think this also explains the typical attraction of lusty people to anxiety (and risk) which is not avoided but "sadistically" transformed into a stimulus, a source of excitement (an act of sadism against self). This characteristic elevation of the pain threshold that may be understood as the basis of both callousness, as a giving up of the expectations of love from others, and the turning against societal standards, we may call *desensitization*.

5. Etiological and Further Psychodynamic Remarks[17]

Constitutionally the ennea-type VIII individual tends to be mesoendomorphic, and on the whole this ego type is the most mesomorphic[18] of all, which suggests that the individual's "choice" of an assertive and pugnacious interpersonal style has been strongly supported by his constitution. It is also one of the most ectopenic[19]—and a corresponding lack of cerebrotonia may be posited as the background of this highly extraversive disposition.

It is possible to imagine that the influence of genetically determined somatotonic temperament on character formation is not simple but indirect, inasmuch as a noisy child or one who is excessively vehement in his desires can easily elicit rejection or punishment which, in turn, will stimulate both self-assertion and rebellion. The following vignette illustrates such indirect effect in regard to what appears to be an inborn adventurousness: "I remember as a four year old child running on the beach toward the infinite. They searched for me in a motor boat, and found me beyond the reach of vision. 'What are you doing here?' 'I am looking at the stars.' Then my father beat me up."

It may be generally said that the ennea-type VIII individual has implicitly decided to seek outside the home a better life, and it is not uncommon to find that he has left home early. A lack of care or even an actual lack of home-like environment may be a factor (as in delinquent children in areas of great poverty), and also it is my impression that violence in the home is more frequent than in the life histories of other

---

[17]In his chapter on antisocial personality in Cooper et al.'s *Psychiatry*, William H. Reid reviews some evidence for organic correlates of this syndrome. "The most reliable data stress autonomic characteristics that indicate lowered levels of baseline anxiety, lessened autonomic reaction to some forms of stress, and changes in speed of autonomic recovery from such stress." According to him "no early developmental experience, or set of experiences, is highly predictive of later sociopathy," though he adds that "the most important single issue with respect to fathers appears to be whether or not they are 'sociopathic'." For "antisocial fathers have been consistently associated with antisocial or criminal behavior in offspring in a statistical sense."

[18] i.e., one in which the constitution is mostly "athletic" and secondarily "visceral."

[19]That is, low in ectomorphia—that is to say the slender aspect of constitution.

characters, and in such cases it is easy to understand the development of insensitivity, toughening up, and cynicism.

Yet in other instances the factors leading to disappointment in parental love are not so evident, notably when one among several children manifests these characteristics and others do not. We may think that in such instances a common experience of punishment has been experienced and interpreted differently so that one brother becomes submissive in the expectation of parental love and the other, more humiliated and angry, becomes adventurous in the search for a better environment. Occasionally a factor in the development of this character is identification with another family member, as in the quotation below where pain and the same-type modeling have coincided: "Since I was little I had felt invaded. It was like the invasion of barbarians. Violently assaulted and it was my grandmother who was the boss. My grandmother was distinctly an 'VIII,' and I was her right eye; I was the first and the inheritor of all her story."

In other instances the stimulus for rebellion has been a tyrannical type VI father, which is an understandable background for one who is not only rebellious but who has learned to survive through intimidation.

Though it may be broadly said that ennea-type VIII, like type V, has pessimistically given up on the search for love to the point of cynically doubting good motives and tending to perceive expression of positive feelings as sentimentalism, we may also speak, as in other characters, of a substitution of an original love wish. Just as in type I, search for love becomes a search for respect, and it is in respect that the "proof of love" is felt to be. In ennea-type VIII the "proof of love" is implicitly felt to be in the willingness of the other to be possessed, dominated, used, and—in extreme cases—beaten up. Correspondingly, all these behaviors and attitudes become, in the course of time, love substitutes.

6. Existential Psychodynamics

The over-development of action in the service of struggling in a dangerous world that cannot be trusted is perhaps the fundamental way in which ennea-type VIII character fails to constitute full humanness. To elucidate further its existential interpretation we need to understand the vicious circle by which not only ontic obscuration supports lust, but lust, in its impetuous grasping of the tangible, entails an impoverishment of tender qualities and subtlety which results in a loss of wholeness and thus in a loss of being. It is as if the lusty character, in his impatience for satisfaction, shifts to an excessively concrete notion of his goal as pleasure, wealth, triumph, and so forth—only to find that this reaching, substituted for being, leaves him forever dissatisfied, craving intensity.

The situation may be explained through the paradigm of the rapist—an extrapolation of the lusty predator's approach to life. He has given up the expectation of being wanted, to say nothing of love. He takes for granted that he will only get what he takes. As a taker, he could not succeed if he were to be concerned with the fancy of other people's feelings. The way to be a winner is clear: to put winning before all else; likewise, the way to having one's needs met is to forget the other. The world without others of the more anti-social ennea-type VIII, however, is no more full of true aliveness than that of the schizoid ennea-type V. Just as the schizoid misses the experience of value and being through the loss of relationship, so does the psychopath, in spite of seeming to be contactful, involved, and brimming with intense emotion.

The paradigm of rape can also serve as a background to a further discussion of the semblance of being which the sadistic type fails to know that he is pursuing. The concreteness of a wish that is excessively sensate (here an interest in sexual pleasure not coupled with an interest in relationship) is an image through which we may reflect on how the concretization of the healthy drive for relationship, far from orienting itself to the reality of the situation (as "realistic phallic-narcissists" claim), involves a blatant lack of psychological reality. The situation conveys a sexualization of lust-centered personality as a result of the repression, denial, and transformation of the need for love.

Hidden as it may be behind the enthusiastic expansiveness, jollity, and seductive charm of the lusty, it is the loss of relationship, the suppression of tenderness, and the denial of the love need that result in the loss of wholeness and sense of being.

Ennea-type VIII pursues being, then, in pleasure and in the power to find his pleasure, yet through an insistence on overpowering becomes incapable of receiving—when being can only be known in a receptive attitude. By doggedly claiming satisfaction where a *semblance* of satisfaction can be imagined, much as Nasruddin seeks his key in the market place, he perpetuates an ontic deficiency that only feeds his lusty pursuit of triumph and other being substitutes.

Chapter Five

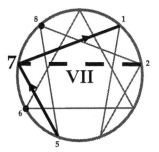

GLUTTONY, FRAUDULENCE, AND "NARCISSISTIC PERSONALITY"

ENNEA-TYPE VII

1. Core Theory, Nomenclature, and Place in the Enneagram

In the Christian world "gluttony" is included among the seven "cardinal sins," yet its usual understanding as a gluttony for food only makes it appear somewhat less sinful than others. It would not be included among the basic sinful dispositions, however, if the original meaning of the term were not—as is the case with avarice and lust—something beyond the literal. If we understand gluttony more broadly, in the sense of a passion for pleasure, we may say that this definitely is a capital sin—

inasmuch as it implies a deviation from an individual's potential
for self-actualization; hedonism is binding upon the psyche and
involves (through confusion) an obstacle in the search for the
summum bonum and a snare. We may say that a weakness for
pleasure constitutes a generalized susceptibility to temptation,
and in this light we can understand Chaucer's statement in his
"The Parson's Tale" to the effect that "He that is addicted to this
sin of gluttony may withstand no other sin."[1]

When I first heard Ichazo's ideas of Protoanalysis, this
was in Spanish, and he used the word "charlatan" for the ennea-
type VII individual (and "charlatanism" for the fixation). This
word also needs to be understood in more than a literal manner:
that the glutton is one who approaches the world through the
strategy of words and "good reasons"—one who manipulates
through the intellect. Ichazo's later word for this personality,
"ego-plan," makes reference to the fact that the "charlatan" is also
a dreamer—indeed, his charlatanism may be interpreted as a
taking (or offering) dreams as realities.   Yet I think
"charlatanism" is more evocative, for planning is a prominent
trait of ennea-types I and III as well, and "charlatanism" conveys
additional meanings, such as expressive ability, the role of a
persuader and manipulator of words, deviously overstepping
the boundaries of his knowledge. More than a mere planner,
ennea-type VII is a "schemer," with that strategic character that
La Fontaine (a bearer of this disposition) symbolized in the fox.

Ichazo characterized gluttony as a "wanting more": I
leave it up to my gluttonous readers to decide which may be the
deeper interpretation. My own impression is that, though this
description is characterologically apt, it points to an insatiability
that gluttons share with the lusty. Also, although it is true that
sometimes gluttons imagine that more of the same would bring
about greater pleasure, it is also true that they more
characteristically are *not* seekers of more of the same, but
(romantically) seekers of the remote and the bizarre, seekers of
variety, adventure, and surprise.

In the language of DSM III, the ennea-type VII syndrome
receives the name of "narcissistic"—yet we must be cognizant of

---

[1]op. cit., p. 602.

the fact that this is a word that has been used by different authors for other personalities as well.[2]

2. Antecedents in the Scientific Literature on Character

It is in the picture that Schneider paints of those that he calls "labile" that I find the closest approximation to our ennea-type VII.[3] I think that in Schneider's classification an ennea-type VII individual might be diagnosed either as that variant of the "hyperthymic" labeled "hypomanic" or as labile. The latter kind of person he describes as "sensitive, highly influenced by the outer world, inclined to self-analysis. Not a depressive, but one who is subject to occasional excesses of sadness or irritation." At a more ordinary level of mental health, he draws attention to a trait of "being easily satiated and bored with things...A restlessness seems to invade this subject, especially in spring; an impulsive longing for variety and novelty...A special manifestation of this personality is the manifestation of vagrancy." He also quotes Stier who has made a special study on desertion: "In all these investigations one finds very different things; partly the fear of punishment or nostalgia, partly the purely social vagabonding of the lonely, partly a romantic love of adventures and the pursuit of novelty."

Since gluttony may be approximately translated into modern terminology as "receptive orality" it is appropriate that as we turn from the literary sources to the psychological ones we begin by considering the orally gratified type of Karl Abraham,[4] characterized by "an excess of optimism which is not lessened by reality experience; by generosity, bright and sociable social conduct, accessibility to new ideas and ambitions accompanied by sanguine expectations."

---

[2]For instance, most of the clinical illustrations in Lowen's book on narcissism correspond to our ennea-type III.

[3]Schneider, Kurt, op. cit.

[4]Abraham, Karl, op. cit.

The following statement from Abraham addresses itself to the characteristic verbal ability of ennea-type VII: "their longing to experience gratification by way of sucking has changed to a need to give by way of the mouth, so that we find in them besides a permanent longing to obtain everything, a constant need to communicate themselves orally to other people; this results in an obstinate urge to talk, connected in most cases with a feeling of overflowing. Persons of this kind have the impression that their fund of thoughts is inexhaustible and they ascribe a special power of some unusual value to what they say."

Whether or not we share Freud's and Abraham's view in regard to the stages in the development of the libido and the role of sexuality in the shaping of character, not only is the syndrome that psychoanalysis labels as "oral-receptive" an observable fact, which corresponds to ennea-type VII psychology (just as passive-aggressive syndrome corresponds to ennea-type IV), but its association with happy breast feeding has been statistically ascertained.[5]

It may be of interest to note that when Freud used the word "narcissistic" in connection with a particular type of individual, his image corresponded to ennea-type VII features and to the narcissistic personality in the DSM III, more than to those of the narcissistic personality disorder as described by Kernberg.

In "Libidinal Types" Freud says: "The main interest is focused in self-preservation. The type is independent and not easily overawed. People of this type impress others as being personalities. It is on them that their fellow men are specially likely to lean. They readily assume the role of leader, give a fresh stimulus to cultural development or break down existing conditions."[6]

In spite of the widespread use of "narcissism" in connection with a characterological disposition corresponding to a variety of our ennea-type V, it is ennea-type VII that receives the label "narcissistic" in the DSM III or, at least, we may say that

---

[5]See "Breast Feeding And Character Formation" by Frieda Goldman-Eisler, op.cit.

[6]Freud, Sigmund, "Libidinal Types," English translation in *Collected Papers*, Vol. 5, p. 249 (London: Hogarth, 1950).

there is in it a juxtaposition of meanings that needs to be pointed out. I will examine the issue in the form of a revision of Millon's description of the narcissistic personality:[7]

"Narcissism conveys a calm and self-assured quality in their social behavior" Millon begins by saying, and in this way definitely portrays an ennea-type VII person rather than the typically awkward, self-doubting, tense ennea-type V.

"Their seemingly untroubled and self-satisfied air is viewed by some as a sign of confident equanimity. Others respond to it much less favorably. To them, these behaviors reflect immodesty, presumptuousness, pretentiousness and a haughty, snobbish, cocksure, and arrogant way of relating to people."

Whereas we may speak of covert arrogance in the case of ennea-type V individuals, this is not suggested by their behavior so much as by the content of their speech. Behavior involving a nonchalant sense of being OK is typical of our "charlatan," in contrast with the awkward shyness of ennea-type V. I continue with Millon:

"Narcissists appear to lack humility and are over self-centered and ungenerous...They characteristically but usually unwittingly exploit others and take them for granted and expect others to serve them without giving much in return. Their self-conceit is viewed by most as unwarranted. It smacks of being uppish and superior without there being substance to justify it."

Though an expectation of receiving not matched by generosity is something that could be applied to avarice, the style is different in gluttony, as is also the level of exploitation. While in ennea-type V the feelings of superiority exist side by side with even greater feelings of inferiority, in the narcissist the balance is the converse: feelings of superiority being more visible and present to the individual's awareness, while feelings of inferiority are hidden, denied, and repressed. Only of the gluttons it may be said, as Millon says of narcissists, that "their behavior may be objectionable, even irrational. And that their self-image is that they are superior persons, extra special individuals, who are entitled to unusual rights and privileges.

---

[7]op. cit.

This view of their self-worth is fixed so firmly in their minds, that they rarely question whether it is valid. Moreover any one who fails to respect them is viewed with contempt and scorn."

The following paragraph from Millon evokes the planning aspect of ennea-type VII as well as the optimism of the oral receptive:

"Narcissists are cognitively expansive, they place few limits on either their fantasies or rationalizations, and their imagination is left to run free of the constraints of reality or the views of others. They are inclined to exaggerate their powers, to freely transform failures into successes, to construct lengthy and intricate rationalizations that inflate their self-worth or justify what they feel is their due, quickly depreciating those who refuse to accept or enhance their self-image." Most characteristic is the observation that "roused by the facile workings of their imaginations, narcissists experience a pervasive sense of well being in their everyday life, of buoyancy of mood and an optimism of outlook. Affect though based often on their semi-grandiose distortion of reality is generally relaxed if not cheerful and carefree. Should the balloon be burst, however, there is a rapid turn to either an edgy irritability and annoyance with others or to repeated bouts of dejection that are characterized by feeling humiliated and empty."

Ennea-types V and VII not only contrast in terms of awkwardness vs. self-assurance but also differ in regard to a mental atmosphere—that is predominantly pleasurable in the former and painful in the latter:

"Narcissists suffer few conflicts. Their past has supplied them perhaps too well with high expectations and encouragements. As a result they are inclined to trust others and to feel confidence that matters will work out well for them." Yet "reality bears down heavily at times. Even the routine demands of everyday life may be viewed as annoying incursions by narcissists. Such responsibilities are experienced as demeaning for they intrude upon the narcissist's cherished illusion of self as almost godlike, alibis to avoid 'pedestrian' tasks are easily mustered since narcissists are convinced that what they believe must be true and what they wish must be right. Not only do they display considerable talent in rationalizing their social inconsideredness but they utilize a variety of other intrapsychic mechanisms with equal facility.   However, since they reflect minimally on what others think, their defensive maneuvers are transparent, a poor camouflage to a discerning eye. This failure to bother dissembling more thoroughly also contributes to their being seen as cocksure and arrogant."

I think it will be relevant to include here some reflections of David Shapiro[8] on the impulsive styles in general, since these apply as he himself remarks, both to "most of those persons usually diagnosed as impulsive characters or psychopathic characters" (VIII), and "some of those who are called passive neurotic characters and narcissistic characters"(VII).

While we may say that one is a tough impulsive and the second a soft one, in both of them we may speak of "an impairment of normal feelings and deliberateness and intention." He includes those conditions described as passive in his discussion because of "the formal qualities of the two sorts of conditions, that marked by impulsiveness and that marked by extreme passivity, shows them to be very closely related. In fact I believe it would be in keeping with the formal similarity of the two sets of conditions to speak of a general passive impulsive style on the experience of impulse...It is an experience of having executed a significant action, not a trivial one, without a clear and complete sense of decision, motivation, or sustained wish. It is an experience of an action, in other words, that does not feel completely deliberate or fully intended.

"These are not experiences of external compulsion or submission to moral principles," he explains, "but experiences of wish. " Yet "experiences of exceedingly abrupt, transient and partial wish, wish that is so attenuated as to be hardly comparable to the normal experience of wanting or deciding, and so attenuated as to make possible or even plausible a plea of 'guilty but without premeditation'." Thus the typical statement "I don't want to do it but I just can't control my impulse" which Shapiro comments may be translated as "I don't feel I ought to do it and I would shrink from doing it deliberately, but if quickly and while I'm not looking my feet, my hands or my impulses just do it I can hardly be blamed" in passive characters frequently

---

[8]op. cit.

takes the form of "I didn't want to do it, but he pressed and somehow I just gave in."

Just as the Freudians have become aware of this ennea-type VII syndrome in the light of their theoretical assumptions, Jung and his successors have been acquainted with it in the light of their own frame of reference. This eminently future-oriented type is characterized by intuition: "The capacity for intuiting that which is not yet visible, future possibilities or potentialities in the background of a situation." I quote from Jung's *Psychological Types:*[9]

"The intuitive is never to be found in the world of accepted reality-values, but he has a keen nose for anything new and in the making. Because he is always seeking out new possibilities, stable conditions suffocate him, he seizes on new objects or situations with great intensity, sometimes with extraordinary enthusiasm only to abandon them cold bloodedly... it is as though his whole life vanished in the new situation. One gets the impression, which he himself shares, that he has always just reached a final turning point... Neither reason nor feeling can restrain him or frighten him away from a new possibility, even though it goes against all his previous convictions...he has his own characteristic morality, which consists in a loyalty to his vision and in voluntary submission to its authority... Naturally this attitude holds great dangers, for all too easily the intuitive may fritter away his life on things and people, spreading about him an abundance of life which others live and not he himself."

Jung's characterization of ennea-type VII as introverted intuition is only incompletely confirmed through testing, for we recognize the personality pattern in Keirsey and Bates's[10] portrait of an INTJ (introvert with more intuition than sensing, more thinking than feeling and a predominance of judgment over perception). They observe that INTJ are the most self-confident of all the types, that they look to the future rather than the past, and that they are both builders of systems and appliers of theoretical models.

---

[9]Jung, C.G. op. cit.
[10]op. cit.

"To INTJs, authority based on position, rank, title or publication has absolutely no force. This type is not likely to succumb to the magic of slogans, watchwords, and shibboleths As with the INTP, authority per se does not impress the INTJ...

"No idea is too far fetched to be entertained. INTJs are naturally brainstormers, always open to new concepts and, in fact, aggressively seeking them.

"INTJ manipulates the world of theory as if on a gigantic chessboard, always seeking strategies and tactics that have high pay off... theories which cannot be made to work are quickly discarded by INTJ....

"INTJs tend, ordinarily, to verbalize the positive and eschew comments of a negative nature."

I find that ennea-type VII matches the personality associated in homeopathy to *Sulphur*. According to D. Demarqwue's *Concordances Homeopathiques* (published by the Centre d'Etude de Documentation Homeopathique) "the character manifestations found in subjects that are sensitive to Sulphur are not pathogenic. They exist, aside from any important episode of sickness. Gaiety, optimism, the enjoyment of life are not, of course, pathological symptoms, neither is selfishness nor an inclination for philosophical speculation."

Could not the same be said of the oral-optimistic ennea-type VII, by a person without psycho-therapeutic sophistication? It is a fact that type IV and type V seem sicker than the happy characters—type VII, type III, type II, and type IX. Yet pathology or not, homeopathic experience has recognized the ennea-type VII pattern: a selfish enjoyer with a love for explaining and generalization.

Turning to *Matière Medicale Homeopathique* by Michel Guermonprez, Pinkas, Tork, (Doin Editeur, Paris, 1985), I find "cyclic behavior, euphoria, imagination, inaction, irritability, selfishness" as characteristics of those for whom *Sulphur* is the remedy of choice. "Cyclic behavior" is then explained as an alternation of euphoric phases ("sociable, optimistic, *charlatan*") and depression.

Particularly interesting, in view of our conception of ennea-type VII as a charlatan, is the observation: "the student believes that he knows everything and does everything well, while being in fact lazy, confusing and negligent." Also "Illusion of a superior intelligence: systems, techniques, synthesis, inventions, exuberant but erroneous theoretical imagination. Metaphysical and philosophical speculation. *Mythomania*: beautifully illustrated frauds."

Along with recognizing that the characteristics of *Sulphur* people in the experience of homeopaths are the best match to type VII, I notice a difference in emphasis between their view and Coulter's description (which originally inclined me to connect *Sulphur* to ennea-type V) for in Coulter's character description of *Sulphur* hedonism is not prominent. Since the ennea-type conscious homeopaths I have questioned confirmed the correspondence of *Lycopodium* to type VI, I have deemed Coulter's *Sulphur* the closest to type VII among the *Polychrests*. I have inquired further and reconsidered the possibility that the loquacious *Sulphur* ("philosopher" in rags) might correspond to type VII, and I have been pleased to learn of the association of *Sulphur* to euphoria, which has confirmed this alternative hypothesis. There is still a difference between my conception of ennea-type VII, and the homeopathic picture: the emphasis on selfishness in the latter. While I have spoken of type VII as a fox whose selfishness is well hidden under a lambskin, homeopathic literature I have consulted doesn't seem to pay attention to the fox's clothing. Or rather, it only reports that there are exceptions to *Sulphur's* self-interest. Says Coulter[11]: "Some *Sulphurs*, moreover, demonstrate a complete lack of interest in material things or financial matters. They can be almost simple-minded in this respect. They are not slow, but their heads are so far in the clouds, they are engrossed in thought, that the 'real life' around them passes by unobserved."

To clarify this it is necessary to point out that only the self-preservation subtype of ennea-type VII is visibly an opportunist with a keen nose for advantages; in the social subtype self-interest is more hidden behind a friendly brotherliness, while the sexual subtype is that of a dreamer whose interests are not of this world.

---

[11] Coulter, Catherine R., op. cit., Vol. 1, p. 159, quoted with permission of the author.

3. Trait Structure

Gluttony

Ennea-type VII individuals, are more than just open minded, exploratory: their search for experience takes them, characteristically, from an insufficient here to a promising there. The "insatiability" of the glutton is, however, veiled over by an apparent satisfaction; or more precisely said, frustration is hidden behind enthusiasm—an enthusiasm that seems to compensate for dissatisfaction as well as keeping the experience of frustration away from the individual's awareness.

Whether in the question of food or in other realms, the gluttony of the glutton is typically not for the common, but, on the contrary, for that which is most remarkable, for the extraordinary. In line with this is the characteristic interest in what is magical or esoteric itself, a manifestation of a broader interest in what is remote—either geographically, culturally, or at the fringes of knowledge.

Also, an attraction to that which is beyond the boundaries of one's own culture reflects the same displacement of values from here to there; and the same may be said of the typical anti-conventional tendencies of type VII. In this case, the ideal may be in a utopian, futuristic, or progressive outlook rather than in existing cultural models.

Hedonistic Permissiveness

A pair of traits inseparable from the gluttonous pleasure bias, are the avoidance of suffering and, concomitantly, the hedonistic orientation, characteristic of ennea-type VII personality. Intrinsically connected to these traits are permissiveness and self-indulgence. In connection with permissiveness it may be said that it not only describes a trait of the individual with regard to himself, but a characteristic *laissez-faire* attitude toward others; such permissiveness sometimes even becomes complicity when gluttons seductively become friends of other people's vices.

Closely related to self-indulgence is the trait of being "spoiled," usually employed in reference to an attitude of entitlement to gratification. Also the "play-boy" orientation to life falls in here, and, indirectly, the exaggerated sense of okayness that the individual develops as a protection of hedonism against pain and frustration: the "optimistic attitude" that not only makes him and others OK, but the whole world a good one to live in. In some cases we may speak of a "cosmic okayness," in which the individual's contentedness is supported by a view of the world in which there is no good or evil, no guilt, no shoulds, no duties, and no need to make any efforts—for it is enough to enjoy.

Rebelliousness

Of course, without rebelliousness self-indulgence would not be possible in the inhibiting world of present civilization. The main things to be said of type VII rebellion are that it manifests most visibly in a keen eye for conventional prejudices and that it usually finds a humorous outlet. Also, the rebelliousness is mostly embodied in an anti-conventional orientation while intellectual rebellion goes hand-in-hand with a good measure of behavioral acquiescence. This characteristic makes type VII people the ideologists of revolutions, rather than the activists.

Ennea-type VII is typically *not* oriented towards authorities. It might be said that the glutton has "learned" early in life that there is no good authority, yet adopts toward authority an attitude that is diplomatic rather than oppositional. An aspect of implicit rebellion is the fact that the type VII individual mostly lives in a non-hierarchical psychological environment: just as type VI perceives himself exaggeratedly in terms of his relationships to superiors and inferiors, type VII is "equalitarian" in her approach to people. Neither does she takes authority too seriously (for this would militate against her self-indulgence, permissiveness, lack of guilt, and superiority) nor does she present to others as an authority, except in a covert way which seeks to impress while at the same time assuming the garb of modesty.

Lack of Discipline

Still another trait that is both independent enough to be considered as such and yet dynamically dependent on gluttony and rebellion, manifests through the lack of discipline, instability, lack of commitment, and the dilettantish features of ennea-type VII. The word "play-boy" reflects not only hedonism but the non-committed attitude of an enjoyer. The lack of discipline in this character is a consequence of his interest in not postponing pleasure—and, at a deeper level, rests on the perception of pleasure-postponement as lovelessness.

Imaginary Wish-Fulfillment

The cathexis of fantasy and orientation to plans and utopia, are part of the gluttonous bias that, like a child at the nipple, clings to an all too sweet and non-frustrating world. Closely related to the above and also an escape from the harsh realities of life is the attraction towards the future and the potential: gluttons usually have a futuristic orientation for through an identification with plans and ideals, the individual seems to live imaginatively in them rather than in down-to-earth reality.

Seductively Pleasing

There are two facets in the ennea-type VII personality, each of which has given rise to the popular recognition of the character ("happy" and "amiable" respectively) and which together contribute to the characteristically pleasing quality of type VII character. Just as ennea-type VII is a glutton for what is pleasant and has come to feel loved through the experience of pleasure—he seems bent on fulfilling the pleasure-gluttony of those he wants to seduce. Like type II on the antipodes of the enneagram, type VII is eminently seductive, and is bent on pleasing through both helpfulness and a problem-free, cheerful contentedness.

The amiable aspect of this character is alluded to by such descriptors as "warm," "helpful," "friendly," "obliging," "selflessly ready to serve," and "generous." Gluttons are very good hosts and can be great spenders. In the degree to which generosity is a part of seductiveness and a way of buying love rather than a true giving, it is counterbalanced in the psyche of the glutton by its corresponding opposite: a hidden but effective exploitativeness that may manifest as a parasitic tendency and perhaps in feelings of entitlement to care and affection.

The state of satisfied well-being of ennea-type VII rests partly on the priorities of an enjoyer, partly on the glutton's knack for imaginary fulfillment. Yet, "feeling good" also serves the ends of seductiveness and seductive motivation may at times make type VII especially cheerful, humorous, and entertaining. The good humor of type VII makes other people feel lighted-up in their presence, and this contributes effectively to the pleasure they cause and the attractiveness of being near to them, to the extent that happiness is, at least in part, seductive and definitely compulsive. The happy bias of ennea-type VII (as in the case of type III) is maintained at the expense of the repression and avoidance of pain, and results in an impoverishment of experience. In particular the "cool" of type VII involves a repression of such anxiety as chronically feeds the attitude of taking refuge in pleasure.

Narcissism

Another group of traits that may be discerned as an expression of seduction may be called narcissistic. It comprises such descriptors as "exhibitionist," "knows better," "well informed," "intellectually superior." Sometimes this manifests as a compulsion to explain things, such as Fellini seeks to portray in movies where a narrator constantly puts into words everything that is taking place.

We may speak of a "seduction through superiority" which most usually takes the form of intellectual superiority, though (as in Moliere's Tartuffe) it may involve a religious, good, and saintly image. The apparent lack of grandiosity in such saintly image is sometimes manifest even in the case of those who actively seek to assert their superiority, wisdom, and kindness. This falls in line with the fact that gluttons tend to form equalitarian brotherly relationships rather than authority relations. Because of this, their pretended superiority is implicit rather than explicit, masked over by a non-assuming, appreciative, and equalitarian style. As in the case of pleasingness, the superiority of ennea-type VII expresses only a half of the glutton's experience; the other is the simultaneous perception of self as inferior, and the corresponding feelings of insecurity. As in ennea-type V, in both cases splitting allows the simultaneity of the two sub-selves, yet while it is the deprecated self that is in the foreground in type V, it is the grandiose self that has the upper hand in narcissistic personality.

A psychological characteristic that is important to mention in connection with the gratified narcissism of the "oral-receptive" is charm, a quality into which converge the admirable qualities of ennea-type VII (giftedness, percep-tiveness, wit, savoir-vivre, and so on) and its pleasing, non-aggressive, vaseline-like, cool, and contented characteristics. Through charm the glutton can satisfy his gluttony as effectively as a fisherman succeeds with bait, which implies that pleasing and charm are not just seductive but manipulative. Through his great charm the glutton can enchant others and even himself. Among his skills is that of fascination—hypnotic fascination even—and charm is his magic.

Along with the narcissistic facet of ennea-type VII it is necessary to mention the high intuition and frequent talents of type VII, which suggests that such dispositions may have favored the development of their dominant strategy (just as the adoption of the strategy has stimulated their development).

Persuasive

We may think of ennea-type VII as a person in whom love seeking has turned to pleasure seeking and who in the necessary measure of rebellion that this entails, sets out to satisfy his wishes through becoming a skillful explainer and rationalizer. A charlatan is of course one who is able to persuade others of the usefulness of what he sells. However, beyond the intellectual activity of explanation, which can become a narcissistic vice in type VII, persuasiveness rests in one's own belief in one's wisdom, superiority, respectability, and goodness of intentions. Thus only artificially can we separate traits that exist in close inter-wovenness: being admirable serves persuasiveness, as also does pleasingness.

The qualities of being a persuader and a knowledge source usually find expression in type VII in becoming an adviser at times in a professional capacity. Charlatans like to influence others through advice. We may see not only narcissistic satisfaction and the expression of helpfulness in charlatanism but also an interest in manipulating through words: "laying trips" on people and having them implement the persuader's projects. Along with a manipulative motivation to influence others we may consider the high intelligence, high verbal ability, capability of suggesting, and so forth, that usually characterize type VII individuals.

Fraudulence

We have discussed the polarity of feeling OK (and better than OK) and of being at the same time driven by an oral passion to suck at the best of life. We have spoken of a rebelliousness as described in Fritz Perls' observation that "behind every good boy one may find a spiteful brat." We have encountered in ennea-type VII a confusion between imagination and reality, between projects and accomplishments, poten-tialities and realizations. Then, we have encountered a pleasingness, a persona-hiding anxiety, a smoothness hiding aggression, a generosity hiding exploitativeness. The word "charlatan" of ennea-type VII in its connotation of fake knowledge and confusion between verbal map and territory has thus an appropriateness to the character beyond mere persuasiveness. Taken broadly, it conveys a more generalized fraudulence (to which all the above add up). Indeed the conceptual label "fraudulence" may be more appropriate than the symbolic or metaphoric "charlatanism" for the ennea-type's fixation.

4. Defense Mechanisms

More than one defense mechanism seems particularly pertinent to hedonistic-narcissistic character.

To say that the type VII individual learns early in life to excuse the indulgence of his wants through "good reasons" implies that the mechanism of rationalization acquires an important strategic function in his life.

Rationalization was described by Ernest Jones as the invention of a reason for an attitude or action the motive of which is not acknowledged. Though it is not always regarded as a defense mechanism, there is enough reason to claim that it is, for even though it does not entail the inhibition of impulse (but, rather, the opposite), it does involve a distraction of attention from the "real reasons" for a person's attitudes and actions, and in making such actions appear as good and noble, it satisfies the demands of the superego.

As Matte-Blanco[12] writes: "Dissipating suspicion concerning the significance of an action, it facilitates the pacific maintenance of repression, and thus it can be considered a manifestation of it."

Rationalization is the more striking, in that it operates and constitutes a way of life—an "explainer" uses persuasion to get around obstacles to his pleasure. Rationalization may be contemplated, however, as a rather elementary defense mechanism that supports the more complex one of idealization. Just as rationalization has not been universally regarded as a defense mechanism, the same is the case with idealization, prominent in ennea-type VII psychology.

First of all there is self-idealization, which in the mind of the type VII person is linked with the denial of guilt and also with the narcissistic attitude and its claims. It may come across as self-propagandizing, even though the self-congratulating individual believes in his idealized version of himself.

---

[12]Matte-Blanco, Ignacio, op. cit.

Idealization also operates importantly in relation to people, and particularly in regard to the mother and mother surrogates. (Just as type VI males tend to be father lovers or father idealizers, tender-minded type VII individuals are characteristically devoted to their mothers and rebellious in the face of authority wielding fathers. In relation to authority figures in general, type VII seems to have adopted a de-idealizing attitude, implicit in its non-hierarchic orientation.)

It is possible to say that the optimistic attitude characteristic of type VII and the joyful mood that is habitual to them would not be possible without the operation of idealization in regard to the world in general and the more significant people in it. In relationship with others as in connection with oneself, optimism entails the suspension of criticality and blaming, and an assumption of lovingness as well as loveability. There is a strong bias toward the feeling expressed by the slogan "I'm OK, you're OK." Beyond that, there is a tendency to entertain a "cosmic optimism"—the sense that everything is all-right in the world and that there is no need to struggle.

Beyond rationalization and idealization, we may also mention a relevance of the defense mechanism of sublimation and type VII psychology, inasmuch as sublimation is defined as a turning of instinctual energy to socially desired ends, and the glutton is characteristically one whose self-interest has been re-labeled as altruistic motivation. The operation of sublimation helps us to understand the orientation of gluttons towards fantasy, which involves a substitution for the real goal of their impulses by images, plans and the cathexis of their own resourcefulness (i.e., in virtue of which, furthermore, they tend to accumulate tools for doing rather than simply doing).

5. Etiological and Further Psychodynamic Remarks[13]

In Sheldonian terms ennea-type VII individuals tend to be predominantly ectomorphic with endomorphia as the secondary component, yet as a whole seem to be the most balanced in the distribution of the three components. This matches a personality in which intellectual and spiritual interests exists side by side with social extroversion and an active or even restless disposition. Perhaps a constitutional predisposition through a balance between the intellectual, emotional and active orientations explains the intuitiveness of ennea-type VII (highlighted by Jung in his picture of the type). Yet I think it likely that the highly strategic type VII arises most commonly from a background factor in which a good intellectual endowment and genetically determined verbal ability are also present. Just as it is natural for an inborn fighter to settle on "moving against" people in the case of type VIII, it is natural for one who is clever and good with words to become an explainer in his approach to getting his way.

It is appropriate to begin the consideration of the environmental aspect of the nature/nurture equation with the

---

[13]The section on etiology written by Kernberg in his chapter on the narcissistic personality disorders in Cooper et al. is longer than most, yet more conjectural in content. He begins by stating that "the theories proposed by Rosenfeld, Kohut and me coincide in pointing to the essentially psychodynamic etiology of these disorders and in focusing on the pathology of self-esteem regulation as the key pathogenic issue." He summarizes Kohut's view stating that narcissistic psychopathology "derives from the traumatic failure of the mother's empathic function and from the failure of the undisturbed development of idealization processes." Which "bring about a developmental arrest, a fixation at the level of the archaic infantile grandiose self and an endless search for the idealized self-object needed to complete structure formation..." In Kernberg's own view "some time between the ages of 3 and 5 years, the narcissistic personality, instead of integrating positive and negative representations of self and of objects 'on the road to object constancy' puts together all the positive representations of both self and objects as well as the idealized representations of self and objects. This results in an extremely unrealistic and idealized idea of himself and a pathologic, grandiose self. Fostering the development of a pathologic grandiose self are parents who are cold, rejecting, yet admiring."

issue of breast feeding, for there is evidence of the correlation between prolonged and happy breast-feeding and a trusting and optimistic personality.[14] As in the case of the relation between unsatisfactory breast feeding and the oral-aggressive shown in the same study, I think that we may consider the finding paradigmatic for a more general relation between happiness in early childhood and cheerful optimism in later life. It is common for ennea-type VII people to report prolonged childhood satisfaction.

When we look at the life history of the cheerful and trusting individual, however, we find that there frequently has been a fall from paradise even more distinct than in the case of type IV, so a regression to the passive and trusting attitude of the child at the breast has taken place in response to the frustrations of later life. Just as type VII does not want to see the harsh aspect of life, it seems that the child has not wanted to deidealize his mother or sometimes his father. Memory in such a case supports fantasy to deny suffering.

I have described such a transition from a happy early childhood to a less happy situation in the life of a type VII individual in *The Healing Journey*.[15] I was a witness to my patient's remembrance (in the course of psychotherapy) of the idyllic relationship he had sustained with his nanny before he was old enough to share his meals with his parents and was exiled from the warmth of his nanny's kitchen to the cold atmosphere of the dining-room, when he was for the first time exposed to sustained contact with his not-so-welcome mother.

Other examples may be less dramatic, such as the following: "At home child rearing ended at the age of two, then we came under the care of our aunt and our parents became like phantoms... I was breast fed until I was two without any kind of schedule. My mother went along with my father in his journeys and they took me with them until I was three, then they left me in the house of an aunt to begin my schooling." Or: "My mother was very over-protective and I began speaking early and was graceful and sweet. School was a shock for me. I was completely

---

[14]Goldman-Eisler's, Ruth, op. cit.

[15]Naranjo, C., *The Healing Journey* (New York: Pantheon Books, 1974).

unprotected before aggression. I was a victim of my class. I sought refuge in a world of fantasy." Still another: "For me the family was great, life flowed very well, and I had no cares. I think it is at school that I began to be problem ridden."

A frequent element in the life stories of ennea-type VII people that I have heard is that of an outrageously authoritarian parent vis-a-vis whom a soft manner of rebellion seemed most appropriate. Most commonly this happened with type I fathers whose excessive dominance and sternness was experienced as lovelessness and not only contributed to an implicit judgment to the effect that authority is bad, but to the experience of an authority that is too strong to be met head-on, and also to a correlative misconception of love as indulgence (i.e. as being free from discipline). Mothers have often been experienced as over-protective and permissive (commonly type IX).

"What got my father most nervous about me is that I did not confront him, but I did what I felt, in spite of his rules. My father was physically imposing, I did not face him, but there was no way in which he would control me."

In response to the question, "What circumstance led you to develop a strategic disposition in face of your parents and life in general?," one subject explained how his parents were always right and this would have overwhelmed him if he had not cheated.

The seductiveness of ennea-type VII is usually apparent in relation to the parent of the opposite sex, and type VII men are most commonly mother oriented (just as type VI men are mostly father oriented). There may be a sense of competing with father in the protection of mother, or caring for her to compensate what hurt father has caused her. "My mother was very seductive and she always presented my father as an ogre, an intimidating man."

Of course it is also true for ennea-type VII that the presence of a similar character in the family has been a factor: "At home it is as if there were 'VII' values, for the things that I heard there are so fantastic and marvelous that it seems you are in another world. Now I can see it better. My father is a crazy VII, for him there is not such a thing as a pound of meat, only cows. We have an industrial refrigerator. Bedrooms, little by little, become pantries. Aside from that he has everything; in an imaginary place, he does. It is as if he has a magical bag and everything becomes reality. I was celebrated for being graceful. My mother used to say that I was not beautiful, but I could conquer the world through charm. Everybody laughs at home and there is freedom to show one's craziness. My mother likes very much when people express themselves very well and values culture."

Another factor I have noticed in the story of "oral optimists" as a whole is the frequency with which the father is fearful. In a little piece of research, in seven out of eight instances the father was either VI, VII or V. In another, four out of five responded in the affirmative to the question, "Did you adopt a weak and gentle position because you lacked an example of healthy aggression, because you lacked the image of a strong father?"

Type VII tends to become a pleasure-seeker to the extent that love becomes equated with the indulging of his wishes. Also the love search becomes a narcissistic striving to the extent that the means of attracting love—being ingenious, funny, and clever, for instance—develop into autonomous motives, and the pursuit of a charming and amiable superiority, an end in itself. Thus as in other personality orientations, a particular facet of love becomes a love substitute, and an obstacle towards a satisfying love life.

6. Existential Psychodynamics

As in other character types, the ruling passion is supported, day after day, not just by memories of past gratification and through past frustration, but through the interference that character entails on healthy function and on self-realization.

As in the case of the other passions, we may understand gluttony as an attempt to fill an emptiness. Gluttony, just as (oral-aggressive) envy, seeks outside something that it dimly perceives that it lacks inside. Only unlike envy (in which there is pronounced awareness of ontic insufficiency), gluttony fraudulently covers up the insufficiency with a false abundance comparable to that of pride. (In this way the passion is acted out without full self-awareness).

Ontic deficiency is not only the source of hedonism (and pain avoidance) however, but also its consequence; for the confusion between love and pleasure fails to bring about the deeper meaningfulness than that of the immediately available. A sense of inner scarcity is also, of course, supported by alienation of the individual from his experiential depth, which occurs as a consequence of the hedonistic need to experience only what is pleasing. It is nurtured also by the implicit fear that permeates the type in its soft accomodatingness—a fear not compatible with the living of one's true life. Also manipulativeness (however masked by amiability this may be), presupposes a loss of true relationship, a divorcing of oneself from the sense of community, and the fradulent sense of community, that is part of seductive charm, does not completely mask over that emptiness.

Finally the orientation of gluttony to the spiritual, the esoteric, and the paranormal, while seeking to constitute the exact answer for the ontic deficiency that lies at core, only serves to perpetuate it—for, by seeking being in the future, in the remote, the imagined, and the beyond, the individual only assures his frustration in finding value in the present and the actual.

Chapter Six

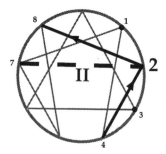

PRIDE AND THE HISTRIONIC PERSONALITY

ENNEA-TYPE II

1. Core Theory, Nomenclature, and Place in the Enneagram

In Christianity pride is not only regarded as one of the deadly sins, but the first and most serious one—more fundamental than the others. In that great monument of the Christian vision, Dante's *Divine Comedy*, we find Lucifer—whose pride prompted him to say "I" in the presence of the Only One—at the center of hell—itself shaped as a cone sloping to the center of the earth. This enormous cavity, according to Dante's myth, was created by the weight of the prideful angel upon his fall from heaven. In line with religious orthodoxy, Dante assigns to pride the innermost pit of hell, and correspondingly (according to inverse sequence of the sins in hell and purgatory) the first circle on the slopes of the mount of purification. On Mount Purgatory, where the pilgrims escalate successive terraces in the traditional sequence of the sins, the cornice of pride is the lowest, nearest to the mountain's foundation.

Dante's near-contemporary Chaucer in *The Canterbury Tales*[1] gives us a good but incomplete characterological allusion to proud people in "The Parson's Tale," which is essentially a preaching on the sins. He mentions among the "evil branches that spring from pride": disobedience, boasting, hypocrisy, scorn, arrogance, impudence, swelling of the heart, insolence, elation, impatience, contumacy, presumption, irreverence, obstinacy, and vainglory. The picture that these traits create characterizes an individual who not only asserts his own value, but also does so with an aggressive self-elevation vis-a-vis others and a disregard for established values and authorities.

True to life as Chaucer's portrayal may be, it fails to convey the whole range of the manifestations of pride-centered character. Fundamental to it is the strategy of *giving* in the service of both seduction and self-elevation. The "official psychology" of ennea-type II has failed to properly describe this characteristic false generosity in the character, for the descriptions of hysterical character have emphasized impulsive egocentricity, whereas it would be more exact to speak of a complementarity of egocentricity and seeming generosity. The account of hysterical character also tends to interpret the eroticism of hysterical personality as a phenomenon of ultimate sexual origin, whereas it may be truer to regard eroticism as a means of seductiveness inspired by a love wish.

The view of pride as more sinful than other inclinations may be a good teaching strategy to counteract proud people's lightness about their way of being, yet this is not the view of the body of psychological knowledge that I am presenting in these pages. According to Protoanalysis, all the passions are of an equivalent seriousness and though one is regarded as more fundamental—accidia or psychological deadness —this is not a statement concerning degrees of sinfulness or a ranking

---

[1]*The Canterbury Tales*, modern English version by J.U. Nicholson (New York: Garden City Books, 1934).

according to prognosis. The position of point 9 at the top of the enneagram, rather, evokes the fact that laziness may be regarded as a neutral middle point of the spectrum of the passions and that active unconsciousness, though present in every fallen mind, is in the foreground of the ennea-type IX phenomenon.

We may envision pride as a passion for self-inflation: or, in other words, a passion for the aggrandizement of the self-image.

The corresponding fixation or fixed and implicit preconception involved in pride, Ichazo successively called "flattery" and "ego-flat"—not only in reference to flattery towards others, but to the self-flattery implicit in self-aggrandizement. The word has the disadvantage of evoking a person whose behavior is mostly that of flattery—whereas the reality is that of a personality given not only to flattery but, in similar measure, to disdain. The person flatters those who through nearness gratify his pride, disdains most of the rest in haughty superiority. More than anybody else, the proud practice something that Idries Shah has called M.C.O.—"mutual comfort operation."[2]

From its position in the enneagram we see that pride stands in the "hysteroid" corner of it, aligned with the preoccupation with self-image that is the essence of vanity. In all three character ennea-types at this corner—II, III and IV—we may say that there operates a mistaken sense of "being" in what others see and value, so that it is the self-image rather than the true self upon which the psyche gravitates, out of which action flows, and on which is supported a person's sense of value.

Points 2 and 4 stand in opposite positions in regard to point 3, and involve internal gestures of expansion and contraction of the self-image, respectively. Whereas envy tends to sadness, pride characteristically is supported by a happy internal atmosphere: ennea-type IV is "tragic," ennea-type II "comic."

Just as with other sets of antipodal characters in the enneagram there is an affinity between those at points 7 and 2. Both the gluttons and the proud are gentle, sweet, and warm

---

[2]Idries Shah, *Reflexions* (London: Zenith Books, 1968).

people; both may be said to be seductive; and they are both narcissistic in the general sense of being delighted with themselves. Also, both are impulsive; moreover, they use seductiveness in the service of their impulsiveness, yet they do this in different ways: the proud seduces emotionally and the glutton intellectually.

The main contrast between the two characters is that, while the glutton is amiable and diplomatic, the proud can be either sweet or aggressive (so that, as I have sometimes remarked, their motto might be "make love *and* war"). Their narcissism also differs. We may say that the former is sustained through an intellectual apparatus: the activity of charlatanism in the broad sense of the word. In ennea-type II it is supported by a more naive falling in love with oneself, an emotional process of self-loving through identification with the glorified self-image and repression of the deprecated image. Also, the narcissism of the glutton is more inner-directed, in that he becomes an arbiter of his own values, as Samuel Butler has stated in describing one of his characters as "a messenger from his church to himself."[3]: Ennea-type II is more outer-directed, so that there is more admixture of borrowed values in the glorified self-image.

A polarity also exists between ennea-types II and VIII, pride and lust, in that both are impulsive and also arrogant— though ennea-type II adopts more often an attitude of being so good as not to need to compete, whereas the lusty is intensely competitive and visibly arrogant. The characterological constellation of ennea-type II is acknowledged in current psychology under the labels of "hysterical" or "histrionic" personality, yet I am not aware of any discussion of pride as a major aspect of its dynamics.

---

[3]Samuel Butler, *The Characters* (Cleveland: Case Western University, 1970).

2. Antecedents in the Scientific Literature on Character

Describing those "in need of esteem" Schneider quotes Koch concerning certain psychopaths with "an ego inconveniently transposed to the place at the center of things" and individuals with "a fatuous and prideful intent of making themselves visible."[4]

According to Kraepelin there is in these people an "increased access to emotions, lack of perseverance, being seduced by novelty, exaltation, curiosity, gossip, fantasy, tendency to lying, great excitability, sudden ups and downs in enthusiasm, sensibility, deep fickleness, selfishness, boasting, pride, wish to be at the center, absurd abnegation, susceptibility to be influenced, hypochondriac representations, insufficient wills to health in spite of all their laments, a tendency to scenes and romanticisms and impulsive behavior that can go as far as suicide."[5]

Further describing the character in question Schneider quotes Jaspers for whom the central trait among these individuals is "seeming to be more than what they are." "The more that theatricalness is developed the more that there lacks in these personalities true emotions: they are false, incapable of durable or deep affective relations. There is only a stage of theatrical and imitative experiences; this is the extreme of hysterical personality."

As with many of the psychopathological syndromes, we find an exaggerated version of type II described by Kraepelin under the label of "Psychopaths in need of Affection." In his book on psychopathic personalities[6] Kurt Schneider, commenting on Koch's description of the same, adds: "It is easy to recognize that this is no different from hysterical character."

---

[4]Schneider, K., *Die Psychopathischen Personalichkeiten* (Vienna: Deuticke, 1923).

[5]op. cit.

[6]Schneider, K., op. cit.

Reading "Hysterical Personality," by Easser and Lesser,[7] I find the observation that "Freud and Abraham originally described the basic character traits of obsessive character, but there has been almost no attempt to systematize the concept of hysterical personality." Though it is true that the erotic orientation of ennea-type II is coherent with Freud's concept of erotic personality (when in his late statement he distinguishes super-ego and ego-driven characters from a character with the predominance of the id), ennea-type II is not alone as an id's character, however, for the same term could be applied to ennea-types VII and VIII.

From a survey of Lazare on the history of "The Hysterical Character In Psychoanalytic Theory"[8] throughout time, I learn that "although the textbooks of general psychiatry at the turn of the century described the hysterical character, it was not until 1930 that the first psychoanalytic description of hysterical character was presented and discussed by Franz Wittels." Indeed, I have been surprised that "not withstanding the fact that Freud's vocation was awakened through the consideration of hysteria, the hysteria he was dealing with seems not to have existed in the context of hysterical character as we today understand it. (Furthermore, Freud hardly makes any comments on character in his early cases—where he concentrates nearly exclusively on symptoms and past history)."

Wilhelm Reich[9] describes the hysterical character as having the following traits:

Obvious sexual behavior
A specific kind of body agility
An undisguised coquetry
Apprehensiveness when the sexual behavior seems
    close to attaining its goal
An easy excitability
A strong suggestibility

---

[7]"Hysterical Personality: a revaluation" in *Psychoanalytic Quarterly*, 1965, 34, pp. 390-402.

[8]Lazare, A., G. L. Klerman, and D. Armor, "Oral, Obsessive and Hysterical Personality Patterns: Replication of Factor Analysis in an Independent Sample," *Journal of Psychiatric Research*, 1970, 7, pp. 275-290.

[9]Reich, Wilhelm, *Character Analysis* (New York: Simon and Schuster, 1961).

A vivid imagination and pathological lying.

Lazare, by collecting the information from what he regards the three most important papers appearing between 1953 and 1968 (by Lesser, Kernberg, and Setzel) arrives at the following list of personality traits:

Self-absorption
Aggressive exhibitionism with inappropriate
    demanding nature
A "coldness" which reflects primitive narcissistic need
Sexual provocativeness
Impulsivity
Emotional Lability

Undertaking to distinguish the sicker from the healthier manifestations of hysterical character, he noticed that "the healthier hysteric is apt to be ambitious, competitive, buoyant and energetic. She is more apt to have a strict punitive super-ego as well as other obsessional personality traits which are likely to be adaptive. The sick hysteric in contrast experiences little guilt." I am of the opinion that his "healthier" cases correspond to our ennea-type III, and only the "sicker" (i.e., more impulsive, labile, and provocative) to our ennea-type II.

Seeking to clarify hysterical character as distinct from hysteria, Easser, in the paper quoted above, discusses six cases and concludes that the presenting problems revolved in the main about sexual behavior and the real or fantasized sexual object. They all complained of disillusionment and dissatisfaction with their lovers. This followed a shattering of a romantic fantasy. They all expressed concern over their passion-ate sexuality and their fear of the consequence of such passion.

"Unconsciously they were motivated to compete with women, to seduce and conquer men and to achieve security and power vicariously through the passionate engagement of the man with themselves...The fantasies usually involved an irresistible, magnetic body that was to be exhibited to conquer the male and exclude all other women. The burlesque queen, the femme fatale, the diva served to portray this image. The other major presenting complaint was the sense of social shyness and apprehensiveness which contrasted with active social involvement... this continued apprehensiveness was asso-ciated with severe humiliation and shame should rejection occur. They obtained pleasure in entertaining others and assumed the role of hostess with graciousness as long as they held the center of the stage through ingratiation and seductiveness as a rule, through temper tantrums when necessary."

In conclusion, the author finds the following traits to be more intimately associated with the hysterical personality: Labile emotionality, direct and active engagement with the human world, a poor response to frustration, and over-excitability.

In the DSM III, ennea-type II is found under the label of "Histrionic Personality Disorder" for which the following diagnostic criteria are given:

A. Behavior that is overly dramatic, reactive, and intensely expressed, as indicated by at least three of the following:

1) self-dramatization, e.g. exaggerated expressions of emotions
2) incessant drawing of attention to oneself
3) craving for activity and excitement
4) over reaction to minor events
5) irrational, angry outbursts or tantrums

B. Characteristic disturbances in interpersonal relationships as indicated by at least two of the following:

1) perceived by others as shallow and lacking genuineness, even if superficially warm and charming
2) egocentric, self-indulgent, and inconsiderate of others
3) vain and demanding
4) dependent, helpless, constantly seeking reassurance
5) prone to manipulative suicidal threats, gestures, or attempts

In *Disorders of Personality* Millon[10] mentions the important feature that "usually these individuals show little

----

[10] op.cit.

interest in intellectual achievement and careful analytic thinking, though they are often creative and imaginative...though they adopt convictions strongly and readily, their judgment is not firmly rooted and they often play hunches."

In this book he discusses histrionic personality immediately after dependent personality (ennea-type IV), and I think it is of interest to quote his description of the former in contrast to the latter:

"Histrionics are no less dependent upon others for attention and affection but, in contrast to dependents, take the initiative in assuring these reinforcements. Rather than placing their fate in the hands of the others, and thereby having their security in constant jeopardy, histrionic personalities actively solicit the interest of others through a series of seductive ploys that are likely to assure receipt of the admiration and esteem they need. Toward these ends histrionics develop an exquisite sensitivity to the moods and thoughts of those they wish to please. This hyperalertness enables them to quickly access what maneuvers will succeed in attaining the ends they desire. This extreme 'other-directedness,' devised in the service of achieving approval, results, however, in a life-style characterized by a shifting and fickle pattern of behaviors and emotions. Unlike dependent personalities, who anchor themselves usually to only one object of attachment, the histrionic tends to be lacking in fidelity and loyalty. The dissatisfaction with single attachments, combined with a need for constant stimulation and attention, results in a seductive, dramatic, and capricious pattern of personal relationships."

Although Jung's descriptions of psychological types are not as rich in observations bearing on interpersonal styles as others, it is hard to doubt that, as he formulated the extraverted feeling type, he had cases of type II before his inner eye:[11]

"Examples of this type that I can call to mind are, almost without exception, women. The woman of this type follows her feeling as a guide throughout life...Her personality appears adjusted in relation to external conditions. Her feelings harmonize with objective situations and general values. This is

---

[11]Jung, C.G., op. cit.

seen nowhere more clearly than in her love choice: the 'suitable' man is loved, and no one else; he is suitable not because he appeals to her hidden subjective nature... but because he comes up to all reasonable expectations in the matter of age, position, income, size, and respectability of his family, etc....

"But one can feel 'correctly' only when feeling is not disturbed by anything else. Nothing disturbs feeling so much as thinking. It is therefore understandable than in this type thinking will be kept in abeyance as much as possible...every conclusion, however logical, that might lead to a disturbance of feeling is rejected at the outset...

"But since actual life is a constant succession of situations that evoke different and even contradictory feelings, the personality gets split up into many different feeling states...this shows itself, first of all, in an extravagant display of feelings, gushing talk, loud expostulations, etc. which ring hollow...As a result of these experiences the observer is unable to take any pronouncement seriously. He begins to reserve judgment. But since, for this type it is of highest importance to establish an intense feeling of rapport with the environment, redoubled efforts are now required to overcome this reserve.

"Hysteria, with the characteristic infantile sexuality of its unconscious world of ideas, is the principal form of neurosis in this type."

I think that the picture described in homeopathic literature of the *Pulsatilla* personality competes with any account of ennea-type II given in psychological literature.[12]

"The constitutional type, found predominantly in women and children, is generally delicate and pretty... and a physique that can fluctuate easily in weight loss and gain, with the fat tending to a shapely plumpness rather than the flabby or formless fleshiness of *Calcarea carbonica*.

"Like the flower swaying in the wind, *Pulsatilla* symptoms are characteristically changeful.... we will examine in detail five seminal mental characteristics: sweetness, dependence, companionability, flexibility, and a gentle

---

[12]Coulter, Catherine R., op. cit., Vol. 1, all excerpts from pp. 199-225 reprinted by permission of the author.

emotionalism." All of these descriptors correspond with the characteristics of ennea-type II individuals. Coulter continues:

"Traditionally regarded as a female remedy...and in these pages referred to in the feminine, it can also be unhesitatingly administered as a constitutional remedy to boys and men who manifest the typical sweet and gentle manner....

"*Pulsatilla*'s sweetness and desire to please do not exclude an under-lying ability to look after her own interests; it is just that she realizes early in life that sugar catches more flies than vinegar. She likes being fussed over and is content to pass even the simplest responsibilities on to others. To be sure, she graciously thanks those who help her, offering her own affection in return as good and legal tender...."

Dependence in the *Pulsatilla* individual manifests as clinging in the child and, sometimes, in adults who don't mature, as helplessness and childlikeness: "As the child grows into adolescence, dependence begins to be directed away from the family and toward the opposite sex. *Pulsatilla* is attractive to men, being the highly feminine young woman whose whole manner flatters the ego... In her dependence, however, she can place severe demands on the time, solicitude and emotional reserves of friends, relatives, and acquaintances. In family, amorous, and even friendly relationships, she seeks ever more support until, at length, others feel they are captives...."

Coulter presents *Pulsatilla*'s companionability as a positive quality, while flexibility can be constructive or, more negatively, can manifest as indecisiveness, as in poring over grocery-store produce to make a selection or vacillating as to what items to order from a restaurant menu. Coulter's description of *Pulsatilla*'s emotionalism corresponds very strongly with ennea-type II:

"*Pulsatilla*'s fifth characteristic, *emotionalism*, is marked by fluctuation, self-pity and sentimentality.... *Pulsatilla* has been aptly called the 'weathercock among remedies' (Boericke) due to her fluctuating, readily swayed nature and her changeable, sometimes 'whimsical' (Hahnemann) or 'capricious' (Hering) moods....

"Ruled by her sensibilities, *Pulsatilla* is essentially non-intellectual. Of course, as with any constitutional type, some are more and some less intelligent, but she generally operates in a highly personal and non-intellectual mode.... *Pulsatilla* is not interested in facts, statistics, scholarly ideas or theories. Her mind feels more comfortable dealing with the particulars of everyday life and human relations.... Influenced by her emotions, she systematically interprets abstractions and generalities in personal terms—in the light of her own thoughts, feelings or preferences."

3. Trait Structure

Pride

While a number of descriptors might be grouped together as direct manifestations of pride—i.e., the imaginary exaltation of self-worth and attractiveness, "playing the part of the princess," demanding privileges, boasting, needing to be the center of attention, and so on—there are others which may be understood as psychological "corollaries" of pride, and to them I now turn.

Love Need

The intense love need of ennea-type II individuals may be sometimes obscured by their characteristic independence— particularly when in the presence of frustration and humiliated pride. The proud person can rarely be fulfilled in life without a great love. The excessively romantic orientation of type II toward life can be understood as the result of an early love frustration associated with a loss of support in one's experience of personal value. Just as the need to confirm an inflated sense of worth overflows into an erotic motivation, pride overflows in the need for love (in turn expressed through physical and emotional intimacy), for the need to regard oneself as special is satisfied through the love of another. The need for intimacy of ennea-type II makes of the person a "touchy feely" type and at a subtler level leads to an intolerance of limits and invasiveness. Also, the strong need for love of the proud makes them "over-involved" in relationships and possessive. Theirs is a possessiveness supported in such seductiveness as has inspired the expression "femme fatale" (which suggests that seductiveness serves a destructive power drive).

Hedonism

Hedonism may also be understood as a trait related to the need for love, in that the wish for pleasure can be usually seen as a substitute for pleasure. Indeed these persons typically need to be loved erotically or through delicate expression of tenderness in the measure to which they equate being loved with being pleased, like in Grimm's fairy tale of "The Princess and the Pea," whose noble blood is discovered in the fact that she is distressed by the pea under the mattress. The affectionate and tender type II individual can become a fury when not indulged and made to feel loved through pampering such as is characteristic of a spoiled child.

The compulsive pursuit of pleasure of the ennea-type II person naturally supports the gay persona of histrionic people, with its pretended contentedness and animation. It is reflected, also, through a propensity to be frustrated and when not specially pleased (through attention, novelty, stimulation), through a low tolerance to routine, discipline, and other obstacles to an irresponsible, playful life.

Seductiveness

It is understandable that the histrionic individual bent on the pursuit of love and pleasure is also keenly interested in being attractive. Such persons *work* for it, we might say, and are, above all, seductive. There are traits that we can, in turn, understand as tools of seductiveness—whether erotic or social. Thus the histrionic person is affectionate. Those who are in need of affection, because of being secretly insecure in regard to it, are, in turn, warm, supportive, sensitive, empathic... even though their display of love may have inspired epithets such as "superficial," "fickle," "unstable," and so forth. The support seductively offered by the individual is typically what may be called "emotional" support or perhaps "moral" support in the sense that one is an unconditional friend, yet may be not as helpful a person as may be suggested through the expression of feelings. (Ennea-type III and others can be more helpful when it comes to doing something practical.) Thus their seductiveness entails not only a histrionic love display but also a failure to deliver and, motivationally speaking, a "giving to get" kind of generosity.

Flattery, too, may be valued as a means of seduction exhibited by ennea-type II individuals. It must be pointed out that type II only flatters those seen as worthy enough to be seduced.

Eroticism is thus one of the vehicles of seductiveness. If we look at the erotic inclination of the histrionic individual as something that serves a broader purpose of proving personal significance (rather than in biologistic Freudian terms), we can, I think, understand both eroticism and pride better.

Assertiveness

Along with an intense love need and its derivatives, we may say that dominance is also a characteristic of ennea-type II and constitutes a derivative of pride. Rather than the harsh, tyrannical demandingness of ennea-type VIII and the moralistic dominance of ennea-type I, who exacts his due as an authority, type II gets his or her wishes met through daring assertiveness— *chutzpah*. It is the assertiveness of one who at the same time is supported in a good self-concept and propelled by a strong, uninhibited drive—which contributes to the aura of vitality of this adventurous character. (As I have remarked already, proud character involves a rare combination of tenderness and pugnacity.)

Another descriptor belonging to this category of assertiveness is willfulness, a trait of "having to have one's own way" even at the expense of an emotional "scene" or broken dishes.

Nurturance and False Abundance

Of great significance to the structure of proud character is the repression of neediness that pride involves. Much as we may be dealing with a zestful individual, who seems to be compulsively pursuing excitement and high drama, the person is typically unaware of the neediness that underlies this compulsion to please and to be extraordinary.

The proud are supposedly OK and better than OK, and to sustain this they must indeed pursue their pleasure in a compensatory manner. Yet nothing would be less OK than to be in need of love—for pride in the course of personality development has been particularly attached to an image of self as a giver rather than as a receiver: one who is filled with satisfaction to the point of generous overflowing.

Repression of neediness is not only supported by hedonism, but also by vicarious identification with the neediness of others, of those towards whom the individual extends sympathy, empathy, and seductive nurturance. Thus we may understand the frequent attraction of ennea-type II to children: they represent not only an unconstrained wildness, but also little ones in need of protection. They sustain the proud in the sense of having much love to offer, as well as covertly satisfying their love need.

Histrionism

I could have written at the head of this trait cluster "histrionic implementation of the idealized self-image," in reference to what may be abstracted as an over-riding strategy in ennea-type II of which false love and false self-satisfaction are a strong form of expression. The affectionate characteristic, however, can be seen as only one of the facets of the typical ideal image the proud enacts and identifies with.

Such image also contains the *happy* characteristic that we have already encountered in the analysis of seductiveness, an independence that involves the denial of dependency needs, and also a characteristic for which the word "free" might be an approximate term, if we understand it to be not the true freedom of liberation from characterological structures, but the freedom of willfulness, impulsiveness, and wildness. This freedom is an ideal of impulse gratification that exists not only in the service of hedonism, but also as an avoidance of the humiliation of having to submit to somebody else's power, societal rules and all manner of constraints. Ennea-type II is not only too proud to conform to such rules, but is rebellious to authority in general— often in a mischievous and humorous way.

Also "intensity," which can be considered, along with wit, a means of attracting attention (and which feeds on the pursuit of pleasure), can be understood as an ingredient in a larger than life self-image. It is not only an addiction but also a form of posing and sustaining the illusion of positivity. The histrionic posing of ennea-type II is in contrast to the efforts of type III to implement the idealized self through achievement and performance--just as her histrionic manipulation (through scandalous expression of emotion) is in contrast with type III's explosiveness, which supervenes upon the breakdown of over-control.

Impressionable Emotionality

While ennea-types IV and II are distinctly the most emotional in the enneagram, type II can be regarded a more specifically emotional type, in that ennea-type IV emotionality frequently coexists with intellectual interests, while type II is usually not only a feeling type, but an anti-intellectual one.

4. Defense Mechanisms

The association between hysterical personality and simple repression is not only the earliest relationship reported between a defense mechanism and a neurotic disposition but the one most thoroughly documented and agreed upon. When the word repression is used to mean a specific defense mechanism rather than as a symptom for defense, it stands for a defense mechanism where the ideational representative of impulses is impeded from becoming conscious. What this selective elimination from consciousness of the cognitive aspect of the experience of wishing implies, is a state of affairs in which the person acts upon his or her impulses without acknowledgment of such impulses—which amounts to an attitude of irresponsibility and impresses us as deception.

The boundary here between not knowing what one does and pretending not to know, is as difficult to draw as it is difficult to distinguish a hysterical condition from malingering. Just as it might be said that clinical hysteria is unconscious malingering, we may say that repression is unconscious "not wanting to know," a pretense that has become acceptable through the decision to deceive not only the world but oneself as well. Of course this can be accomplished only through a certain dulling of the intellect, through a sort of vagueness, a loss of precision or clarity, which goes hand in hand with (or rather is sustained by) a de-valuation of the cognitive sphere. This explains the emotional characteristic of the type, supported in a constitutional disposition.

In the case of every defense mechanism, unconsciousness seems to require a compensatory phenomenon. Just as unconsciousness of destructive or passive tendencies in ennea-type I is maintained through a conscious pursuit of goodness and an anti-hedonic bias, we may ask whether there is also a compensation for the loss of awareness of needs in ennea-type II. The answer lies, I think, in an intensification of the *feeling* states associated with impulse. Just as there exists a mechanism of intellectualization, that serves to distance oneself from one's feelings, we may say that here there is an "emotionalization" or "emotionalism," that facilitates the process of distracting attention from the awareness of need or, more exactly, "the intellectual representation of instinct."

But not only is there an emotional amplification in this type, there is also a characteristic impulsiveness, a pushiness in the interpersonal relation, an impatient need for satisfaction and a childlike inability to defer gratification. It is as if the experience of *unconscious* satisfaction failed to bring about *true* satisfaction; as if satisfaction without the awareness of need failed to bring the individual to a sense that the need has been met and resulted in an insatiable thirst for intensity.

It is easy to see how unawareness of needing—and particularly unawareness of needing love—supports pride, for if pride is built upon self-worth, what measure of worth presents itself more naturally to a child's mind than being worthy of the love of her parents? To the extent that the proud is implicitly saying "I am worthy of love, and feel loved," she is saying, "My love wish is satiated, I am not frustrated in my love thirst." Yet this image of self as not wanting necessarily clashes with the ongoing acknowledgment of want—and the gap is made up by "histrionics."

The connection between repression and the "universal giver" or "Jewish mother" aspect of type II is similar: it is not congruent to hold in the mind simultaneously the awareness of emotional neediness and of overflowing givingness. For a specialist in the manipulation and seduction of others through giving, it would also be "dangerous" to acknowledge one's own wishes, for then "givingness" would be suspected for what indeed it is in its characteristic excess: a giving to get or a giving motivated by a personal need to identify oneself with the position and role of a giver.

To end, let me remark that to speak of a repression of neediness is practically equivalent to speaking of a repression of the psychological atmosphere of envy—and just as in the case of ennea-type I we understood anger as a reaction-formation to gluttony, we may in this case understand pride as a transformation of envy through the joint action of repression and histrionic emotionalism. Just as for the perfectionist it is self-indulgence that is most avoided, in the proud and histrionic character nothing is more avoided than the love thirst and the sense of unlovability that are characteristics of envy. Thus we may say that through a combination of repression and histrionic emotionalism envy is transformed into pride, and (to speak in Murray's terms) succorance[13] into nurturance.[14]

---

[13]To solicit sympathy, affection, or emotional support from others.

[14]To engage in behaviors that provide material or emotional benefits to others.

5. Etiological and Further Psychodynamic Remarks[15]

The body build of ennea-type II is typically more rounded than ennea-type I and also softer than ennea-type III, and so it is possible to think that a genetically determined endomorphia supports the viscerotonic need for affection. Since physical beauty is more common in type II than in any other character, it is also possible to speculate that this and perhaps a constitutionally-given playful disposition are "seductive" beyond any attempt of the child to be seductive—particularly as a stimulus to a seductive parent.

As in the case of type IV, type II is much more common in women than in men, and however true it may be that Daddy's favorite little girl has an attractiveness that makes him want to caress her and speak to her tenderly (and in the little girl's reaction there is a conscious or unconscious erotic ingredient) I think that the seduction scenario observed by Freud at the beginning of his career represents a typical manifestation rather than the heart of the matter (just as in the case of the anal character the biological interpretation, however evocative, fails

---

[15]In spite of agreeing with Kernberg's contention that we should draw distinction between histrionic personality and hysterical personality proper, I think that his condensed account concerning the family dynamics of hysterical patients (in Cooper et al.'s *Psychiatry*) fits the case of the histrionic better than that of the hysterical sensu strictu. He reports that psychoanalytical literature "conveys a growing consensus that women with hysterical personality disorder come from rather stable families with the following characteristics. Their fathers are described as seductive, often combining sexual seductive and over-stimulating behavior toward their daughters with abrupt and authoritarian and at times sexually puritanical attitudes toward them: seductiveness during childhood typically shifts into prohibition against sexual and romantic involvements in adolescence. These patient's mothers are described as domineering and controlling of their daughter's life in subtle and pervasive fashions, often conveying the impression that they were attempting to realize their unfulfilled aspirations through their daughters. At the same time these mothers were effective and responsible at home and in their community functions. "I also think that it is essentially to the type II that Marmor's observations generally apply concerning "the realization that there were indeed patients with predominantly oral conflicts centering around pathologic dependency, passivity, and above all, evidence of severe disturbances in preoedipal mother-infant relations."

to address itself to the more important issue of interpersonal strategy). I am convinced that the parent's favorite is eminently a seducer and only secondarily one who puts eros into seduction, and I think the more modern turn in psychoanalysis to lean towards a pre-oedipal view of the histrionic personality is correct —for just as in the grown-up's desire to be caressed there lingers the baby's desire to be held by a tender mother, also in the "spoiled, adorable and demanding" five year old there lingers an oral frustration that is here finding a compensation.

Here is how a student of protoanalysis described her situation growing up:

"I was my father's bride. He made me believe that I was the woman of his life, and that was a lie. He loved me so much...but he didn't marry with me, he was married to mother. I was happy with my father, the pity is that it had an end."

Here is another account reflecting the special father-daughter bond:

"My father called me his 'sign.' He said I had a special mark on my neck that only he could see, and because of that I was magnificent and unique. I believed it."

Not every type II person remembers a childhood as a happy, loved, and pampered princess or an adorable, favorite son. In some we hear a story of deprivation, and on occasion this surfaces after some therapeutic exploration. It is possible to bring the person to see how the time of becoming a little princess was preceded by one of emotional pain. In these cases it seems as if the child wanted to be specially reassured of mother's or father's love through being specially cared for, delighted in, and tolerated in her whims or bouts of crying. It is as if the child were saying: "*Prove* to me that you really love me!," and as the demand for *special* expression of love were essentially a reaction to having felt rejected.

Thus, for instance, a patient says: "For my mother I was ugly, dirty, ordinary...and I could not allow any of her view to get into me, for I would panic at sinking into this ugly image. It is in this way that I defended myself with pride and through feeling the center of the universe." In this case it can be seen that the imaginary reconstruction of the self can precede and be more fundamental than the seeking for an external alliance to confirm the proud self-image. It also suggests that the compensation for

oral frustrations of infancy involves not only the denial of
frustration, but also a compensatory assertiveness. Just as this
person asserted being the center of the universe, another had to
adopt an attitude of "don't step on me" in face of two very hard
brothers, and still another says: "I had a twin who was a model
child, and I was the opposite. I rebelled. I reacted with prideful
rebellion in face of my mother's rejection."

A transition from frustration to a self-satisfied and self-
satisfying stance, and self-image generally can be seen, among
women, as a shift from the experience of relative rejection by the
mother to the development of seductiveness in view of becoming
father's favorite.[16]

"My mother was dry and skinny. My father was
immense, happy, with a round face and with a very beautiful
skin. It was no help for my becoming fat. Who doesn't like it let
him go to the skinny and dry ones."

The following example involves a variant: "I did not
receive attention, I felt abandoned by my mother[17]. I had two
fathers. My fantasy has been more that of Cinderella than that of
a princess. I had to expect my prince, who was my father, who
had abandoned me. And this has been a clear fantasy always. It
was with my second father that I was the favorite, in spite of not
being his daughter. I have much of my mother's perfectionism,
but I was also very seductive. With that mother there was no
help to being in the shadow."

Hearing ennea-type II histories I have noticed something
akin to a breaking of the will that seeks compensation in
willfulness. Frustration is transformed in the compulsive search
for freedom that characterizes this character's intolerance for
rules and boundaries. As a woman has said: "Whims were the
proof of love." An instance of this is an acquaintance who
remembers that when she was taken away from mother's to her
grandmother's house as a child, she was promised many
beautiful things to lure her, overcoming her reluctance. Later,

---

[16]Perhaps related to the experience of early frustration is the discovery I have
received from a group of type II women that most of them felt that at least one of
their parents were disappointed in that they were not the opposite sex.

[17]Apparently ennea-type I.

feeling betrayed, she demanded ever more beautiful things, seeking her compensation with a "vengeance."

Here is another quote on egocentrism as a compensatory love thirst:

"There were economical differences and I began to work at fourteen, and I think whims were demands through which I charged what I felt was due to me."

It is not surprising that often type VII fathers appeared in the history of ennea-type II women, which makes sense given their typical seductiveness, gaiety, orientation to pleasure, and family orientation. Just as in type I the desire for love becomes a search for respect, in type II the love-wish becomes a search for intimacy and the expression of tender feelings through words and caressing. In one case as in the other the secondary search interferes with the primal satisfaction. Not only, in this case, because the development of the "seductive apparatus" makes the person less than complete and thus less lovable, but also because to feel loved a person needs to be in touch with his/her love-wish, and this is repressed in the proud along with their denigrated self-image.

A feature of early life history coherent with the position of superiority and giving of ennea-type II that I have observed is that of becoming a mother's helper vis-a-vis the care of siblings. I illustrate with a fragment of a report by a group of type II women:

"All of us carried a lot of adult responsibility as very young children; became the little mother in the house or the mother in the house at early ages. And we kept, we strove to keep our parents happy, so that our needs would be met. If parents were happy, then we got some love and attention and approval, but if not, then we were the ones that had the wrath poured on us or whatever. It was a safer environment to be in if parents were happy. Most of us expressed ourselves in a way that said that we were providing for one parent what the other parent wasn't in some ways, became the companion for the father if the mother wasn't that or vice versa in many activities."

The following individual report suggests that an ennea-type II can seek to be a "good little girl":

"After you established a certain level of performance it became expected and after that you had to do a little more because you did make them happy, but after a while that was just expected, so in order to make them happy you had to do more." And so they had to keep the performance extraordinary. While it may be said of a type II girl that she is a "good little girl" just as the type I girl is, the difference is that in this case performance occurs in an atmosphere of wish fulfillment rather than frustration.

Another factor in early childhood history that had been brought to my attention is some measure of over-protectiveness and over-possessiveness by one of the parents—a problematic side of being a favorite related to the thirst for freedom and which has led some to become independent at an early age. It is common for type II girls who did not have freedom to be with friends, come from large families and have been told: "You know you got siblings to play with, you don't need anybody else," and to be relatively confined."

6. Existential Psychodynamics

If we understand pride as the result of an early love frustration that was equated in the child's mind with worthlessness (so that the impulse to worthiness and toward being special amounts to a compulsive repetition of the original maneuver of compensating for that early lack), it may be a mistake to continue to interpret pride as the elaboration of a love need. This may amount to putting the cart before the horse, since the intense love need of ennea-type II individuals is rather a consequence of pride than a more deeply seated antecedent. In line with the manner of interpretation undertaken thus far, which seeks to replace libido theory in the understanding of neurotic wants with an existential one, we can look at pride (as each of the passions) as a compensation for a perceived lack of value which goes hand-in-hand with an obscuration of the sense of one's being—the natural, original, and truest support for one's sense of personal value.

We may say that, despite superficial elation, vitality, and flamboyance, there lurks in proud character a secret recognition of emptiness—a recognition transformed into the pain of hysterical symptoms, into eroticism and clinging to love relationships. Not withstanding the usual interpretation of this pain as a love pain, it may be more exact to regard it as no different from the universal pain of fallen consciousness, beyond type-bound characteristics. If we do so, we can understand that it may be transformed not only in libido, but that, interpreted as a sense of personal insignificance, it sustains the will to significance that is in the nature of pride.

Such an interpretation is useful, for it orients us to look for what in the present life of the individual is perpetuating this "hole" at the center of the personality. How this hole arises is not difficult to understand, for, as Horney has remarked, embracing the pursuit of glory amounts to something like selling one's soul to the devil—inasmuch as one's energy becomes involved in the realization of an image rather than in the realization of one's self.

The sense of being rests in the integrated wholeness of one's experience, and is not compatible with the repression of one's neediness any more than it is compatible with the failure to live one's true life (while occupied in dramatizing an ideal image for a selected audience of supporters). Excitement may capture one's attention and serves as an ontic pacifier from moment to moment, but only in a superficial level of awareness. The same may be said of pleasure. The individual fails to be as he or she is while driven to seek pleasure and excitement instead while trying to live in the continuous ecstasy of being the center of attention.

False abundance, thus, is doomed to be, after all, an emotional lie that the individual does not fully believe—for otherwise he or she would not continue to be driven to fill up frantically the hole of deeply felt beinglessness. If it is ontic deficiency that supports pride and, indirectly, the whole edifice of pride-centered character, ontic deficiency is, in turn, brought about by each one of the traits that constitutes its structure: a gaiety that implies (by repression of sadness) a loss of reality; a hedonism that, in it's chasing after immediate gratification, only affords a substitute satisfaction and not what growth requires; the compulsive indiscipline that goes along with this hedonism, with its free and wild characteristics of "hysteria," which also get in the way of accomplishing such life goals as would bring about a deeper satisfaction.

In conclusion, in recognition of this vicious circle whereby ontic insufficiency supports pride, which through its manifestation, in turn, supports ontic insufficiency, lies therapeutic hope; for the aim of therapy should not stop at providing the good relationship that was absent in early life: it can include re-educating the individual toward self-realization and the daily elaboration of that deep satisfaction that comes from an authentic existence.

Chapter Seven

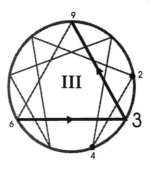

VANITY, INAUTHENTICITY, AND "THE MARKETING ORIENTATION"

ENNEA-TYPE III

1. Core Theory, Nomenclature, and Place in the Enneagram

Vanity is a passionate concern for one's image, or a passion of living for the eyes of others. Living for appearances implies that the focus of concern is not in one's own experience, but in the anticipation or fantasy of the experience of another, and thus the insubstantiality of the vain pursuit. Nothing could be more appropriately called "vanity of vanities," of which the preacher in Ecclesiastes speaks, than living for an ephemeral and insubstantial image (rather than out of oneself).

To speak of vanity as a living for a self-image is not different than speaking of narcissism, and indeed we may regard narcissism as a universal aspect of egoic structure, mapped on the right corner of the enneagram. Yet, since the word "narcissism" has been used in reference to more than one personality syndrome, and mostly since the publication of DSM III in reference to our ennea-type VII, I have not included it in this chapter heading.

Vanity is present especially in the "hysteroid" region of the enneagram (comprising ennea-types II, III, and IV), yet in the case of pride, as we have seen, it is satisfied through a combination of imaginative self-inflation and the support of selected individuals, while in ennea-type III, instead, the person mobilizes herself to "prove" objectively her value through an active implementation of the self-image in the face of a generalized other. This leads to an energetic pursuit of achievement and good form as defined by quantitative or generally accepted standards.

The difference between ennea-types III and IV lies mostly in the fact that the former identifies with the image that it "sells," while the latter is more in touch with the denigrated self-image and is thus characterized by the experience of a vanity never fulfilled. As a result, ennea-type III is cheerful, ennea-type IV depressive.

As mentioned in the introduction, Ichazo spoke of "deceit" rather than vanity as the passion of ennea-type III, relegating vanity to the sphere of the fixations. Throughout most of my teaching experience I have chosen, rather, to consider vanity as a passion akin to pride, while seeing in deception the cognitive core or fixation in ennea-type III character. The word "deceit" is not the best to evoke the particular manner of deception that goes with vanity, however—different from the lying of ennea-type II or the conning of VIII, for instance; rather than a lack of truthfulness in regard to facts (ennea-type III may be a faithful, factual reporter) there is in vanity a lack of truthfulness in regard to feelings and pretense.

In contrast to the comic vein of ennea-type II and the tragic vein of ennea-type IV, the characteristic mood of ennea-type III is one of neutrality or feeling control—where only "correct feelings" are acknowledged and expressed.

Though pride (*superbia*) and not vanity is included among the traditional capital sins of Christianity, it seems that both ideas are commonly juxtaposed—as is suggested by the common iconography that depicts pride through a woman looking at a mirror (as in Hieronymus Bosch's "Seven Deadly Sins").

It is interesting to observe that the characterological disposition involved in ennea-type III is the only one not included in DSM-III—which raises the question as to whether this may be related to the fact of its constituting the modal[1] personality in American society since the twenties.

2. Antecedents in the Scientific Literature on Character

Kurt Schneider proposes the expression "hyperthymic" for individuals who "are predominantly joyful and active." He says that "hyperthymic personalities are gay, frequently kind, active, balanced and with an unshakable optimism. As an immediate consequence of that, they lack in depth...too self-assured."[2]

In view of the prominence of the vanity type in the U.S., it may be significant that the corresponding personality syndrome has escaped the committee that produced the DSM III. Along with the comparative difficulty of discriminating character traits that are prevalent and implicitly valued in the culture as a whole, we may understand this omission also as a consequence of the fact that ennea-type III individuals are characteristically satisfied with themselves, since the essence of their psychological aberration is the confusion of the self-image that they sell (and others buy) with what they are.

---

[1]A statistical-technical term meaning the most frequent by contrast to an average.

[2]op. cit.

Perhaps the better known description of ennea-type III was that of Fromm[3] who claimed to discover it as a personality orientation beyond the three classically discerned by psychoanalysis (the "receptive," the "oral aggressive" or "exploitative," and the "anal" or "hoarding orientations"). Believing it to be a modern development, secondary to the arising of the modern market, Erich Fromm called it "the marketing orientation."

"The market concept of value, the emphasis on exchange value rather than use value, has led to a similar concept of value with regard to people and particularly to oneself."

A basic feature in the marketing orientation is that of concern with self-presentation in a "personality market."

"One has to be in fashion on the personality market, and in order to be in fashion one has to know what kind of personality is most in demand. This knowledge is transmitted in a general way throughout the whole process of education, from kindergarten to college, and implemented by the family. The knowledge acquired at this early stage is not sufficient, however: it emphasizes only certain general qualities like adaptability, ambition, and sensitivity to the changing expectations of other people. The more specific picture of the models for success one gets elsewhere. The pictorial magazines, newspapers, and newsreels show the pictures and life stories of the successful in many variations.

"Pictorial advertising has a similar function. The successful executive who is pictured in a tailor's advertisement is the image of how one could look and be, if one is to draw down the 'big money' on the contemporary personality market.

"The most important means of transmitting the desired personality pattern to the average man is the motion picture. The young girl tries to emulate the facial expression, coiffure, and gestures of a high-priced star as the most promising way to success. The young man tries to look and be like the model he sees on the screen. While the average citizen has little contact with the life of the most successful people, his relationship with

---

[3]Fromm, Erich, *Man for Himself: An Inquiry into the Psychology of Ethics* (New York:Holt,Rinehart and Winston,1964).

the motion picture star is different. It is true that he has no real contact with them either, but he can see them on the screen again and again, can write them and receive their autographed pictures. In contrast to the time when the actor was socially despised but was nevertheless the transmitter of works of great poets to his audience, our motion-picture stars have no great works of ideas to transmit, but their function is to serve as the link an average person has with the world of 'the great.' Even if he cannot hope to become successful as they are, he can try to emulate them; they are as his saints and because of their success they embody the norms for living."

While Fromm gives us a view of a "social psychoanalyst," Horney has given us a more explicit clinical report[4]. She uses for the character the name "narcissistic," and comments:

"I use the term narcissism with some hesitation, because in the classic Freudian literature it includes rather indiscriminately every kind of self-inflation, egocentricity, anxious concern with one's welfare, and withdrawal from others. I take it here in its original descriptive sense of being 'in love with one's idealized image.'

"More precisely the person is his idealized self and seems to adore it. This basic attitude gives him the buoyancy or the resiliency entirely lacking in other groups. It gives him a seeming abundance of self-confidence, which appears enviable to all those chafing under self-doubts; he has no (conscious) doubt; he is the anointed, the man of destiny, the prophet, the great giver, the benefactor of mankind. All of this contains a grain of truth. He often is gifted beyond average, with early and easily-won distinctions, and sometimes was the favored and admired child. This unquestioned belief in his greatness and uniqueness is the key to understanding him. His buoyancy and perennial youthfulness stem from this source. So does his often-fascinating charm. Yet clearly, his gifts notwithstanding, he stands on precarious ground. He may speak incessantly of his exploits or of his wonderful qualities and needs endless

---

[4]Horney, Karen, *Neurosis and Human Growth* (New York: W.W. Norton & Co., 1991).

confirmation of his estimate of himself in the form of admiration and devotion. His feeling of mastery lies in his conviction that there is nothing he cannot do and no one he cannot win. He is often charming indeed, particularly when new people come into his orbit. Regardless of their factual importance for him, he must impress them. He gives the impression to himself and others that he 'loves' people. And he can be generous, with a scintillating display of feeling, with flattery, with favors and help—in anticipation of admiration or in return for devotion received. He endows his family and his friends, as well as his work and plans, with glowing attributes. He can be quite tolerant, does not expect others to be perfect: he can even stand jokes about himself, so long these merely highlight an amiable peculiarity of his, but he must never be questioned seriously."

Though Fromm and Horney have had great influence on our culture in general, the fall into oblivion of the type may be a reflection on their limited influence in today's professional world. In today's psychotherapeutic practice ennea-type III is usually diagnosed in Bioenergetic terms as Lowen's "rigid." In Johnson's account[5] of rigid character it is the splitting of the loving response from the sexual response that is emphasized:

"Wherever sexuality is cut off or split from the loving response some of the natural human loving is lost. In this sense the rigid can not truly love." More generally he observes that the rigid "is more able than any other character to attract, achieve and be self-sufficient. Her illusion is that she can buy love with this accomplishment but, because she can not let true love in, all that she really gets is attention...Love-sex relationships are the most consistently troubled parts of life. She may, for example, find she can be sexually attracted to but not love one man while she can love another but experience no sexual arousal with him. Or, she may find herself sexually attracted to unavailable men but lose interest when these same men become available. Alternatively, she may be very skilled, satisfying and satisfied in the initial seductive phases of love relationships, but unable to sustain any of that as the relationship becomes more intimate.

---

[5]Johnson, Stephen M., Ph.D., *Characterological Transformation: The Hard Work Miracle* (New York: W.W. Norton & Co., 1985).

Typically, the rigid compromise is the most effective, best defended, and culturally most approved...As a general rule, the more purely rigid people in our culture seek psychotherapy only when their spouse threatens to leave, their children begin to act out, or a heart attack or other illness threatens the workability of the compromise."

The ennea-type III syndrome is the most usual background for what is diagnosed as type A personality: achieving, competitive, ever stressed, and prone to cardiac diseases.

Practitioners of Transactional Analysis are also acquainted with this syndrome, at least in some of its manifestations. In Steiner's *Scripts People Live*,[6] for instance, we·see a picture of a "Creeping Beauty": "She has standard attributes of so called 'media beauty'...she sees herself as deceiving everyone who thinks she is beautiful and thinks they are fools for buying the deception."

We also find a description of a "Plastic Woman": "In an effort to obtain strokes, she encases herself in plastic: bright jewelry, platform heels, foxy clothes, intriguing perfumes, and dramatic make-up. She tries to buy beauty and OKness, but never really succeeds. She feels chronically one-down of 'media beauty' women whom she idolizes in women's magazines and the movies....When superficial beauty can no longer be bought and pasted on, she ends up depressed: she gets no strokes that she truly values, either from herself or from others. She may try to fill the void with alcohol, tranquilizers, or other chemicals. As an older woman, she often fills her life with trivia and her house with knick-knacks."

I recognize the ennea-type III pattern in Kernberg's[7] description of hysterical personality. I quote from his description of its manifestation in women: "A dominant characteristic in women with hysterical personality is their emotional lability. They relate easily to others and are capable of warm and sustained emotional involvements—with the important exception of an inhibition in their sexual responsiveness. They

---

[6]op.cit.

[7]Kernberg, Otto, op.cit.

are usually dramatic and even histrionic, but their display of affects is controlled and has socially adaptive qualities. The way they dramatize their emotional experiences may give the impression that their emotions are superficial, but exploration reveals otherwise: their emotional experiences are authentic. These women may be emotionally labile, but they are not inconsistent or unpredictable in their emotional reactions. They lose emotional control only selectively, vis-a-vis a few closely related persons concerning whom they have intense conflicts, especially of a sexual and competitive nature."

He adds that: "even though hysterical women are prone to emotional crisis they have the capacity to 'snap out' of such crises and evaluate them realistically afterwards" and that "they may cry easily and tend toward sentimentality and romanticism, but their cognitive capacities are intact." This is in contradiction with Shapiro's observation[8] of "a cognitive style of hysterical patients characterized by their tendency toward global perception, selective inattention, and impressionistic rather than accurate representations"—all of which, I think, fits the histrionic ennea-type II well.

While men with a hysterical personality may be differentiated from those with histrionic personality also in terms of the more restricted field of lability and impulsiveness ("while maintaining the capacity for differentiated behavior under ordinary social circumstances"), and they are also characterized "by a pseudo hypermasculine quality, a histrionic accentuation of culturally accepted masculine patterns, usually a stress on independence and superiority over women, combined with childlike sulkiness when such aspirations cannot be fulfilled."[9]

I do not find the ennea-type III characterological pattern among Jung's descriptions of psychological types, although it is unquestionably an extroverted type with well developed sensing

---

[8]Shapiro, David, op.cit.

[9] I disagree with Kernberg's contention that this is the pattern that used to be called "phallic-narcissistic," for Reich's description resembles more closely the more exaggerated masculinity dominance and impulsiveness of ennea-type VIII.

and thinking.[10] Examining the description of test profiles I find the pattern in the portrait of an ESTP (an extroverted sensing, with predominance of thinking over feeling, and perception over judgment). Keirsey and Bates[11] describe them as men and women of action:

"When someone of this personality is present, things begin to happen. The lights come on, the music plays, the game begins...If only one adjective could be used to describe ESTPs, resourceful would be an apt choice.

"Their attractive, friendly style has a theatrical flourish which makes even the most routine, mundane event seem exciting. ESTPs usually know the location of the best restaurants, and head waiters are likely to call them by name.

"They carry on amusing repartee, and laughter surrounds them as they recount from their endless supply of clever jokes and stories.

"The ESTP's mate may in time come to feel like an object —the female a chattel, and the male a negotiable commodity. Relationships usually are conditional, and the condition is the consideration of what the ESTP is to gain in the relationship.

"...They are masters at using these observations to 'sell' the 'client' The eye of the ESTP is ever on the eye of the beholder, and all actions are directed towards this audience.

"ESTPs are ruthless pragmatists and often offer the ends as justification for whatever means they see as necessary...

"ESTPs are outstanding as initiators of enterprises that bring people together to negotiate. They make invaluable itinerant administrators who can pull troubled companies or institutions out of the red very quickly, and with style! They can sell an idea or project in a way no other type can...."

It seems appropriate that the brilliant and active ennea-type III personality be associated in homeopathy with *Phosphorus*.[12]

---

[10]Unlike ennea-type VIII where sensing is prominent and thinking is usually not.

[11]op.cit.

[12] Coulter, Catherine R., op. cit., Vol. 1, all excerpts on *Phosphorus* from pp. 1-17, reprinted by permission of the author.

"Anyone who has been by the ocean at night has seen the flecks of sparkling *Phosphorus* dancing in the foam or gleaming in the swells. This restless element captures the attention, and the *Phosphorus* individual has a similar eye-catching impact. He attracts by his sparkling appealing manner and his bright intelligent face."

Catherine R. Coulter describes *Phosphorus* individuals, both men and women, as neat, graceful, and refined, with clear skin sometimes porcelain-like or translucent: "Emotionally, *Phosphorus* is sympathetic, responsive, and sensitive to another's wavelength. The whole manner betrays a readiness to establish warm communication with his interlocutor, and he immediately senses how best to establish rapport. Finely intuitive in his dealings with people, he predisposes others toward himself by little verbal kindnesses, warm praise, or touching consideration, and at times by almost undue generosity. When assistance is required, he will drop whatever he is doing and be the first to arrive....

"*Phosphorus* is gregarious and needs people around to feel whole, well, and happy....*Phosphorus* is highly impressionable and susceptible to his emotional environment... Disagreeable or unpleasant feelings can make him physically ill, bringing on trembling stomach and head pains, or palpitations. Even pleasurable emotions affect him similarly...."

Coulter describes at length not only the vivacity and sociability of the type, but also the qualities of vanity and narcissism present in the ennea-type III character:

"The *Phosphorus* sparkle proceeds not only from eager responsiveness to others and love of life but also from *self-love*. He considers himself more sensitive and refined, more intuitive, more entertaining, more gifted, more spiritual than others. He can be quite fascinated with himself and view his person as the center around which others revolve.... *Phosphorus* does not dominate aggressively yet still manages to divert attention to himself. Usually, however, he does it so subtly that others hardly realize what is happening, or so entertainingly that they do not object... Liking of self must be considered a healthy characteristic...But carried to an extreme, it reveals a negative side, a self-limiting narcissism....

"He has a performer's temperament. Beneath his genuine sociability lies the need for an audience, whether of one or of thousands, for whom he is prepared to supply entertainment and affection and to give his all. For he needs others' appreciation and attention to bring out the best in his own nature and to feel alive."

3. Trait Structure

Attention Need and Vanity

If we regard the substitution of appearance for self as the fixation of ennea-type III, what are we to regard, then, as the ruling passion in this character?

It is my impression that the most characteristic emotional state and at the same time the one that underlies the characteristic interest in display to the point of self-falsification is a need for attention: a need to be seen, that was once frustrated and seeks to be satisfied through the cultivation of appearance. Other than the felt sense of wanting to be seen, heard, appreciated, there is in type III character a corresponding sense of loneliness that arises, not only from the chronic frustration of the need to be for others, but also from the fact that whatever success is met with needs to be credited to a false self and to manipulation. Thus there lingers the question "would I be loved for myself if it were not for my accomplishments, my money, my pretty face, and so on?" The question is perpetuated by the fact that the individual is not only moved by a fear of failure in his rushing around in the pursuit of achievement, but is also plagued by fear of self-exposure and rejection if she were to reveal herself to the world without a mask.

I have included the expression "concern with appearances" in the clustering of type III descriptors along with "vanity," which not only makes reference to a passion to appear, but also involves a capitulation to cultural values and a substitution of internal direction with extrinsic direction and valuation. I have also included as part of the vanity cluster "perfectionism in regard to form," "imitativeness," and "chameleon" (in virtue of which, for instance, vanity in the counterculture may cultivate a self-image of striking lack of concern for personal appearance).

Not only a passion for the modulation of appearance is involved in the psychology of ennea-type III. A skill to the effect of achieving the aims of vanity typically supports it in the individual's psyche. Thus, beautiful women are more likely to embrace the strategy of brilliance (and the corresponding existential mistake of confusing their attractiveness with their true self). In addition to characteristics reflecting a generalized desire to please and attract, such as refinement, considerateness, or generosity, some traits stand out because of their prominence which I discuss below: achievement drive, social skill, and concern with personal appearance.

Achieving Orientation

Ennea-type III strives for achievement and success, and this may imply striving for wealth and for status. Since a number of traits may be understood as instrumental to this aim and drive, I will consider them under this general heading.

a) The ability to do things expeditiously and with precision is characteristic of these individuals and makes for both good secretaries and good executives. In the service of efficiency thinking tends to be precise and there is often a leaning towards mathematics. A fast tempo is also characteristic and has probably developed in the service of efficiency as well as out of a desire to stand out through special efficiency. Also in the service of efficiency is an orientation to life that is both rational and practical—an orientation often seen in the personality of those who take up engineering as a profession. Though there is interest in science, the peculiar bias of the character would be best described as scientism—that is to say, a tendency to undervalue thinking that is not logico-deductive and scientific. Along with this, one usually sees a high valuation of technology, and the broader trait of being systematic and skilled in organizing one's activities or those of others.

b) Also related to the high achievement drive is a measure of ruthlessness in human interactions when it comes to a choice between success and considerateness. Ennea-type III individuals are not only pleasers, but frequently described as cool (i.e., a "cold cookie") and calculating, and they use others as well as themselves as stepping stones to their goals.

c) Closely related to the pursuit of success are also the traits of control over self as well as over others, and dominance. These are typically observed in parents in their behavior toward their children, whom they may overpower through unsought advice and the insistence on having things done their way (even in the case of choices that would be more fitting for the children to make on their own).

d) Another important trait within this personality syndrome that stands out as a means to achievement and winning is competitiveness—a trait connected in turn to ruthlessness, to the cultivation of efficiency, and to the use of deception, bluffing, self-promotion, slander, and other behaviors discussed below under "image manipulation."

e) The traits of anxiety and tension are an understandable result of exaggerated striving for achievement and the implicit fear of failure. The rise of blood pressure in response to stress goes along with them and makes of these people the well known "type A personalities."

Social Sophistication and Skill

Another group of traits that stands out among the descriptors of type III brings together the characteristics of being entertaining, enthusiastic, bubbly, sparkling, conver-sationally active, pleasing, needing applause, and witty. This generalized trait might be called "social brilliance" or "social performance." Concern with status might be regarded as an indulging motivation in these. "Tell me who you associate with, and I'll tell you who you are."

Cultivation of Sexual Attractiveness

A trait similar in nature to the previously mentioned ones are those that have to do with self-beautification and the conservation of sexual attractiveness—traits that are most specially evoked by the image of the mirror in the traditional iconography of vanity. (Generally speaking, no other women are so dependent on cosmetics as those of type III). Just as cultivated sexual attractiveness goes hand-in-hand with frigidity, there is, more generally speaking, a special kind of vain beauty: a cold porcelain, doll-like beauty—formalistic and yet emotionally hollow.

Deceit and Image Manipulation

In the case of the two generalized traits of sexual attractiveness, social brilliance and achievement, we are in the face of different *appearances* through which the individual seeks to satisfy the thirst to be, and which at the same time veil over his existential vacuum. For while the passion to display oneself may be understood as the outgrowth of an early need for attention and validation, it can also be understood as the consequence of a confusion between being and appearance, and the corresponding confusion between extrinsic validation and intrinsic value. Since deceit is what we may call the fixation, that is, the cognitive defect in ennea-type III, I have separately grouped some descriptors that have to do more specifically with it, such as: "becoming the mask," "believing in what they sell," "affected," "false," and "phony." Most characteristically, we should include here deceptive emotional experience. Deception goes beyond emotional experience proper, however, for it involves rationalization and other maneuvers.

The words deception or simulation may be used as pointers to a central feature of this personality organization, used in connection with self-deception (believing in the idealized image that is presented to the world) as well as in connection with simulation before an outer audience (as in bluffing or hypocritical kindness). Yet it is the identification of the person with the role and with the mask—the loss of the sense of merely playing a role or putting on a mask— which causes what is seen by others to come to be perceived as one's reality.

Ennea-type III not only cares for appearance but also has developed a skill in presentation; presenting others, presenting things and ideas. The special flair for selling and advertising that characterizes these individuals would seem to be a generalization of an ability that was originally developed in the service of "selling" and promoting themselves. Thus they not only are interested in such things as their clothing and cosmetics and exhibiting good manners, they are expert packagers of goods and information and excel in the advertising industry. The trait of promoting others, explicitly or implicitly, can be akin to a complementary one: the ability to present things or people in a bad light, to manipulate their image in an adverse way—which may be done not only through slander but also through a sophisticated social skill whereby it is possible to seem nice while back-stabbing an opponent or competitor.

Other Directedness

Closely related to this group of traits having to do with concern about appearance and the skill in self-preservation is another having to do with the values according to which the ideal self is shaped. These are characteristically neither intrinsic nor original but external to the individual, who is the most other-directed among all the characters and has developed a skill in conducting an implicit and ongoing "marketing research" in the entourage as a point of reference for his thinking, feeling, and action.

The trait of identification with prevalent values embodies both other-directedness and the chameleon quality of type III in general, i.e., his or her readiness to change in attitude or appearance according to fashions. Related to this other-directed characteristic, in turn, is the progressive but conservative disposition of ennea-type III—a disposition not unqualifiedly conservative, as in type IX, but a combination of conformity with a striving for progress or excellence (that results in an orientation to what is modern and avant-garde) without being radical. In practice what is both modern and shows itself to be modern without throwing traditional values into question is scientific progress and thus again a root of technocratic orientation that is so characteristic of ennea-type III psychology.

Pragmatism

Typical of ennea-type III (in contrast with the more distinctively emotional neighbors in the enneagram) is the characteristic conveyed through traits of rationality, and a systematic orientation to things, also implicit in their being described as "calculating." The expression of these traits is not only intellectual, for the control over self that it entails can be manifested   also as being organized and keen, practical, functional and expedient. It is in the service of efficiency that we can understand the more rational skills which typically give type III an engineering or an entrepreneur mentality and manifest also in an orientation to technology and technocracy.

Active Vigilance

At a higher level of abstraction than both the cognitive and behavioral sharpness or effectiveness, there are still more general traits related to achievement that I have called hypervigilance and activity.

The type III person is not only hypervigilant but incapable of surrender, of self-abandonment; he or she needs to have everything under control and has learned early in life to cope in an attitude of self-reliance, out of the feeling that others are not taking care of him or her properly. Because of this we can not separate the trait of hyperactivity that makes the type III person an "ego-go" from either stress or a deep distrust in life— distrust that things might go well without being in control over them. The same can apply to hypervigilance; it is part of a stressful coping born of an anxiety about things going all right and distrust in surrendering to the "organismic self-regulation" of one's psycho-mental being. The underlying lack of trust in type III contrasts with its superficial "polyannish" optimism (which regards everything as not only OK but wonderful) and constitutes one of the factors through which ennea-type III is prone to anxiety.

Superficiality

The trait that an outsider may describe as superficiality is in the individual's awareness more likely to manifest as a sense of not having access to the depth of her feelings, as an identity problem—in the sense of not knowing who he or she is (beyond roles and tangible characteristics) and not knowing his or her true wants (beyond pleasing others and being effective). Although the person may not consciously thirst after a missing depth, the presence of dissatisfaction is apparent in the very intensity of the rushing for accomplishment or the labors undertaken to be pleasing and acceptable. To the extent that the thirst for being is displaced into an outer search, the individual does not allow the opportunity even to acknowledge it—thus perpetuating the chronic error.

4. Defense Mechanisms

Central to type III is identification with an ideal self-image built as a response to the expectations of others, and thus we may assume that in early life this involved identification with parental wishes, values, and behaviors.

Unlike introjection, which refers to *feeling* like another, identification is defined as a process through which the person *adopts* the characteristics of another and is thus transformed, to some extent, after an external model. However true it may be that the adoption of parental traits is a universal characteristic of human development, it is also clear that an imitativeness that orients itself to outer models is most characteristic of type III values. Unlike the situation of introjection, in which the person seems to cling excessively to an early identification, it is most typical of the adult expression of vanity to identify, not with significant individuals of the past so much as with an updated and *constructed* image of what is regarded as socially desirable. Thus, in the elaboration of a personal self-image the type III individual seems to conduct an implicit marketing research to know the expectation of the generalized other. It is this "computed" image of what is valued and desired that the individual pretends to be and seeks to implement with characteristic effort.

Also the mechanism of rationalization is prominent in type III psychology (as also in type VII). But most characteristic —aside from identification—is the mechanism of negation: that by which something is declared not to be the case (in anticipation of somebody's realization that it is). This maneuver, implicit in Shakespeare's "The lady doth protest too much," and also the target of the French saying "Qui s'excuse, s'accuse" (who justifies himself, gives himself away) is closely related to self-image maintenance and is, of course, a direct expression of deception.

5. Etiological and Further Psychodynamic Remarks[13]

Constitutionally ennea-type III exists in the context of somatotonia and, correspondingly, a good measure of mesomorphia. As a whole, the ennea-type III population may be the highest in mesomorphia after that of type VIII and that of the counter-phobic character[14]1. It is not surprising that an athletic constitution supports the active and energetic character of type III. It seems to me likely that physical beauty and general

---

[13] According to Kernberg in Cooper et al.'s *Psychiatry* "there is as yet no evidence for genetic predisposition to the personality disorders within the hysterical-hystrionic spectrum," yet the "persistent failure to differentiate the hysterical from the hystrionic personality disorders in empiric studies...weaken the currently available contributions to the genetics of these personality disorders." Freud's obeservation that hysteria involves an infantile conflict at the phallic-oedipal stage is mostly applicable to our ennea-type III. Also those of later psychoanalytical writers stressing the predominance of the Oedipus complex and of castration anxiety and penis envy as dynamic features of the hysterical personality.

[14] The sexual variety of type VI.

intelligence may also be among the factors leading to the implicit choice of vanity as a way of psychological survival.

Though it is common to hear that type III individuals felt stimulated during the time of their growing up to comply with parental expectations and ideals, it is also very common to find that their desire to attract attention to excellence in one form or another has arisen in reaction to an earlier experience of not having been seen or heard enough; thus it would seem that the wish to be brilliant has been a reaction to the fear of being ignored.

"I was the youngest of five. There was no place for me so I had no other resource than shining to get attention."

A factor that I have noticed often in women in the situation of not being seen or acknowledged enough is the presence of a type V father.

Also frequent in ennea-type III life histories (especially in the preservation subtype) is a sense of not being able to count on anybody which has stimulated the child's autonomy. Efficiency in this case does not only stem from a desire to attract parental love through a good performance; it also arises from the need to care for oneself. "I had to seek safety for myself and my sisters. Fighting at home was continuous." "I had to take care of myself. The conflict level at home was such that my attitude became 'everything is fine here'."

It is not uncommon for a type III person to come from a family in which there was illness or some kind of chaos, the situation in which a great problem (such as father's alcoholism) competed with the attention that parents might have given to the child, and contributed to the child's incentive to take care of itself.

Often, too, there are memories of situations conveying to the child that it was unsafe to say the truth or reveal his or her feelings and wishes.

"A childhood memory that I have that just sprang into my mind, to confirm and affirm deceit was: We had apple trees and whenever we would eat the green apples, we would get the diarrhea. And my mother had forbidden us to eat the green apples. And she went out to hang up the clothes and found apples with bite marks in them. And so she promised anyone,

"If you tell the truth, you will not be punished. Who ate the green apple?" Well I had taken a bite out and so did my sister. So I admitted it. I got the spanking and my sister got a penny out of the sugar bowl. To me, I was so confused and I thought, "Well what's the point of telling the truth. So you learn then to be deceitful."

The self-controlled characteristic of type III can be understood not only in view of survival and image manipulation: there is often behind it all a story of stern discipline. Speaking for a group of three women of the same character, one of them said: "We all could identify with the strap. If we didn't get it someone else got it. And I remember for me that was always a real horror, you know, you'd do anything to not 'get it' and so then the good behavior kind of thing and sometimes not knowing what it was for, but the strictness again. That things had to be a certain way. It wasn't perfectionism, but it was proper not to, I think it had a touch of shaming, but it was a sense of being shamed if you didn't do it the way it was to be done."

It is not uncommon for the type III individual to have a type III parent, in which case we may think that the concern with appearances has arisen through identification. "My mother turned me into a doll: ballet lessons, dressing up nicely, not raising my voice, no laughing, no feeling...She died when I was nine and my father continued her task." At times, seduction was an added incentive in mimesis: "My father was a very dignified man. He was retired, but he had a white shirt and he wore gold rings and a blue serge suit always. He was very, very proper. And this came off on me as a role player. He was a role player."

"Parents always needed to look good to the neighbors, parents always needed to look good. You know, we needed to look good as *three's*, but we had a *three* parent, and so that *three* parent passed on that they always had to look good and so we were their product and so we had to look good." The most common ennea-type among mothers of type III individuals is type IV and in these cases it is possible to speak of a rebellious disidentification—a desire *not* to be a complaining and problematic person, but one that acts independently causing others the least trouble. This may coincide with a situation in which the child feels that it cannot afford to have problems since it is put in the role of having to take care of mother.

It may be said that throughout the character development of type III the search for love has led to a motivation to perform well and eventually the wish to please and to be acknowledged, becoming autonomous, obscures the original love wish. Also there is a striking sexualization of the love wish so that being loved is equated with being attractive and successful.

6. Existential Psychodynamics

Just as in the schizoid character the existential issue is most apparent to the subject—who is keenly aware of the experience of inner emptiness—it is in the case of the ennea-type III style that the existential issue of an inner vacuum is most observable to *outsiders*, who typically see vain persons as superficial, empty, or "plastic." The tendency of the vain to ignore the impoverishment of their experiential world brings them close to type IX in which, as we will see, ontic obscuration —through its very centrality—is most ignoring of itself. Their similarity in this regard fits the relationship between them on the enneagram according to which vain identification with appearance is the psychodynamic root of pathological self-forgetfulness.

The fact that type III is not to be found in DSM III and that type IX is only imperfectly congruent with one of the syndromes in it suggests that the recognized pathologies constitute a more external or visible layer of psychopathology than is entailed in these two; ennea-type III and ennea-type IX may live very ordinary and perhaps successful lives without clearly recognizable interpersonal defects, harboring mainly a spiritual psychopathology—loss of interiority and of true spiritual experience.

When aware of "something missing inside" a type III individual is likely to verbalize this perception of emptiness as a not knowing who he or she is—i.e., an identity problem. The wide recognition of the identity issue together with the sense of its universality reflects, I think, the prevalence of ennea-type III in American culture.

What "not knowing who I am" generally means in a type III individual is, "All I know is the role that I enact—is there something else besides?" The individual has come to realize that his or her life is a series of performances and that identity has rested thus far in identification with professional status and other roles. Together with realizing "this is not me" or "these roles don't amount to anybody" there is a sense of being out of touch with some hidden or potential self. Along with an intuition of an ignored self or individuality, there is usually, also, the sense of not knowing one's true wishes and feelings—a sense that dawns upon them to the extent that they begin to recognize fabricated feelings, and the extent to which choices are not inner directed but supported in outer models.

While in more socially-oriented individuals there is a "butterfly" quality to their status-seeking drivenness, and it is obvious that their self-alienation has resulted from an excessive concern with the image that they sell in face of the public eye, in the more sexually oriented ones an equivalent process takes place in regard to the search for "sexual applause" behind the cultivation of sex-appeal. The passion to please and attract polarizes the attention of the person towards the surface of her being at the expense of focus on the depth of erotic and emotional experience—bringing along in women the frequent complication of frigidity.

That something similar may happen to men is reflected in an insightful account that Jodorowsky has in a short magazine article on a sexual superman who has hundreds of hands and thousands of fingers in each of which there is a sexual organ or a tongue, who can achieve the highest standards of sexual performance, yet whose focus on effectiveness tragically leaves him with no attention left to enjoy.[15]

Given the prominence of the existential issue in ennea-type III (understandable in view of its place in the enneagram) it is useful to go beyond the interpretation of the passion for applause as a substitute for love, or as the indirect expression of

---

[15]"La vida sexual del hombre elastico." In *Metal*, No. 47 (Spain).

a love wish. True as that may be and important to acknowledge, I think we need to consider that the chronic struggle of ennea-type III to obtain "narcissistic supplies" is supported by a self-created impoverishment that arises, precisely, from the diversion of psychic energy towards performance and living through the eyes of others.

The way in which the frantic agitation of "ego-go" creates the loss of being—which, in turn, fuels the search for being in the realm of appearances—is, I think, worthy of due consideration; for, if it is true that truth can set us free, true insight in this vicious circle can liberate the individual's energy and attention to focus on that habitually avoided—and potentially painful—interiority.

In his or her frantic agitation in pursuit of achievement, status, or applause, and in the corresponding inability to pause to look within, the ennea-type III person seems to be repeating to herself that very American injunction "Don't just stand there, *do* something." This is just the sort of person who needs to be told, "Don't just do something, *stand* there."

It is important also for psychotherapists to understand that these "masked" people who usually have difficulty in being alone and in extricating themselves from over-acting achievement can particularly benefit from the task of *facing* themselves and from bearing the "loss of face" entailed by not looking into the social mirror.

Because interiority is so foreign to them, something seemingly nonexistent from the point of view of a world centering on form and quantity, meditation—particularly meditation that emphasizes non-doing—may seem most uninteresting and meaningless to them. Through closer observation of this meaninglessness of "just sitting" with enough intellectual conviction or personal trust to engage in the task, however, it is possible that further focus on boredom or meaninglessness might lead to some perception of the tragedy of an incapacity to be nourished through a living sense of existence.

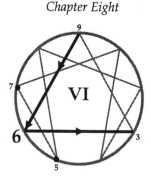

Chapter Eight

COWARDICE, PARANOID CHARACTER, AND ACCUSATION

ENNEA-TYPE VI

1. Core Theory, Nomenclature, and Place in the Enneagram

Ichazo's words for the passion and the fixation of ennea-type VI, as mentioned in the Introduction, were "timidity" and "cowardice" respectively.

Timidity may be taken to mean an anxious hesitation or inhibition of action in the presence of fear, but if this is so, then the meaning is not very different from that of "fear" which I am using to designate the ruling passion in this character.

If we use fear or cowardice to designate the ruling passion of ennea-type VI, however, we need to point out, as in the case of anger and other emotions, that this important emotional state need not be directly manifested in behavior. It may be, alternatively, manifest in the over-compensation of a conscious attitude of heroic striving. The counter-phobic denial of fear is no different in essence from the covering up of anger through excessive gentleness and control, the covering up of selfishness through excessive yielding, and other forms of compensation manifested throughout the range of characters, particularly in some of the sub-ennea-types.

More characteristic than fear and cowardice, in many ennea-type VI individuals, may be the presence of anxiety—that derivative of fear that might be characterized as fear without the perception of external or internal danger.

Even though fear is not among the "deadly sins," the transcendence of fear may be a cornerstone of the true Christian ideal inasmuch as this involves an *Imitatio Christi* to a point that is necessarily heroic. It is interesting to observe, however, that the Christian ideal shifted from that of the early martyrs to one pervaded by attitudes which Nietzsche criticized under the epithet of "slave morality" (though lately, in South America at least, the church has become heroic again to the point of martyrdom).

Unlike the Greek notion of virtue (*arete*) which emphasized courage, as Nietszche pointed out, the ideal of Christian society supports an excessive obedience to authority and an imbalance in the direction of Apollonian control over Dionysian expansiveness.

Just as we may witness a degradation in Christian consciousness along the specific path of courage to cowardice, we may speak of a degradation in its understanding of faith. While faith is, in Protoanalysis, the psychocatalyst that lies as a gate of potential liberation from the bondage of insecurity, this is an altogether different thing from what the word has come to mean in average religious discourse: which is a firm holding on to a set of beliefs.

As I will elaborate in the psychodynamic analysis, I think that the cognitive counterpart of fear may be found in an attitude of self-invalidation, self-opposition and self-blaming—a becoming an enemy to oneself—that seems to imply that it is better to oppose oneself (siding with anticipated opposition outside) than to meet an outer enemy. The DSM III definition of paranoid character is narrower than ennea-type VI, for the latter comprises three different varieties of paranoid thinking that involve different ways of dealing with anxiety. The phobic character of psychoanalysis, now echoed in the DSM III "avoidant" personality and also in "dependent" personality disorder, is another; yet there is also a more obsessive style, usually diagnosed as a mixed personality disorder, between the paranoid and the obsessive.

2. Antecedents in the Scientific Literature on Character

In Kurt Schneider's classification of personalities, it is the description of the fanatic that fits our ennea-type VI, though it fails to describe the whole range of the character.

We may say that paranoid or suspicious character is a subtle form of what in the extremity of mental pathology was already known to Kraepelin as paranoid schizophrenia. Addressing the pre-morbid character of paranoid schizophrenics Kraepelin mentions,[1] along with the sense of being an object of hostility, and so on, the observation that it involves "a combination of uncertainty with excessive valuation of self, which leads to the patient being forced into hostile opposition to the influences of the struggle for life and his seeking to withdraw himself from them by inward exaltation."

Today's widely shared conception of paranoid character became enriched through Freud's studies and observation of paranoid schizophrenia. What Freud said of the latter, particularly in reference to the famous Schreber case, has been extended to the characterological syndrome corresponding to it. While not many today continue to uphold the sexual interpretation of paranoia as a defense before homosexual

---

[1]Kraepelin, quoted in Schneider, op. cit.

surrender to a parent, Freud's broader interpretation indeed has been confirmed in general experience: that paranoid hatefulness is a defense against love. I think that this view is correct if we understand such a defense against "love" not as one primarily directed at instinctual or erotic love but a defense against the temptation of a seductive "love through surrender" that fear inspires in the growing child.

While the "weak" (outwardly coward) individual offers loving obedience to parental authority and the "compulsive" or dutiful subtype obeys an abstract principle through legalistic or ideological obedience, the "strong" and fanatical subtype of suspicious character (usually called paranoid) defends himself from the temptation to surrender just as vehemently as he is counter-phobic. He protects himself from doubt, ambiguity, and indecision through a "true believer" excessive certainty. While the acknowledgment of a fight/flight reaction is widespread in the language of experimental psychology, the polarity between the "weak" and "strong" varieties of suspicious character correspond, rather, to a fight/surrender dichotomy that is also present in animal life—familiar from the behavior of dogs (or wolves) who offer their throats to the aggressor as expression of subordination.

Without mention of paranoid character, we find a similar personality disposition described by Kurt Schneider[2] under the label of "fanatics." He observes of fanatics that "their affectivity is restricted, and they may appear 'cold' to others. They have no true sense of humour and are usually serious. They may pride themselves on always being objective, rational, and unemotional."

Another observation of Schneider is that it is typical of all fanatical trouble makers to attribute a "sort of public importance" to their concerns, and that "there is a tendency for the fanatic ideas to issue in schemes and programmes. If the over-valued idea relates to a personal difference or a civil dispute, every effort is concentrated on laying low the offender utterly...."

---

[2] op cit.

Today the DSM III acknowledges an aspect of ennea-type VI psychology under the diagnosis of paranoid personality, except that this DSM III syndrome may be said to represent the pathological form of only one of the possible varieties of fearful disposition.

In DSM III Paranoid Personality Disorder is characterized by the essential feature of "a pervasive and unwarranted suspiciousness and mistrust of people, hypersensitivity, and restricted affectivity not due to another mental disorder, such as Schizophrenia, or a Paranoid Disorder."

Says Millon:[3]"Individuals with this disorder are typically hypervigilant and take precautions against any perceived threat. They tend to avoid blame even when it is warranted. They are often viewed by others as guarded, secretive, devious, and scheming. They may question the loyalty of others, always expecting trickery. For this reason they may be pathologically jealous...They are concerned with hidden motives and special meanings. Often, transient ideas of reference occur, e.g., that others are taking special notice of them, or saying vulgar things about them...They often find it difficult to relax, usually appear tense, and show a tendency to counterattack when they perceive any threat..."

Shapiro contemplates a wider range of suspicious character when he writes of paranoid character in his *Neurotic Styles*.[4] At the beginning of the chapter he observes that "aside from the dimension of severity there are descriptively and quite roughly speaking *two*[5] sorts of people who fall within the category of this style: furtive, constricted apprehensively suspicious individuals, and rigidly arrogant more aggressively suspicious megalomaniac ones."

These correspond to the pugnacious and cold "paranoid personality disorder" of the DSM III and the warmth-seeking avoidant and dependent syndromes in which suspiciousness or doubting are turned mostly inwards and take the form of insecurity. Avoidant personality is distinguished from schizoid

---

[3]Millon, Theodore, op.cit.

[4]Shapiro, David, *Neurotic Styles* (New York: Basic Books, Inc., 1965).

[5]My emphasis.

personality in that an active detachment in the insecure person who doesn't dare to approach others contrasts to the passive detachment of the schizoid, who is a true loner and whose distance betrays not a conscious conflict but indifference.

Whereas the schizoid is best characterized by deficits such as underarousal, undermotivation, and insensitivity, in the case of avoidant personality it is a matter of overarousal, over-motivation, and hypersensitivity. As Millon observes,[6] the essential feature of avoidant personality is "hypersensitivity to potential rejection, humiliation or shame; an unwillingness to enter into relationships unless given unusual guarantees of uncritical acceptance; social withdrawal in spite of desire for affection and acceptance; and low self-esteem." Unlike the schizoid person who has difficulty in attaching himself or herself to others, the avoidant or phobic type is only cautious yet with a great potential for attachment. Also, there is a greater emotionality both in the capacity to experience pain and warmth: "They feel their loneliness and isolated existence deeply, experience being 'out of things' as painful, have a strong though often repressed desire to be accepted. Despite their longing to relate and to be active participants in social life they fear placing their welfare in the hands of others."

The label "phobic" character has been used in psychoanalysis. Thus Fenichel writes,[7] "phobic characters would be the correct designation for persons whose reactive behavior limits itself to the avoidance of situations originally wished for."

Beyond these two varieties of paranoid style (which we might characterize with the traits of strength and weakness respectively) there is still another (corresponding to a third subtype according to instinct dominance) which we might call a "Prussian character" in reference to the stereotype of dutiful and authoritarian German rigidity. We do find its description in Millon's "companion volume" to the DSM III that I have often

---

[6]It was Millon who coined the "avoidant personality" label in *Disorders of Personality*.

[7]Fenichel, O., *The Psychoanalytic Theory of the Neurosis* (New York: W.W. Norton & Co., 1945).

quoted throughout this book—there explained as a "paranoid-compulsive mixed personality":[8]

"Despite their growing hostility and the repudiation of conformity and submissive respect as a way of life, they retain their basic rigidity and perfectionism. They are now all the more grim and humorless, tense, controlled and inflexible, small-minded, legalistic, and self-righteous. These features of their makeup are even more deeply embedded and internalized as a fixed habit system. They may have found it necessary to discard their dependence on others as their primary source of reward, but the remnants of their lifelong habit of overcontrol and faultlessness are not as readily abandoned. Thus, they continue to seek the clarity of rules and regulations, cannot tolerate suspense, and impose order and system on their life. Deprived now of the guidelines of those others they have spurned, these paranoids lean increasingly upon themselves and become their own ruthless slave drivers in search for order and power."

In view of the similarity between these ennea-type VI individuals (who could well be loosely called "obsessive") with the obsessive personality proper (i.e., ennea-type I), Millon seeks to understand the difference between them and proposes that it lies in that these paranoid-compulsives have renounced their dependency aspirations and have given up hope of achieving protection through the good offices of others. Whatever the truth of that, it cannot be questioned that the paranoid are more inner-directed and introverted. Yet "they continue to seek the clarity of rules and regulations, cannot tolerate suspense and impose order and system in their life."

Among Jung's psychological types the most closely matching[9] the ennea-type VI personality is his introverted thinking type, who "is strongly influenced by ideas and whose judgment appears cold, inflexible, arbitrary and ruthless, because it relates far less to the object than to the subject." A covertly suspicious and pugnacious characteristic is observed by Jung, as he remarks: "He may be polite, amiable, and kind, but

---

[8]Millon, Theodore, op. cit.

[9]I find confirmation for the fact that it was ennea-type VI character that Jung had before his mind's eye, as he described his introverted thinking type, in the fact that he considers it embodied in Kant and in Nietzsche.

Jung, as he remarks: "He may be polite, amiable, and kind, but one is constantly aware of a certain uneasiness betraying an ulterior motive—the disarming of an opponent, who must at all costs be pacified and placated lest he prove himself a nuisance."

The fanatical aspect of the type is also observed by Jung: "In the pursuit of his ideas he is generally stubborn, head strong, and quite unamenable to influence."[10]

In the realm of test profiles I find the counter-phobic variety of ennea-type VI represented in the ENTJ.[11]

In Keirsey and Bates[12] it is an interest in authority that dominates the picture of this personality: "If one word were used to capture ENTJ's style it would be commandant. The basic driving force and need of ENTJs is to lead...." They also point out that "ENTJs have a strong urge to give structure wherever they are—to harness people to distant goals."

"Their empirical, objective, and extraverted thinking may be highly developed; if this is the case, they use classification, generalization, summarization, adduction of evidence, and demonstration with ease."

I do not find a single personality description in homeopathy matching ennea-type VI, but two. Though on the basis of Coulter's portrait of the *Lycopodium* personality in homeopathy I had found it the best approximation to the ennea-type VII pattern, I cannot help heeding the unanimous view of homeopaths I know in Mexico and Spain, and also the opinion of Dr. Iain Marrs in his otherwise favorable and even enthusiastic review* of my book in a homeopathic journal in Canada. Since they agree that *Lycopodium* is a type VI medicine, I have turned

---

[10]Jung, C.G., op. cit.

[11]Extraverted individual with predominance of intuition over sensing, thinking over feeling, and judgmentalism over an interest in perception for itself.

[12]op. cit.

* "Character and Neurosis / An Integrative View," Claudio Naranjo, M.D.— review by Iain Marrs, in *Simillimum*, Fall, 1995, Vol. VIII, no. 3.

once more to Coulter's chapter[13] to see whether in her description there may not be a juxtaposition of type VI and type VII observations. I find that, rather, most of her description refers to a "divergent type" that "graces contemporary homeopathic practice." I think that it is clearly the classical type that ennea-type conscious homeopaths have had in mind, however:

"The classic picture of *Lycopodium* found in the homoeopathic literature is as follows: the patient is thin, muscularly weak and lacking in vital heat; the hair is prematurely gray or balding; deep furrows (from much thought and worry) line the forehead; the sunken skin of the face is sallow and earthcolored, with premature wrinkles; the worried expression may make him look older than his years; the child will resemble a wizened little old man, while the young man may appear distinguished but somewhat whitened. The mind may be developed at the expense of the body. and yet the opposite is also found: mental degeneration, early senility, failing brain power, weak memory. Finally, the individual has been described as melancholy, morose, despairing, defiant, suspicious, inclined to take things ill, excessively irritable, misanthropic, cowardly, and so on. All these characteristics are encountered in the type and must be recognized when present."

Another personality description in homeopathy matching the ennea-type VI is that associated to *Psorinum*—connected to a sense of deficiency, fault, or flaw. One of the deficiencies commonly observed is that of vital heat manifesting in the symptom of chilliness, aversion to open air, and over-sensitivity to drafts. This is very true, I have observed, of the more timid type VI individuals, who not only seek emotional warmth but seem to translate a psychological sense of solitude into a yearning for heating and a tendency to protect his or her body with warm clothes. Also the allergic tendency of *Psorinum* individuals seems to fit what I have observed among the more timid and preservation-oriented type VI individuals. These are the people who are more susceptible to remorse, acknowledged

---

[13]Coulter, Catherine R., op. cit., all excerpts on *Lycopodium* from Vol. 1, pp. 79-123, all excerpts on *Psorinum* from Vol. 2, pp. 161-187, quoted by permission of the author.

to be a *Psorinum* tendency. Kent speaks of "anxiety of consciousness" and Coulter reports a traditional association between *Psorinum* and the notion of original sin. She also reports symptoms of fearfulness, insecurity, dejection, and a sense of being forsaken. She also observers that "duress, combined with inherent weakness and numerous environmental sensitivities can provoke 'irritability'" (one of the symptoms noted by Kent). When this is expressed as an outburst of anger it is likely to lead, in turn, to remorse. More characteristically of the more self-protective form of ennea-type VI is the observation that other patients "may not complain but rather display a needless diffidence and faint-heartedness, being frightened of their own shadow. Such an attitude breeds 'irresolution' (Kent)."

Coulter speaks of the *Psorinum* individual as one "who can bring himself to act only after carefully weighing every step and every conceivable consequence, knowing precisely where he stands and what he thinks" and quotes an intelligent female graduate student whose fear and timidity had been aided by *Psorinum* as observing "I used to fear to act because of all the possible ramifications. But recently I have realized that even if you don't act, there are consequences. So I might as well assert myself more and enjoy it!" Most typical of ennea-type VI is the observation "he worries unduly about events which may never transpire, depleting his limited energy anticipating entirely improbable vicissitudes."

3. Trait Structure

Fear, Cowardice, and Anxiety

A central characteristic among the descriptive traits of ennea-type VI is the peculiar emotion that contemporary psychology has described as anxiety. This may be likened to a frozen fear or a frozen alarm before danger that has ceased to threaten (though it continues to be imagined).

Examining type VI descriptors I find, aside from anxiety, many in which fear is the explicit psychological characteristic: fear of change, fear of making mistakes, fear of the unknown, fear of letting go, fear of hostility and trickery, fear of not being able to cope, fear of not surviving, fear of aloneness in a threatening world, fear of betrayal, and fear of loving. Paranoid jealousy might be included in the same group.

Closely connected to these are the traits that have to do with the expression of fear in behavior: insecurity, hesitation, indecision and tentativeness (a consequence of the fear of making mistakes), being paralyzed by doubt, immobilized, out-of-touch with impulse, avoidance of decisions and the inclination to compromise, being over-careful and cautious, prone to compulsive double checking, never being sure, lacking self-confidence, over-rehearsing, and having difficulty with un-structured situations, (that is to say, those in which there is no set guideline for behavior).

If fear paralyzes or inhibits, the inhibition of impulses feeds anxiety, as was Freud's contention; and we may say that fear is a fear of one's own impulses, a fear to act spontaneously. This "fear to be," to borrow Tillich's expression, is typically complicated by a fear of the outer world and a fear of the future consequences of one's present actions. An additional way in which fear, through immobilization, re-kindles itself is through the sense of impotence that plagues an individual who dreads giving free rein to aggressive or sexual impulses. Not being able to rely on one's power, distrusting one's abilities and the capacity to cope with situations—with the consequent insecurity and the need to rely on others—may be regarded as not altogether irrational but as the result of knowing oneself to be, in a psychological sense, "castrated."

Over-alert Hyperintentionality

Closely related to anxiety but not identical to it is the hyper-alertness entailed by a suspicious and over-cautious disposition. Unlike the confident over-alertness of type III which orients itself to having "everything under control, "this is a hyper-vigilance that is on the lookout for hidden meanings, clues, and the unusual. Aside from constituting a state of chronic arousal in the service of interpreting (potentially dangerous) reality, it serves an excessive deliberation concerning what for others would be a matter of spontaneous choice. I have borrowed Shapiro's word "hyper-intentionality" for the extraordinarily rigid and tense directedness of behavior (of suspicious character) as well as for the exaggerated need to rely on rational choices.

Theoretical Orientation

Fear makes the coward unable to be sure enough to act, so that he never has enough certainty and wants to know better. He not only needs guidance, but also typically (distrusting guidance as well as needing it) solves this conflict through appeal to the guidance of some logical system or of reason itself. Ennea-type VI is not only an intellectual type, but the most logical of types, one who is devoted to reason. Unlike ennea-type VII who uses intellect as strategy, type VI is likely to worship intellect through fanatical allegiance to reason and reason alone —as in scientism. In his need for answers in order to solve his problems, type VI is more than any other a questioner, and thus a potential philosopher. Not only does he use the intellect for problem-solving, but he resorts to problem *seeking* as a way to feeling safe. In his hypervigilance, his paranoid character is on the look-out for problems; he is a trouble-shooter in regard to himself and has difficulty in accepting himself without problems. While there is hope in seeing oneself with problems—the hope of being able to solve them—there is also a trap in problem making that manifests, for instance, as an inability to go beyond the role of patient in the therapeutic process and a difficulty in just letting oneself be.

Not only is the ineffectualness or generalized problem with doing of the more timid type VI individuals a consequence of an excessive orientation to the abstract and theoretical, but seeking refuge in intellectual activity is also a consequence of fearful holding back, indirectness, vagueness, and "beating around the bush."

Ingratiating Friendliness

Other groups of descriptors point to generalized traits understandable as ways of coping with anxiety. Thus we may understand the warmth of most ennea-type VI individuals as a weakness: a way of ingratiation. Even if we do not agree with Freud's interpretation of friendship as paranoid banding together in face of a common enemy, we must grant that there is such "friendship." The compulsive search for protection of cowardly affection falls into this category.

Together with the descriptor "affection" I list in this cluster "seeking and giving warmth," "being a good host and being hospitable," and "generous." "Pathological piety" may be also listed here, along with "exaggerated faithfulness" to individuals and causes. Also the traits of "considerateness," "gentleness," "obsequiousness," and the need for support and validation of the more insecure cowards falls in with the above. I notice that ennea-type VI individuals in whom these traits dominate are also prone to sadness, forlorness, and a sense of abandonment, much as in ennea-type IV.

Related to the ingratiating obsequiousness and the warmth of ennea-type VI is the need for association with a stronger partner, that gives them security yet typically frustrates their competitive inclinations.

Rigidity

Closely related to the affectionate expression of cowardice is an accommodating quality. The trait of obedience itself, however, I have grouped with characteristics of a more generalized dutifulness, such as an obedience to law, a devotion to fulfilling responsibilities as defined by external authority, a tendency to follow rules and to value documents and institutions. Ennea-type VI individuals in whom these traits predominate may be said to have a "Prussian character," in reference to this stereotype of rigidity and organization. The fear of authority and the fear of making mistakes causes them to need clear-cut guidelines as to what is right and wrong, so they are highly intolerant of ambiguity. These guidelines are never those of popular opinion, as in the "other directed" ennea-type III, but the rules of present or past authorities, such as the set of implicit inner rules of Don Quixote, who follows the knight errant in his imagination. Along with the above I have listed the traits "controlled," "correct," "well informed," "hard working," "punctual," "precise," and "responsible."

Pugnacity

An alternative to both the soft, obedient, ingratiating style of coping with anxiety and the rigid, principled, rule-bound style, we find a cluster of traits that may be understood as a pugnacious intimidation through which the individual (as Freud described in connection with the oedipal struggle) competes with parental authority—and later in life uses the position of authority both to feel safe and to obtain what he wants. To the extent that competitive usurpation is involved, there is guilt, fear of retaliation, and a perpetuation of paranoid insecurity. Belonging in this category are, aside from the denouncing of authority and the competitive wish to stand in the place of authority, "argumentativeness," "criticality," "skepticism," and "cynicism."

Along with these I have listed the descriptors "they think they know the right way," "pressuring others to conform," "bombastic," "bluffing," "strong," "courageous," and "grandiose." The trait of scapegoating appears to be related to this "strong" expression of type VI rather than the warm and weak style. We are in the presence of the counter-phobic manifestation of type VI—a strategy comparable to the barking of a dog.

Orientation to Authority and Ideals

What the aggressive, the dutiful, and the affectionate safety maneuvers have in common is their relevance to authority. We may say the fear of ennea-type VI was originally aroused by parental authority and the threat of punishment by the power-wielding parent—usually the father. Just as originally his fear led to sweetness, obedience or defiance (and usually ambivalence) toward his parents, now he continues to behave and feel the same in the face of others to whom he assigns authority or towards whom he (consciously or unconsciously) becomes one.

The pattern of "authoritarian aggression" and "authoritarian submission" noted by the authors of *The Authoritarian Personality* may be mentioned here: type VI manifests aggression towards those below and submission to those above in the authority hierarchy.[14] Not only do they live in a hierarchical world: they both hate and love authority consciously (being, in spite of anxiety in the face of ambiguity, the most explicitly ambivalent of all character types).

In addition to traits of submissiveness, the demand for obedience and love, hate and ambivalence toward authority, ennea-type VI exhibits, to a larger extent than any other, an idealization of authority figures—manifest either in individualized hero-worship, in a generalized attraction to the great and the strong or in an orientation to impersonal greatness, which causes some to over-mythologize life so as to indulge a passion for archetypal sublimity. This penchant for what is larger than life seems not only to underlie a divinization/demonization of the ordinary (observed by Jung in connection with the introverted thinking type) and the perceived sublimity of ideals of fanatics, but is a characteristic of ennea-type VI people in general, who in view of this may be described as "idealistic."

Accusation of Self and Others

Guilt is as prominent in ennea-type VI character as in types IV and V, only that in type VI the mechanism of guilt production goes hand-in-hand with a prominent mechanism of exculpation through projection and the creation of outer enemies. It is not only anxiety, but guilt, we may say, that seeks to be alleviated through ingratiation, through dutiful appeasement of potential accusers, through submission to personal or intellectual authorities, or through an assertive bluffing behind which the individual hides his weaknesses and imperfections. In usurpation of parental authority and becoming

---

[14]Adorno, T.W., et.al., *The Authoritarian Personality* (New York: Harper and Brothers, 1950).

an authority, just as in placating authority, the individual acts not only self-protectively but blame-avoidantly.

We may say that guilt manifested in such traits as defensiveness, self-justification, and insecurity, involves an act of self-accusation, by which an individual becomes an invalidating parent to himself. It is in this act of self-opposition through which an individual becomes his or her own enemy, that I see the fixation proper of type VI, i.e., the cognitive defect that developed as a consequence of fear and has ended by becoming its root. Accusation is not only a type VI characteristic in regard to self, but also to others—perhaps through the operation of projection in the service of avoiding the torment of too much guilt. Not only does ennea-type VI persecute himself and feel persecuted, but also he is a suspicious and critical persecutor—and he may affirm his grandiosity precisely in view of the entitlement that it affords to pronounce judgment on others.

Doubt and ambivalence

To speak of self-invalidation is to speak of self-doubt, just as suspiciousness implies a doubting of others. Beyond the attitude of an accusatory inquisitor of self and other, the word "doubt" brings to mind the uncertainty of ennea-type VI in regard to his views: he both invalidates himself and he props himself up—feeling subtly as paranoid schizophrenics feel in the extreme: both persecuted and grandiose.

To say it differently: he doubts himself and he doubts his doubt; he is suspicious of others, and yet he is afraid that he may be mistaken. The result of this double perspective is, of course, chronic uncertainty in regard to choosing a course of action, and the consequent anxiety, need of support and guidance, and so on. At times—and as a defense against unbearable ambiguity—he may take before the world the position of a true believer who is absolutely sure of things. When not a fanatic, though, ennea-type VI is characterized by ambivalence, more strikingly than any other character; and his most striking ambivalence is that of hating and loving his "authority bearing" parent at the same time.

Intellectual doubt, it seems, is only the expression of that emotional doubt in virtue of which he is torn between his hateful and his seductive selves, the wish to please and the wish to move against, to obey and to rebel, to admire and to invalidate.

4. Defense Mechanisms

The close association between paranoid functioning and projection is so well established that Shapiro[15] observes: "the mental operation or mechanism is so central to our understanding of paranoid pathology and symptoms that it has almost come to define what is called paranoid in psychiatry."

Though "projection" is a word that has been used with a variety of meanings, that which is appropriate in this context is that of attributing to others motives, feelings, or thoughts not acknowledged in oneself. In some cases ("super-ego projection") it is self-accusation that is disowned, through the implicit pretense that punitive ill-will comes from an outer source (as is most striking in the persecutory delusions of psychotics). The sense of being watched, judged, and so on that is part of type VI suspiciousness can also be interpreted in terms of exter-nalization: the mechanism of transferring an intra-personal event to an inter-personal relationship. In other instances, ("projection of the Id") it is the person's unaccepted impulses that are disowned and attributed to others, so that self-condemnation becomes the accusation of another.

In either case, projection may be understood as a mental operation aimed at self-exculpation or blame-avoidance, and thus something in the nature of an escape valve for excessive guilt. The generation of such guilt—which I am proposing to regard the core of type VI psychology—may be understood in relation to the defense mechanism known as "identification with the aggressor."

The psyche of the coward is that which best embodies the meaning of "diabolus," the devil: the adversary, the enemy.[16]

---

[15]op. cit.

[16]This is not to say that accusation is more "devilish" than falsification—as intimated by the devil's appellation of "father of lies."

We may say that the ennea-type VI individual once sought to placate his enemies through becoming an enemy to himself. It is as if he thought to himself that it is prudent to adopt a self-accusing attitude, since in that way he will not run into trouble with authority. Self-accusation typically sees monstrosity where there is only nature, and to the extent that fear is part of the universal neurosis, we carry within us a Freudian Id filled with hostility and destructiveness. This imagining of monstrosity where there is potential spontaneity and the wisdom of the organism not only leads to self-inhibition, but is complicated by the fact that inhibition perpetuates the situation of not knowing oneself, which in turn makes the individual vulnerable to self-vilification.

5. Etiological and Further Psychodynamic Remarks[17]

Though it is possible that within every character type there are some constitutional differences among the subtypes, in no other instance is this more striking than in that of type VI, where the three subtypes clearly embody the three Sheldonian components. While the counter-phobic (sexual), strong, and pugnacious form of ennea-type VI is mesomorphic, the avoidant or phobic (preservation) form shows an overall softer, more endomorphic appearance; while the duty-oriented and fanatic (social) subtype is typically, like Don Quixote, ectomorphic. It would seem that, however universal the childhood experience of anxiety may have been in the early environment, it is the constitutional factor that determines whether this anxiety is met through a wish to be bigger and intimidating to others (in the more aggressive and somatotonic ones); through a desire to form reciprocal protection alliances (in the viscerotonic); or through the wish to find an answer to the problems of life

---

[17] According to Siever's and Kendler's discussion of the etiology of the paranoid personality "there are a number of genetics studies showing it more commonly occurring in the family of schizophrenics and particularly showing a linkage to paranoid psychosis." They quote Colby as summarizing the four major theories that have been postulated concerning paranoid ideation: "Freud's homosexual theory, the hostilities theory (according to which paranoid phenomena result from the projection of intense unconscious hate), a homeostatic theory (the restoration of the equilibrium through the individual's transformation of guilt or inadequacy into the belief that others are threatening him, and a shame-humiliation theory. They also quote Colby's judgment that the shame-humiliation model (according to which the individual rather than permitting the unpleasant affect of shame and humiliation to be experienced, blames others for wronging the self) provides the broadest and most clinically relevant explanation. Summarizing psychoanalytic conceptions on the origin of the avoidant personality, Millon (in Cooper et al., op.cit.) states that an early parental rebuff or indifference seems most applicable in the background of avoidants. Most of what was said, however, seems of questionable specificity to the avoidant personality, in my opinion (for example Horney's observations in connection with moving away from people seem at least as applicable to the schizoid).

"cerebrotonically" through reason or ideology or other authoritative standard.

In addition to perceived lack of affection there is in the background of type VI a fear of punishment, especially the punishment of emotional rebuke. Most striking are the problems of authority, generally in relation to the father who tends to be the authority-bearing parent. Yet in relation to authority, too, the subtypes are differentiated, the avoidant one becoming the most yielding and the counter-phobic one the most competitive and rebellious.

In addition to the fear connected to rejection or punishment by an authoritarian father (frequently type VI or type I) there is also in the childhood of the fearful a contagion of fear through the internalization of an over-protective world view from the mother's side. Bombarded by such statements as: "Be careful, you'll fall down/ Be sure you don't talk to strangers/ Be careful with men—never trust them," the child learns to distrust his own resources and the world around him. Sometimes it is possible to find a life history of invalidation such that the child learns to doubt his perceptions, as in the following:

"But the first seven years of my life that's my ongoing memory, is him coming home, them fighting, my being afraid that they were going to kill each other. One night ...when I was four, it must have been a particularly bad year for his drinking and their encountering each other. Because I have since come up with other incidents from my brothers and sisters. But this one night in particular, well: my brothers had a room, my sisters had a room, and I had a small bed in my parents' room 'cause there wasn't space anywhere else. So, being the youngest, I was always the first one put to bed and whenever my dad would get home, I guess when the bars closed, the fighting would start. I always knew that once I was put to bed, I was to stay there, that you just didn't leave. But this one night the fighting was just really bad. So I found that I would get paralyzed with the fear. But this particular night all of a sudden there was a surge of adrenaline and I flew out of bed and down the stairs. And ... I thought at that moment that my fear had come to realization because my mother was flat on the floor, and my dad was sitting in a chair and I went over to her, but I couldn't rouse her at all, and I looked at my dad and I said, 'She's dead, you killed her.'

And he just, he was in a stupor and he just said, 'No. She's faking and there's nothing wrong. Go back to bed.' And I can remember wanting to stay there, but I was so afraid of him that I went back to bed. And when I went back to bed I think I eventually cried myself to sleep, but the next morning I remember hearing my mother call my one brother and sister to come for breakfast before they went to school. And so I got up real quietly 'cause I didn't want to disturb my father who was sleeping it off. That was usual in the morning, I had to be very quiet. But when I went downstairs, nobody said anything about the night before. And that was so typical. And so it's the whole fear thing, but also the self-doubt. Is it in your head or is it in reality?"

Sometimes inconsistency in parental behavior has contributed to the child's anxiety. Not knowing whether he would be punished or not, for instance, the child had occasion to doubt the outer world before doubting himself. Just as most ennea-type VI individuals have grown up in an atmosphere of strong authority, most of them have been the target of distrust by their parents—and thus we may think that self-doubt is the end result of an internalization.

Another commonly shared experience is being made to feel guilty: "See how much your father works, you should not give him more troubles." Religion may be an important means of accusation and sexuality a common target. Another, causing pain to their parents: "They made me feel very unfair to them through the damages that I caused them while they loved me so much and did so much for me."

A self-victimizing and complaining type VI mother may contribute greatly to such feelings and is a common occurrence in the family of type VI individuals: "My mother was very authoritarian with angry threats and blackmailing (IV); she ate my father up (VI). She always spoke in the plural and always was in the foreground. I always felt from her a great disrespect toward my interests and inclinations, and she hit me a lot. My father used to say that women are absorbing."

A common though not universal experience is the lack of communication between the parents: "At home the only conversation was complaining." "There were always fights at home." "My parents had many discussions, they were always trying to be right." It is easy to see how such conflicts may be echoed in the high ambivalence of the ennea-type VI individual, which is not only an ambivalence in regard to his impulses but one linked to a dual perception of each parent, who is evaluated not only empathetically but through the other parent's eyes.

The search for love becomes differentiated in type VI according to subtypes. The counter-phobic and the aggressively paranoid individual demands obedience, just as he has understood loving his own father as obedience. The avoidant phobic person, on the other hand, has learned to equate love with protection, a source of security to compensate his/her insecurity—a strong person to lean on. The dutiful social type is too uncertain or ambivalent about individual people to give them authority and chooses instead the impersonal authority of a system as parental surrogate, an internal action that may be viewed as implying a competition with parental authority. It is as if he were telling father: "I'd rather follow Christ than follow you, and you'll have to understand that it is better to be a good Christian than simply an obedient son." In shifting his allegiance or loyalty from a parent to a religion, or to reason, he is also shifting his expectation of love from the world of real people to a world of larger-than-life authorities, that exists mainly in a phantasmic reality, like Don Quixote's Dulcinea.

6. Existential Psychodynamics

This is a particularly relevant topic in the case of ennea-type VI in view of the connection between points IX and VI in the enneagram: we may say that the fear to do entails being out-of-touch with oneself, that a lack of grounding in being translates as a fragility or weakness in regard to self-expression.

While ennea-type III is scarcely aware of its self-alienation and types IV and V dwell on it intensely, experiencing it as a sense of insubstantiality, the experience of ontic obscuration in type VI is projected onto the future and carries a sense of fearful anticipation. It has been aptly described by R.D. Laing as the terror of looking within and finding that there is nobody there. There is in this situation neither an ignoring of the issue nor a meeting of it full face, but rather a not-quite-looking, a partial avoidance.

The fragility of the sense of being is also of such quality that it is suitably described by the expression which Laing proposed in connection with ontic obscuration in general: "ontic insecurity." We may say that being-loss in type VI manifests as an experience of threatened being, precarious being. Also Guntrip's expression "ego weakness" seems particularly appropriate for the paranoid nuance of being-loss.

It is possible to think that the excessive concern of type VI with security is not rooted in physical fear or even emotional fear so much as in an excessive clutching at factors of physical and emotional security out of an insecurity that is "not of this world." Unlike the experience of the truly courageous person— the hero who can risk anything, life included, out of an implicit sense of rootedness-in-something-beyond-contingent-existence— the coward projects his ontic insecurity onto the outer layers of existence through either a generalized incapacity to risk or an excessive concern with an authority and power that serves as a guarantee for such risking.

In the case of paranoid character *sensu strictu* it is easy to understand loss of being as a derivative of a search for being— through proximity to "the great" and the nourishing of one's grandiosity—as may be illustrated by the situation of Don Quixote, who in his identification with the ideal of a knight errant of chivalry pursues a life of fancy, incompatible with the all too ordinary (non-grandiose) experience of day-to-day reality.

In other instances it is not the grandiosity of an ideal or internalized image that becomes a being substitute, but the grandiosity of an external authority of the present or the past. In all such cases we may say that there is a confusion of being with authority and the special kind of power entailed by authority.

Just as it is true that at the psychological level proper the ennea-type VI individual gives up his *power* before authority, it is also possible to say that it is the very sense of being that is given up through its projection upon individuals, systems, or ideas endowed with a "greater than life" importance or sublimity.

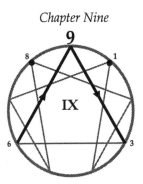

Chapter Nine

PSYCHOSPIRITUAL INERTIA AND THE OVER-ADJUSTED DISPOSITION

ENNEA-TYPE IX

1. Core Theory, Nomenclature, and Place in the Enneagram

The words "laziness" and "indolence" with which Ichazo designated the ruling passion and the fixation (respectively) corresponding to the ennea-type IX, fail to convey what they were originally intended to signify—before "sloth" was introduced instead of the earlier Latin term *accidia*.

Professor Giannini, of the University of Chile, writes, "What Saint Thomas, Gregory the Great, Saint Isidore, Cassian (to cite only the more representative authors) designated as *accidia* is a very complex phenomenon and far from translations such as lack of motivation toward action and other contemporary translations."[1]

In turn, a translation from the Greek "a-chedia" (no care), *accidia* refers to a laziness of the psyche and of the spirit, rather than a tendency to inaction, and so does "indolence" in the context of this book. Such spiritual laziness may be spoken of in terms of a forgetfulness of God or, in non-theistic language, a deafening to the spirit and a loss of the sense of being to the point of not even knowing the difference—a spiritual coarsening. Psychologically, *accidia* manifests as a loss of interiority, a refusal to see, and a resistance to change.

Dorothy Sayers in her commentaries to Dante's *Purgatory* writes that *accidia* "is insidious, and assumes such Protean shapes that it is rather difficult to define." It is not merely idleness of mind, but "that whole poisoning of the will which, beginning with indifference and an attitude of 'I couldn't care less', extends to the deliberate refusal of joy and culminates in morbid introspection and despair. One form of it which appeals very strongly to some modern minds is that acquiescence in evil and error which readily disguises itself as 'Tolerance'; another is that refusal to be moved by the contemplation of the good and beautiful which is known as 'Disillusionment', and sometimes as 'knowledge of the world'."[2]

The combination of loss of interiority and the resigned and abnegated character that goes along with it, results in a syndrome of a good hearted, comfortable "earthiness" that may be exaggerated to the point of literalness and narrowness.

Ennea-type IX is not only one who has not learned to love himself or herself as a consequence of love deprivation, but also one who forgets his love frustration through a sort of psychological pachydermism, an over-simplification, a psychological amputation that makes him the least sensitive and the most stoic of characters. (Ennea-type IX stands opposite to the hyper-sensitives IV and V at the bottom of the enneagram).

---

[1] H. Giannini, "El demonio del Mediodia," in *Teoria*, Dic. 1975, Santiago de Chile.

[2] Dante, *The Divine Comedy, Book 2—Purgatory*, translation by Dorothy Sayers (Middlesex, England: Penguin Books Ltd.,1955).

True as these observations may be, they fail to reflect the manifestations of spiritual laziness outside of hermitages and monasteries, or to evoke its pervasiveness in the world. For it is not a lack of religiosity that characterizes ennea-type IX but rather the contrary—only that this tends to be a religiosity in the social and ideological implications of the word rather than in reference to its mystical core. Ennea-type IX is, as we shall see, the contented and generous type of person whose "sloth" reveals itself not so much in an aversion to spiritual things as in a loss of inwardness, an aversion to psychological exploration, and with a resistance to change that exists side by side with an excessive stability and a conservative inclination. His motto—to himself and others—could be "don't rock the boat."

I imagine that the more dysfunctional among the "overadjusted" are diagnosed today as "dependent," yet dependency is something that ennea-type IX shares with ennea-type IV and, particularly, the avoidant form of ennea-type VI—the explosion of resignation into psychotic depression is much lower today than in Kretschmer's day.

2. Antecedents in the Scientific Literature on Character

Though Kurt Schneider addressed himself to the more deeply disturbed spectrum of the population we may recognize our ennea-type IX in his "abulic psychopath"—in which the main characteristic is "the lack of will and the incapacity to resist outside pressures." These are individuals "easy to seduce by others and by situations. In accordance with their malleable way of being, they are also accessible to good influences... these people who are nearly always kind, don't give the least trouble at the clinical and pedagogical establishments; they are reasonable, docile, laborious and modest." He remarks that they are "model guests in such establishments and yet, after they leave the influences of life take over, so the gains become lost."

Perhaps the best known of the syndromes corresponding to ennea-type IX is that designated by Ernest Kretschmer[3] as cyclothymia. In his study of the pre-psychotic personality of his manic-depressive patients reported in his classic volume *Physique and Character* (after statistical analysis of the data) he observed that the most frequent characteristics of this temperament were the following:

1. Sociable, good-natured, friendly, genial
2. Cheerful, humorous, jolly, hasty
3. Quiet, calm, easily depressed, soft-hearted

What for Kretschmer was the cycloid character became in the work of Sheldon—his intellectual continuator—a variable that people manifest to a different degree and only a minority exhibit in its maximum.

In his *The Varieties of Temperament* Sheldon[4] tells us in "briefest summary" that "viscerotonia is manifested by relaxation, conviviality and gluttony for food, or company or affection or social support. When this component is predominant, the primary motive in life seems to be assimilation and conservation of energy."

I quote below the list of the twenty principal traits of viscerotonia that he singled out in the course of his research of the fifties:

1.   Relaxation in posture and movement.
2.   Love of Physical Comfort
3.   Slow Reaction
4.   Love of Eating
5.   Socialization of Eating
6.   Pleasure in Digestion
7.   Love of Polite Ceremony
8.   Sociophilia
9.   Indiscriminate Amiability
10. Greed for Affection and Approval
11. Orientation to People
12. Evenness of Emotional Flow
13. Tolerance

---

[3] op.cit.

[4] op. cit.

14. Complacency
15. Deep Sleep
16. The Untempered Characteristic
17. Smooth, Easy Communications of Feeling, Extraversion of Viscerotonia
18. Relaxation and Sociophilia under Alcohol.
19. Need of people when Troubled
20. Orientation toward Childhood and Family Relationships.

Without contradicting Sheldon's view that viscerotonia may be observed in different degrees of expression, there can be no doubt to the effect that it is in the sloth type that its expression is maximum, for here viscerotonic traits are not only salient but seemingly the raw material on which the rest of the character is supported. We could say that the extreme extroversion of ennea-type IX not only has a constitutional root, but that constitution serves as a point of support for the defensive evasion of interiority. Arietti[5] has drawn a distinction between two main types of depression, each supported by a different type of personality: The "claiming depression" (our envy type) and the self-blaming type, "where the main emphasis is on self-accusation and self-depreciation." Though Arietti deals mainly with the states of psychotic decompensation, which is opposite to the typical joviality of the indolent, it is possible to recognize the ennea-type IX pattern: we are told that this is a duty bound, hard worker type, with strong patriotic sentiments, conformity with a strong need to belong, and conservative ideas.

At present I observe that ennea-type IX individuals are being classed by Bioenergetics therapists as "masochistic":

"The masochistic body is often noted to be thick, with powerful muscles which are believed to restrain the direct assertion and block the powerful underlying negativity. Characteristically, the masochistic character is overly pleasing and self-sacrificing, while at the same time evidencing passive-aggressive behavior."[6]

---

[5]Arietti, Silvano, "Affective Disorders" in *American Handbook of Psychiatry* (New York: Basic Books, 1974).

[6]Johnson, Stephen M., Ph.D., op. cit.

A "Mother Hubbard" Script is described in Transactional Analysis.[7]

"She spends her life nurturing and taking care of everyone but herself. She chronically gives much more than she receives and accepts the imbalance because she feels she is the least important of her family and her worth is measurable only in terms of how much she supplies to others."

Of the DSM III[8] categories, the one most congruent with ennea-type IX is "dependent personality," described in terms of the following characteristics:

"A pervasive pattern of dependent and submissive behavior, beginning by early adulthood and present in a variety of contexts, as indicated by at least five of the following:

1. is unable to make decisions without an excessive amount of advice or reassurance from others
2. allows others to make most of his or her important decisions, e.g., where to live, what job to take
3. agrees with people even when he or she believes they are wrong, because of fear of being rejected
4. has difficulty initiating projects or doing things on his or her own
5. volunteers to do things that are unpleasant or demeaning in order to get other people to like him or her
6. feels uncomfortable or helpless when alone, or goes to great lengths to avoid being alone
7. feels devastated or helpless when close relationships end
8. is frequently preoccupied with fears of being abandoned
9. is easily hurt by criticism or disapproval.

Millon characterizes the syndrome by the fact that: "the dependent persons' 'centers of gravity' lie in others, not in themselves. They adapt their behaviors to please those upon whom they depend, and their search for love leads them to deny thoughts and feelings that may arouse the displeasure of others."

---

[7] I quote from "Banal Scripts of Women" by Wickoff, in Claude M. Steiner, *Scripts People Live* (New York: Bantam Books, 1975).

[8] op. cit.

According to Millon "dependents are notably self-effacing, obsequious, ever-agreeable, docile and ingratiating... They deny their individuality, subordinate their desires, and hide what vestiges they possess as identities apart from others."[9]

Though anyone acquainted with cyclothymia would characterize it as extroverted, in Jung's description of psychological types, ennea-type IX is most closely approximated by the introverted feeling type which he notices predominantly in women:

"Their outward demeanor is harmonious, inconspicuous, giving an impression of pleasing repose, or of sympathetic response, with no desire to affect others, to impress, influence, or change them in any way... Although there is a constant readiness for peaceful and harmonious coexistence, strangers are shown no touch of amiability, no gleam of responsive warmth, but are met with apparent indifference... Faced with anything that might carry her away or arouse enthusiasm, this type observes a benevolent though critical neutrality...Any stormy emotion, however, will be struck down with a murderous coldness"[10]

On revising this chapter just after the publication of Lorna Benjamin's *Interpersonal Diagnosis and Treatment of Personality Disorders*,[11] however, I see that her understanding of dependent personality disorder is essentially that of our phobic (self-preservation subtype of ennea-type VI). If her understanding reflects that of the professional world in general, it seems to me that ennea-type IX has become to the collective eye of the American medical world as invisible as ennea-type III.

If we turn from Jung's to von Franz's[12] descriptions, however, I notice that it is her extraverted sensation type[13] in

---

[9]Millon, Theodore, op. cit.

[10]Jung, C.G., op. cit. There seems to be a measure of juxtaposition in Jung's description between ennea-types IX and V, since insistence on the scant expression of emotion, while appropriate, fails to reflect the equally characteristic affability of the cyclothomic character.

[11]Benjamin, Lorna Smith, *Interpersonal Diagnosis and Treatment of Personality Disorders* (New York: Guilford Press, 1993).

[12]Von Franz, Marie-Louise, and James Hillman, *Lectures on Jung's Typology* (Dallas: Spring Publications, Inc., 1979).

which we find the best match to ennea-type IX and its typical paucity of inner experiences:

"The extraverted sensation type is represented in someone whose gift and specialized function is to sense and relate in a concrete and practical way to outer objects...it has the best photographic apparatus, as it were; he can quickly and objectively relate to outer facts. This is why this type is found among the good mountaineers, engineers and business people, all of whom have a wide and accurate awareness of outer reality in all its differentiations...Jung says that such people very often give an impression of being rather soulless. Most people have met such a soulless engineer type, where you have the feeling that the man is absolutely dedicated to engines and their oils, and sees everything from that angle...Intuition is also completely lacking; that is for him just the realm of crazy fantasy."

Turning to test profiles, I find ennea-type IX recognizable in the portrait of an ISTJ (with introversion-sensing-thinking-judgment dominance), characterized by "decisiveness in practical affairs," and " guardians of time-honored institutions." I quote Keirsey and Bates:[14]

"If only one adjective could be selected, dependable would best describe this type."

"Whether at home or at work, this type is rather quiet and serious...the thought of dishonoring a contract would appall a person of this type...they perform their duties without flourish or fanfare; therefore, the dedication they bring to their work can go unnoticed and unappreciated."

"ISTJ's interest in thoroughness, details, justice, practical procedures and smooth flow of personnel and material leads this type to occupations where these preferences are useful. For example, ISTJs make excellent bank examiners, auditors, accountants, or tax examiners... They would be capable of handling the duties of a mortician, a legal secretary or a law researcher."

---

[13]The description of which in Jung matched our ennea-type VIII.

[14]op. cit.

"As a husband or wife, the ISTJ is a pillar of strength. Just as this type honors business contracts, so do they honor the marriage contract."

We can also recognize ennea-type IX characteristics in a different profile, however: that of an ESFJ (with extraversion-sensing-feeling-judgment dominance), depicted by Keirsey and Bates as the most sociable of all types:

"Harmony is a key to this type...ESFJs are the great nurturers of established institutions, such as the home, the school, the church and civic groups...ESFJs are hurt by indifference and need to be appreciated both for themselves and for the abundance, typically in the form of services, they give to others...conscientious and orderly, ESFJs may become restless when isolated from people." They "are likely to be aware of and enjoy discussing events and problems in the lives of their colleagues; but when conversation turns to abstractions of philosophy or science, the ESFJs may become restive."

"ESFJs want family decisions settled efficiently and quickly, and want family living routinized, scheduled, and correctly executed. They do not rebel against routine operations, are devoted to the traditional values of home and hearth, respect their marriage vows, and are the most sympathetic of all types."

In the experience of homeopaths the character corresponding to ennea-type IX has been clearly recognized, and its qualities of stability and neutrality have been compared to the properties of that of Calcium carbonate that is still used to paint white walls. The Calcium carbonate of the remedy is taken from the middle layer of the oyster shell, and the mollusc too is seen as related to the human type: "First, there is the animal itself—cold, pale, moist, limp, inactive. Second, there is the shell—thick, impenetrable, fixed to a rock, protecting the completely defenseless creature within. Third, within this otherwise undistinguished creature there grows a pearl of polished and delicate beauty, born through steady concretion around an irritating grain of sand...."[15]

I quote further from Catherine R. Coulter: "*Indolence* or 'inertness' (Hering) is a key characteristic. Recall the inactive

---

[15]Coulter, Catherine R., op. cit., Vol. 1, all quotations on *Calcarea* from pp. 39-46, reprinted by permission of the author.

oyster, the most passive member of the mollusc family, only opening and closing its shell to take in food or to reproduce....

"In general, *Calcarea* may retain a certain immaturity or undeveloped quality, even in adult life. He usually empathizes readily with children, and sometimes he is more comfortable with them than with adults...In fact, he often wants to remain a child—preferring its slow, protected, tranquil existence to the striving competitive world of adulthood....*Calcarea*'s inertia is traceable to 'lack of determination' (Hahnemann) and the absence of such other qualities as ambition, energy, and drive. The individual is rendered inactive by being too easygoing, too resigned, or he may consider striving and work to be as unnecessary for others as they are distasteful to himself. He may thus be a failure by ordinary standards...because he will not push or compete in a world where a certain amount of pushing and competition is required."

The picture of mental laziness is explicit: "The type puts off, is easily distracted, tarries, and fiddles with little things, unable to get down to the serious business at hand. He wears himself out with minutiae, so as to postpone undertaking the larger task....

"*Calcarea* can also present the polar opposite of the traditional picture of indolence [in which] what is stressful to *Calcarea* might be a part of another's normal routine.... Thus *Calcarea* is sometimes lethargic, apathetic, and phlegmatic, and at other times an immoderate worker who perseveres in order to overcome, or over-compensate for, his fundamental slowness and inertia. Indeed, this diligence can sometimes reach the point of 'exaggerated' or 'insane industry' (Kent), where he works day and night without letup...."

3. Trait Structure

Psychological Inertia

When I seek to bring order into the list of type IX descriptors through classification according to felt psychological commonality, I find that one of the conceptual clusters implies a trait that could be understood as a "paucity of inner experiences," to use Horney's expression in a paper of the same title, a lack of fire, a phlegmatic lack of passion. Along with these terms we may link "narcotization" (also introduced by Horney) and "thick-skinned" (a desensitization in the service of "long suffering"). An intellectual expression of the defensive loss of inwardness is a lack of subtlety and of imagination; an emotional consequence, a deadening of feelings, which may be either apparent (in an excessively phlegmatic disposition or in lack of communication about self) or hidden (under a genial or jovial disposition).

At the cognitive level, the most decisive aspect of it is the person's deafening to his or her inner voices—a loss of instinct well hidden by the apparent animalization (just as a pseudo-spontaneity of sexual and social freedom coexists with an inner deadening).

Not wanting to see, not wanting to be in touch with one's experience is something akin to cognitive laziness, an eclipse of the experiencer or inner witnessing in the person. In line with such eclipse of cognition in the light of a predominantly active disposition is a trait that may be called "concretism," the expression of which ranges from literalness to an excessively earth-bound attitude, a Sancho Panzaesque concern for survival and practicality at the expense of the subtle and the mysterious —a loss of openness to the unexpected and to the spirit.

Over-Adaptation

If spiritual laziness or *accidia* is the passion in ennea-type IX, the interpersonal life strategy and associated life view may be seen in a cluster having to do with "over-adaptation," "self-denial," "self-neglect," "inattention to personal needs," and "an over-controlled disposition"—which I am including in the same group—for it is not possible to adjust (to say nothing of over-adjusting) without the ability to take hold of oneself and inhibit one's impulses. It is against the background of this disciplined and controlled aspect of type IX (a trait that it shares with ennea-type I with somewhat less intensity) that we can understand the alcoholic propensity of this character as well as the passion for eating. Both illustrate a compensatory indulgence of physical appetites that does not constitute an intensification of aliveness.

Other descriptors corresponding here are "deliberate" and "responsible." A type IX individual is not only one who ends up "carrying the bucket," but a dependable as well as generous person ready to carry a large load over his or her shoulders. If in most cases the failure to embody the ideal of loving one's neighbor as oneself comes from loving oneself more than one's neighbor, in ennea-type IX, the situation appears as the opposite, for the over-adjusted postpone their own good and the satisfaction of their needs in an excessive yieldingness to the demands and needs of others.

It is easy to understand the connection between the two above-described traits: excessive adaptation to the world would be too painful to endure without self-forgetfulness.

Resignation

Both self-alienation and abnegated over-adaptation involve resignation—a giving up of oneself, an abdication from oneself and from life. It is as if the individual endorsed a strategy of playing dead to stay alive (yet becoming tragically dead-in-life in the name of life). Though resignation underlies over-adaptation it deserves to be considered by itself in view of the prominence of traits involving laziness in regard to one's needs, contentedness, and giving up or not standing up for one's rights.

Generosity

Related to a predominant orientation towards adapta-tion, in addition to a generalized "goodness of nature," "kind-ness," "helpfulness," "forgivingness," and, above all "abnegation," may be considered the "heartiness" of ennea-type IX, the friendly conviviality and the extraverted jollity of the "cyclothymic." It would seem that such jollity is part of an attitude of taking oneself lightly in order not to weigh upon others, just as friendliness is supported by the ability to be for the other more than for oneself. The convivial and hypomanic aspect of the "viscerotonic" was well known to Dickens, who gave us a wonderful portrayal of it in Mr. Micawber in *David Copperfield*. The over-adjusted individual characteristically likes children, is fond of animals, enjoys gardening. In his relation to others he is usually a good listener, ready to be helpful, sympathetic, and comforting, perhaps commiserating.

Ordinariness

Ennea-type IX individuals are frequently described as unassuming. Their self-concept is likely to be low—which often involves a resignation in terms of narcissistic needs. Their concern about excelling or shining is also low, and they may neglect their personal appearance. A characteristic ordinariness, a plainness and simplicity seem to derive from the giving up of the concern to excel and shine. (Type IX wants neither to shine, like type III, nor to be the best as type I). Though individuals with this character seem to have given up the wish for recognition, there is a deep and unconscious love thirst in their abnegated resignation and an implicit wish for love retribution. The sense of worth as well as the sense of existence of type IX is satisfied, not through applause, but rather, through vicarious participation, a living through others: lost identity becomes an identity by symbiosis with family, nation, party, club, team, and so on. We might speak of interiority through participation, either at the sentimental, the familial, or the larger group level.

Robotic Habit-Boundedness

Different traits emerging from the clustering of descriptors have to do with being "robotic." The over-adjusted are creatures of habit. They are bound by custom and regularity, as Sheldon observes of viscerotonics in general. They are

excessively concerned with the preservation of their balance. As
a corollary, they tend to be conservative and tradition-directed to
the point of rigidity. The same trait of psychological inertia may
be thought to underlie an excessive attachment to the familiar, to
the group norms or "how things are done."[16] Robotization, of
course, can be seen as a consequence of loss of interiority, of
alienation from self. On the whole we are struck by the paradox
that this most painstaking and long suffering way of being in the
world is rooted in a passion for comfort: a psychological comfort
purchased at such high price that, as intimated above,
bioenergetics practitioners brand ennea-type IX individuals as
"masochistic."

Distractibility

From what has been said it is clear that ennea-type IX
approaches life through a strategy of not wanting to see, and this
results in an over-simplification of the outer and inner world, a
diminished capacity for psychological insight and also an
intellectual laziness: a simpleton quality, characterized by
excessive concreteness and literalness. It is not surprising that a
loss of inwardness and insight entail a spiritual consequence—a
loss of the subtlety of awareness required to sustain the sense of
being beyond the manyfold experiences in the sensory-motor
domain.

That a perturbation of consciousness is involved in these
various obscurations seems confirmed in the fact that ennea-type
IX people describe themselves as distractible, confused,
sometimes with a bad memory. It seems to me that it is common
for type IX to break things or have personal accidents, and I
think this observation may be the basis for the statistical fact of a
correlation between death by car accidents and obesity. The
nature of their attention problem seems to be a difficulty of
concentration—which causes awareness to escape from the
center of the experience realm toward its periphery. This
distractibility of attention is assisted, however, by the

---

[16]Also, and perhaps as a compensation—in view of their over-adaptiveness—
they are characteristically hard-headed and stubborn in a narrow-minded and
prejudiced manner that they also share with ennea-type I.

individual's deliberate pursuit of distractions, as if driven by the desire not to experience or not to see. TV, newspapers, sewing, cross-word puzzles, and activity in general—in addition to sleep —serve the purpose of narcotization or "numbing out."

4. Defense Mechanisms

When I first presented my views on the correspondence between character structure and dominant defense mechanisms, I did not find a fully appropriate term for the characteristic way in which the ennea-type IX person distracts herself from inner experiences through attention to the outer world. The most appropriate I found and that which I adopted was Karen Horney's word "narcotization"—for her meaning is not only a loss of awareness but, more precisely, a "putting oneself asleep" through an immersion in work or in stimuli such as TV or reading the papers. Later I was to realize that this self-distracting maneuver is partly described by Erving Polster through the term introduced into the Gestalt therapy vocabulary as "deflection."

"Deflection is a neurotic mechanism[17] for turning aside from direct contact with another person. It's a way of taking the heat off the actual contact. The heat is taken off by circumlocution, by excessive language, by laughing off what one says, by not looking at the person one is talking to, by being abstract rather than specific, by not getting the point, by coming up with bad examples or none at all, by politeness instead of directness, by stereotyped language instead of original language, by substituting mild emotions for intense ones, by talking about rather than talking to, and by shrugging off the importance of what one just said. All of these deflections make life watered down. Action is off-target; it is weaker and less effective. Contact can be deflected either by the person who initiates the interaction or by the respondent. The initiating deflector frequently feels that he is not getting much out of what he is doing, that his efforts don't bring him the reward he wants. Furthermore, he

---

[17]Some in the Gestalt movement today prefer, somewhat pedantically to my taste, "boundary disturbance."

doesn't know how to account for the loss. The respondent, who deflects another person's effect almost as if he had an invisible shield, often experiences himself as unmoved, bored, confused, blank, cynical, unloved, unimportant and out-of-place. When deflected energy can be brought back on target, the sense of contact is greatly heightened."[18]

While Polster's description makes reference to a watering down of interpersonal contact, however, I think that the defense mechanism involved in type IX's psychology is one in which a similar process takes place in regard to self-contact or contact in the broadest sense of the term. (Thus, for instance, I recall somebody who may be called a "TV addict" who listened to the news during mealtimes. I mostly thought of it as distracting from the personal situation around the table, but occasionally my attention would be roused by some particularly important piece of international news. Yet I soon observed that every time that something truly important was discussed, it was impossible to listen since he began to talk or, sometimes, switched channels to football). The mechanism of attending to the peripheral rather than the truly important may be seen as the basis of a generalized "defensive extroversion" in the "auto-intraceptive" type IX. I propose that it be simply called "self-distraction."

Another psychological mechanism that is particularly prominent in type IX is one which Kaiser postulated as a "root of all emotional disturbances" and described as a fantasy of fusion and as an unrealistic carry-over into the adult life of the early symbiotic relationship with mother. The concept is echoed in the Gestalt therapy notion of "confluence," described as a "boundary disturbance," but could be called a defense mechanism just as well, inasmuch as it constitutes an attempt to reject from awareness the fact of one's isolation, aloneness, and individuality. I quote from the Polsters:[19]

"Persons who live in unhealthy confluence with one another do not have personal contact. This, of course, is a common blight of marriages and long friendships. The parties to

---

[18]Polster, Erving and Miriam, *Gestalt Therapy Integrated* (New York: Vantage Books, 1974).

[19]Polster, Erving and Miriam, op. cit.

such confluence cannot conceive of any but the most momentary difference of opinion or attitude. If a discrepancy in their views becomes manifest, they cannot work it out to a point of reaching genuine agreement or else agreeing to disagree. No, they must either restore the disturbed confluence by whatever means they can or else flee into isolation. The latter may emphasize sulking, withdrawing, being offended, or in other ways putting the brunt upon the other to make up; or, despairing of restoring the confluence, it may take the form of hostility, flagrant disregard, forgetting, or other ways of disposing of the other as an object of concern.

"To restore interrupted confluence one attempts to adjust oneself to the other or the other to oneself. In the first case one becomes a yes-man, tries to make up, frets about small differences, needs proofs or total acceptance; one effaces his own individuality, propitiates, and becomes slavish. In the other case where one cannot stand contradiction, one persuades, bribes, compels or bullies.

"When persons are in contact, not in confluence, they not only respect their own and the other's opinions, tastes, and responsibilities, but actively welcome the animation and excitement that come with the airing of disagreements. Confluence makes for routine and stagnation, contact for excitement and growth."

5. Etiological and Further Psychodynamic Remarks[20]

Sometimes ennea-type IX individuals are markedly endomorphic—the "whales" of Sheldon's atlas are rarely found in connection with other characters—and it may be said that as a

---

[20] Writing on the etiology of the dependent personality (in Cooper et al.'s *Psychiatry*) Esman states that "no known biological foundations can be associated with this syndrome, but it is possible that certain innate temperamental variants may predispose to its development." He also quotes Mahler suggesting that such children fail to resolve the "rapprochment crisis" of the second year, experiencing intense separation anxiety and maintaining, therefore, a clinging attachment to the mother that interferes with a normal evolution of a differentiated self and object representations."

whole the group is the most endomorphic in the enneagram. It is also the most ectopenic, and in this we may see a constitutional predisposition to the lack of inwardness in type IX character.

Sheldon observes a lack of distinct features, not only in the endomorphic body build but also in the viscerotonic personality, though whether this is a constitutional given in the realm of temperament or a secondary development is difficult to say, for it has been claimed that symbiotic character[21] arises from a difficulty in the individuation phase in development; yet it is possible that this developmental characteristic is itself constitutionally influenced, for Sheldon observes a lack of distinct features, not only in the endomorphic body build but also in the viscerotonic personality.

Though Millon has suggested that the dependency in subjects with dependent personality may derive from an excessive maternal care, this is definitely not what I have observed in ennea-type IX individuals, who typically come from a large family where parental attention was divided among many siblings or from very busy households in which hard work absorbed much of the mother's energies. Such antecedents are congruent with the resignation of the so-called dependent personality and the great effort to deserve love implicit in their self-denying, over-giving behavior. Only after the course of psychotherapy does type IX understand the love starvation of his childhood and the degree to which he has "naively" protected his parents from deidealization, persevering in a childlike over-trusting naiveté.

While a constitutional viscerotonic endowment may support the contented disposition of ennea-type IX, it is often clear from childhood circumstances that there was not another way out for the child than yielding to circumstances. Sometimes it was not that mother's warmth was lacking, but circumstances prevented her from being more available, and the child perceived that complaining or calling attention to oneself would be of no help. On other occasions the child feels in a precarious position in the family, and this gives a sense that by complaining one might lose what little one has. In the following extract from

---

[21]That may be considered equivalent to the sexual subtype of the over-adjusted. See Johnson's book *Characterological Transformation*.

an autobiographic report we find two unusual yet paradigmatic events having contributed to the "solution" of over-adjustment: an exotic cultural pattern and extreme brutality.

"My early childhood was divided up. When I was six months I was given away to my great grandmother, that's part of the early culture of the Zamoros. So I never knew my parents until I was nine years old when the war broke, and my Aunt thought that she should return me to my parents in case anything happened during the war. And already I was rejected and abandoned, and when I came back to my family, my brothers and sisters did not accept me, they thought I was an intruder to the family. So...my mother is quiet but domineering. My father is a drunkard and when he comes home, we know when he's coming home because he will be singing from work. We know what we are supposed to do; that we should disappear, and I always get the blame 'cause I am the oldest of thirteen children and anything that goes wrong in the family, I get the blame. I will get the spanking, and then my father will give me the belt, and I will give it to my brothers and sisters to let them know that I am the boss when my parents are not around, that they should listen to me. My mother is quiet but very domineering in her quietness. She controlled my father and, well, one thing about my father, we children never saw him raise his hand to my mother, but my mother would wait until he sobered up and then talk to him, and then he'd come home the next day the same thing—drunk from work. One thing I can say about my dad, that he never spent the money for his drink, he'd always bring the check home. He's a good provider and his friend would give him the drink. He never raised his voice on my mom. And we'd never see them quarrel. During the Japanese time he worked very hard, and yet when we'd collect the food the Japanese came and took the food from us. And my mother would go and collect some more of the food, we all went and helped her pick potatoes and all kinds of things, and a few days later the Japanese would come. So we were deprived of food at that time. I was nine years old. And toward the end of the two years we were in the Japanese camp, the Japanese collected all the men, eighteen up, and took them, before the Americans came in, and my father was one of them, but he escaped and the rest of the men that were taken, they were killed on the way. And my mother hid me just before then because the Japanese were collecting them all up and put them in a cave and threw hand grenades in and killed them 'cause they were afraid that there would be an uprising. And they were going to finish us all but the Americans came in."

Though the events in this story are rare they are paradigmatic: it is clear that the girl in it had grounds to become resigned, i.e., she had to cope in situations where there was nothing she could do. When I said this to her after listening to her report, her immediate comment was: "That's why I'm always saying 'I'm OK'. I deceive people by laughing things off."

An element that often appears in the stories of ennea-type IX is an expectation that they contribute to what work there is to do at home. A woman says, for example: "You always had to milk the cows, morning and night...another trait in both of my parents was the work before you play, you don't show emotions, you suffer it out, you stick it out, you don't complain by being sick."

A common variety of that situation is becoming mother's helper with younger siblings as in the following example: "I have a brother that's two years older than I, and then it's myself—and I was the baby for five years—and then my sister was born. And I don't know how that came about, but it seemed like I fell into being *responsible for my sister*, as a five-year old already, and that just came to me a couple years ago when I experienced some resentment against her, and I was trying to figure out why, and then it came to me that I kind of lost my childhood at that point. I remember one incident when she must have been a toddler maybe three or four years old, and we were standing on a busy street. My mother was in the store shopping, and we were waiting for my dad, and I had her by the hand and I would have been maybe eight years old then and all of a sudden she saw my dad coming and she broke loose and ran into this busy street, and the thing that I remember—my dad saw her too and he just ran out and stopped the traffic, or else she would have been run over. And the first thing that I thought of was if she had been hurt it would have been my fault. Now, it's a very strong impression. I don't think my parents ever gave me that, I don't remember that they did. But anyway...So then four years later another little girl came along, and by that time I was really ready to be the mother and I guess I took it on—both parents coming from large families where it was taken for granted that each child would take care of the younger ones. I think that we just fell into it. It wasn't that I really had to, because Mom didn't work outside of the home and she could have really handled it quite easily I think. But that's where I think I got the idea of the self-forgetfulness and putting myself aside and not ever feeling real free to have fun and do what I wanted to do, because there I was always looking after the kids, keeping an eye on them and making sure that they were okay."

Regarding the personality of parents, it is common to find types IX and I, particularly in combination. The former influence, of course, has acted a model of self-giving, the second has brought in perfectionistic demands: "My mother was very puritanical and perfectionistic. Being good was the way of avoiding spanking." "I always received the message that it was not allowed and that in addition, one had to be ready for a time when it would be even less allowed."

Even though over-adjusting is very opposite to rebellion, it is interesting to observe that rebellion toward a parent may have constituted a motive in adopting this style, as for instance in the following report by a young man: "My mother (I) has always reproached my father (IX) before me, and I think that it has been a rebellion toward her that has made me what I am, because I always had to do what she wanted. It was also an expression of love toward him. He was not present a lot. He worked out of town and whenever he appeared there were problems according to my mother. But I, as a child, remembered beautiful things in connection to my father."

It is easy to understand why sometimes a type IV mother appears often in type IX histories; as in the case of a perfectionistic parent, this has involved demands and the need to defer to somebody else's need. In the following example this element appears along with another common feature in the childhood of ennea-type IX, that of seeking to be a pacifier between the parents: "I always remembered my mother disparaging my father saying that he was lazy, that he had to work, that she had managed things, etc. But I could not believe that my father was such a bad person, and I wanted to be like him—peaceful and leisurely. He has little but manages with little. I also need little, just affection. I became like a bridge between them. I tried to make it better between them as a mediator."

While the search for love in other characters has visibly turned into the search for love substitute or into the search for something that was originally perceived as a means to attracting parental care, in the "slothful" it appears to have been a resignation in regard to love and attention. Yet this resignation is only maintained through a loss of inwardness, for compulsive generosity does entail an unconscious expectation of reciprocity. While the unconsciousness of the love wish makes it inappropriate to speak of seduction or baiting, the individual is most grateful when his or her giving is acknowledged, and we may say that her search for love mainly takes the form of this wish to be acknowledged in her givingness and her selfless generosity.

6. Existential Psychodynamics

Just as at the bottom of the enneagram (IV and V) conscious existential pain is maximal, in ennea-type IX, at the top, it is minimal; and while ontic obscuration in type III is better intuited by an outsider who may ask "What is all the rush about?" than by the subject himself, in type IX not even an outsider would guess the loss of inwardness on the individual's part, for his contentedness seems to radiate in such a way that he seems more *there* to others than he himself feels. Precisely in this lies the special characteristic of the ontic obscuration in the indolent, over-adjusted disposition—that it has become blind to itself.

Throughout the elucidation of the loss-of-being in the other characters we have noted how a craving for being, in its impatience, seems to fix itself upon different appearances where there lies an ontic promise. In the case of ennea-type IX, rather, it is not the intensification of "ontic libido" that stands in the foreground but, on the contrary, a seeming lack of craving that gives the person an aura of spiritual fulfillment.

Yet the seeming enlightenment of the "healthy peasant" entails an unconsciousness of unconsciousness, a falling asleep to one's yearning. I cannot understand Ichazo's statement to the effect that in indolence "the trap" is being too much of a seeker. Characteristically, the opposite is true: type IX is not enough of a seeker, despite the subjective sense of being so and despite manifestations of displaced seeking such as erudition, traveling, or collecting antiquities. Indeed such negative transmutation of the transformative urge into impulses oriented toward a less dimensioned venture is typical, and may express itself in a desire to know curiosities. Dickens' Mr. Pickwick is a good literary example in his venturing beyond the outskirts of London, learning languages, and so on.

As I have examined the existential psychodynamics of the different characters thus far, I have been spelling out the contention—expressed by the central position of ennea-type IX in the enneagram of characters—that the "forgetting of self" is the root of all pathologies. While in other instances this transpersonal perturbation seems the background for striking interpersonal consequences, in type IX it is the foreground, and a relative paucity of compensatory consequences gives the impression of interpersonal health, "pseudo maturity." We may say that type IX is less neurotic than other characters in the ordinary sense of the word that makes reference to psychological symptoms proper, and that its perturbation is more purely spiritual.

Even though the being-substitutes of ennea-type IX are not in the foreground—as in the frantic speeded-up psychology of vanity or in the intensity search of the masochistic or the sadistic personalities—this "search for being in the wrong place" is there, as it is in all characters. One of its forms I have called "over-creaturization": a search for being in the realm of creature comforts and survival-related practicalities. Such a person might say, "I eat therefore I am." Another form is the pursuit of being through belonging. For the ennea-type IX individual, the needs of others are his own needs and their joys are his joys. Living symbiotically, he lives vicariously. He could say, "I am you, therefore I exist"—where the "you" can be a loved one, a nation, a political party, a Pickwickian club, even a football team....

Though compulsive abnegation develops in part as a response to the belonging drive, it also serves as function of ontic compensation: "I am because I can do," "I am because I can be useful." Just as being can find substitute satisfaction through belonging, it can also take substitute satisfaction through ownership—as pointed out in the title of one of Erich Fromm's books: *To Have or To Be.*[22]

On the whole, the physical and obvious afford the Sancho Panzas of the world a most satisfying "ontic pacifier," and the search for being in the concrete, seeming most common-sensical, turns out to be the most hidden. It's hiddenness reminds us of Nasruddin's donkey: It is told that Nasruddin was seen at a remote outpost of customs officials crossing the border again and again on his donkey; he was suspected of smuggling something, but never were the customs inspectors able to find anything other than hay in his donkey's bags. When one of them ran into Nasruddin much later in life, at a time when both lived in a different country and had left behind the circumstances of their past, he asked the Mulla what it was that he was surely smuggling so astutely that they were never able to catch him for it, Nasruddin's answer was: donkeys.

While in its highest sense a pointer towards the hiddenness of God ("closer than our jugular vein"), Nasruddin's smuggled donkey can also serve as a paradigm for the invisibility of ignorance and for the singular unobtrusiveness of ennea-type IX neurosis.

---

[22]Fromm, Erich, *To Have or To Be* (New York: Bantam Books, Inc., 1982).

Chapter 10

SUGGESTIONS FOR FURTHER WORK ON SELF

I once heard about somebody who asked Karen Horney what to do about his neurosis and received the answer that reading her books attentively was already doing something.

Also Freud, at the beginning of his therapeutic adventure, believed in the value of sharing with his clients his view of the mind in general and his emerging therapeutic theory. And, of course, psychoanalytic insight originated in an important way from Freud's self-analytic experience, and the value of self-analysis was shared by those in his circle—along with a realistic understanding of its limitations. With the passing of time, however, self-analysis was not only neglected but definitively inhibited by the opinion of practicing psychoanalysts in general.

One exception to the growing opposition of professionals to the effort on the patients' part to analyze themselves was Horney, who wrote her classic on the subject when she was still one of the senior training analysts at the New York Institute of Psychoanalysis. I personally view the widespread injunction of therapists to their patients not to attempt to clarify themselves as an expression of implicit authoritarianism, insecurity, and implicit alliance with a monopoly of experts, and I believe we cannot afford it at a time when our collective predicament depends much on individual human transformation and when we cannot afford not arousing the potential and motivation of individuals to work on themselves to the extent that they can.

While it is true that intellectualization can compete with the therapeutic process inside the individual mind or in a therapeutic relation, I suspect that self-analysis was mostly forgotten as an implicit result of psychotherapeutic authoritarianism in the profession, particularly in the course of the pre-humanistic years. Thus it constitutes also an expression of the monopolistic attitude of psychoanalysis as an institution—which through each individual analyst is saying to the analysands, not only "don't go anywhere else for help," but also "don't try to heal yourself. I'll do it for you."

I take the position here that self-study can be not only a complement to psychotherapy in a professional, individual, or group setting, but can also go a long way with the support of the information in this volume.

Not only have ancient and hallowed traditions enjoined us to know ourselves but, we may say, the self-therapizing impulse (and more generally speaking the impulse to optimize one's consciousness) is a natural, healthy, and wise response to life difficulties. I am well aware of the enormous value of personal relationship in the healing of relationship problems and of the necessity of some persons to undergo, not only a period of therapeutic relationship, but also a period of therapeutic regression in the context of such relationship, before healing can take place—but I want to underscore that even in an interpersonal situation we may say that it is the individual who ultimately does the work. We may say that assisted psychotherapy is a specialized and particularly helpful situation in which to conduct self-study, yet what we discover about ourselves and how we envision what we discover is ultimately up to us. In view of this, I have espoused throughout many years of my life what I call an ethos of "working on oneself,"* and even conveyed a view to the effect that in our critical and turbulent times, psychotherapy should be only viewed as supplementary help and not a substitute for self-care.

---

* Arguing that people should be educated to keep their minds and relationships clean.

It is now several years since I have been giving groups of people not only information such as is contained in this book but also tools to work with each other, supervised along the way, and I know that this process has been extremely significant in the lives of many who had already had many previous experiences with psychotherapy. Yet, in that situation I present ideas such as those in this book in the context of a mere introduction to working on oneself, and the reader may, in view of that, understand to what extent I regard the present book as no more than an introduction to self-study.

Yet, as Karen Horney did in regard to her own work, I have envisaged the process of reading it as already a form of working. In particular I have imagined that the reader, as he or she has moved from one to another hall of portraits deriving from literature, psychology, or my own cumulative experience and its elaboration, would have felt as if she had been walking in a hall of mirrors reflecting back to her different aspects of her personality. For those who still, after reading, ask themselves, "What can I do now with this?" and are not part of an experiential teaching situation or community as I have described, I have written this chapter.

First of all I would like to endorse that aspect of "working on oneself" which is the acknowledgment of the truth about oneself and one's life in spite of the discomfort or pain that this may involve—in other words, intimate confession.

Just as, in Christian language, it is said that the acknowledgment of sin can be the gateway for contrition, purification, and eventual salvation, we may say in more contemporary terms that anyone who fully acknowledges psychological enslavement to neurotic needs will feel a desire for liberation animated by the intuition of a spiritual freedom. In other words, he will intimately aspire or pray to be free from the passionate realm, so as to breathe loftier air.

Together with endorsing this wish for transformation and this turning from the world to the divine, I want to emphasize at the same time that the teaching strategy involved in this work is not only one of self-observational focus, but includes the development of a neutrality vis-a-vis the study of the "machine," a neutrality in which the desire for change is not "acted out" in a precipitated and self-manipulative attempt to "perfect oneself."[1]

Though behavior modification will be the focus of another stage in the inner work, this next stage of actively seeking the development of interpersonal virtue could hardly be tackled without the background of thorough self-awareness. Centuries of institutionalized do-goodism in all the higher civilizations clearly demonstrates that without self-understanding, self-intentional virtue can only be accomplished at the expense of repression and the impoverishment of consciousness.

When one practices the pursuit of self-knowledge in an attitude of prayerful aspiration and objective recognition of one's aberration, and yet at the same time seeks to make space in one's mind for such present imperfections as are unavoidable as a consequence of the imprints of past experience and the inevitable duration of the self-realization process, one comes to discover that self-understanding is sufficient to itself. Indeed, the truth about ourselves can free us, for once we have truly understood something about ourselves, it will change without "our" attempt to change it. True insight into what we do and how we do it transforms our obsolete responses into idiocies which are likely to fall by the wayside or lose power over our essential intentions.

Whatever is valid in regard to awareness of our aberrations in general applies, of course, most pointedly to awareness of our chief feature and ruling passion, which involves the perception of the *gestalt* of one's many traits and their dynamic connection to these central foci.

In writing the nine preceding chapters I have implicitly assumed that the reader, coursing through them, will identify more with some characters than with others, and that for some of them self-recognition in the light of one particular set of traits and dynamics may come both spontaneously and effectively. Indeed, believing that the spelling-out of that character throughout the book can serve as a self-diagnostic instrument and also believing that knowledge of one's chief feature can

---

[1]The subtlety of this orientation, and other key issues, in work-on-self is spelled out in detail by E.J. Gold in his collection of essays, *The Human Biological Machine as a Transformational Apparatus* (Nevada City, CA: Gateways Books, 1985).

make an individual free from its tyranny (as center of the psyche) make me feel very pleased.

For those who have not come to such self-recognition through reading the book alone, self-study oriented to an insight into their "chief feature" will remain as the next most important aspect in the task of coming to know themselves better.[2] Sometimes self-recognition is being resisted as a consequence of not having yet achieved the ripeness to see oneself objectively; in such cases insight will have to await this ripening, and the pursuit of self-recognition is likely to constitute a stimulus for acknowledging psychological realities as they are.

I advise those of my readers who have come to a realization of what the dominant passion is (and the corresponding fixation) to begin a course of additional self-study through the writing of an autobiography that takes into account such insights. This autobiography should include early memories—particularly the memories of painful situations and experiences in early family life; and it should become clear how, throughout the story of childhood, character was formed; particularly, how it was formed *as a way of coping* vis-a-vis painful circumstances.

To those undertaking this exploration, I recommend that they seek to immerse themselves in their memories as they write, and to make sure that their narration does not lapse into abstractions, but that it reflects the sounds, the sights, the recollected actions, attitudes, and feelings of the past. Don't hurry, but welcome the opportunity to be in touch with your memories for whatever time it takes.

When immersing yourself in your experience of the past, seek to cultivate the attitude of an impartial observer. Write as one who merely *reports* on the facts, inner experiences, thoughts, decisions, actions, or reactions of the past. After the story of childhood, observe both your growth and your ego-growth during adolescence, a time when the pain of childhood becomes conscious of itself, a time when the yearning for what was missing in childhood gives shape to the earliest dreams and life

---

[2]To assist in the process I am providing some guidelines to differential diagnosis in an appendix.

projects. After this, as you continue with your life story, you may observe the living-out of these early dreams or ideals.

Make out of the writing of this autobiography a study in the origins and development of your particular character—centered on your particular ruling passion and fixation. When you finish analyzing your past, in terms of this basic structure, you will be in a better position to observe your "machine" in ordinary life and in the here and now.

After the study of your past life, you will be prepared to undertake an ongoing self-analysis from the point of view of these ideas—i.e., an ongoing self-administered Protoanalysis: the processing of daily experience in the light of the psychological understanding discussed in this book. This will involve the discipline of self-observation and also a discipline of retrospection—a chewing-up of recent experience in the light of "work ideas."

Since a relevant work idea, in connection with this discipline, is the recognition of the particular usefulness of attending to "negative emotions," and, since these are painful states caused by the frustration of the passions, it may be said that an inevitable aspect of this work is what Gurdjieff used to call "conscious suffering"—a willingness to stay with such experiences as need to be observed and investigated.

The ideal material to process in one's writing is that of painful and unsatisfactory moments in the day: moments of frustration, guilt, fear, hurt, pride, solitude, and so on. In particular, examine episodes that may be felt as "wrongly lived": times when one feels that one's behavior or words were not what they could have been, and one looks for an alternative, wishing to "re-write" the episode in one's life. It is to these that one should begin to apply the book's information, seeking for the operation of the passion—one's ruling passion, in particular—and seeking also to identify the traits or attitudes, linking this behavior to one's generalized way of being.

In addition to the ongoing writing-up of painful interpersonal episodes and their analysis, one should seek to include more and more the experience of existential pain: i.e., the pain of feeling (perhaps increasingly) one's mechanicalness, the conditioned nature of one's personality, one's lack of ultimate reality and, especially, the lack of a sense of truly being.

We might say that the ordinary condition of the mind is half full and half empty in regard to the sense of being. We are only half conscious of our unconsciousness, only half aware of our disconnection with what should be the core of a human being's experience. Or rather, we might say that we have obscured an old, too painful sense of existential vacuum with a false sense of being that is supported in the various illusions peculiar to each character.

Awareness of endarkenment is the deepest aspect of conscious suffering—yet burning in this pain, for anyone who plunges into it, is the source of the most precious fuel for the work of transformation. I would recommend to those who have thus applied themselves to self-observation and journal writing for 3 or 4 months to re-read what I have written under the heading of "Existential Psycho-dynamics," (in the chapters corresponding to their ego types) and that, drawing on their observations, they write a statement of both corroboration and amplification.

Work of self-observation such as I have been recommending is not only an occasion for the development of an observing self, which is an intrinsic aspect of progress along the path of self-knowledge; growth of the capacity to be a witness of oneself, in turn, is a factor that supports the harvesting of psychological insight.

Of the various disciplines used to develop a self-aware, non-robotic, and centered stance, I particularly recommend, as a beginning, the task of ongoing belly-centered awareness as described by Karlfried von Durckheim in his book *Hara*.[3] Essentially, the practice consists in maintaining throughout daily life a sense of presence at a point about four fingers under the navel, coupled with abdominal relaxation, relaxation of the shoulders, alignment of the body axis to gravity, and breathing awareness.

An additional recommendation to those who share an interest in continuing to use this book beyond its reading, is to further develop their ability to experience the moment without

---

[3]Von Durckheim, Karlfried Graf, *Hara: The Vital Center of Man* (London: George Allen and Unwin, Ltd.,1962).

conceptualization or judgment, which may be done through the practice of *vipassana* meditation.

The combination of self-study and meditation has been one of the constant features of my work, and the natural consequence of a schooling in both Buddhism and the "Fourth Way." After nearly 20 years of experimentation, I have come to the conviction that the most suitable background for self-study proper is that of *vipassana*, with particular emphasis on the mindfulness of sensations and emotions, while the practice of *samatha*, with its emphasis on tranquillity, is the most appropriate for the second stage of the work—where the focus is on behavior and development of the virtues.

A number of books on *vipassana* are in print and may serve both as a stimulus and a basis of wider understanding of the topic, yet I'll finish this set of suggested prescriptions with the following *vipassana* instructions that may be put in practice from this very day on:

- Sit, either on a chair or, preferably, in the half-lotus posture or on a meditation bench.

- Close your eyes and relax. Relax your shoulders, in particular be sure you relax your tongue—more connected to internal dialogues than is usually realized. Let your body hang from your spine and sink, if possible, into your belly. Relax your hands and feet, too.

- Attend to your breath, now.

- Allow your internal animal to do the breathing, if possible, or your lower brain—rather than telling yourself to breathe in and to breathe out in a military fashion.

- Now, add the awareness of the rising and falling of your upper abdomen to the awareness needed to drop muscle tensions and to be in touch with your breathing. Seek actually to sense the abdominal wall at the epigastrium (i.e., the triangle region under

the tip of the sternum and between the descending
lower ribs) as it rises and falls within each breathing
cycle. Be in touch with your "solar-plexus" as your
abdominal wall rises and falls with each breathing
cycle.

While the above may be sufficient practice for several
meditation sessions, it is only a back-bone of the *vipassana*
practice proper. Once you have attempted it and developed
some proficiency at it, regard your breathing as a reminder to
ask yourself, with every in-breath the question, "What do I
experience now?" In this manner, the meditation exercise
becomes one of an ongoing awareness of mental events without
forgetfulness of the breath or of the abdominal focus.

The question "What do I experience now?" need not be
put in words, of course. The very act of breathing can be taken as
the equivalent of a wordless question, or a wordless reminder to
be in touch with whatever is happening in the body, feelings,
and subtler aspects of the mind.

While the above corresponds to contemporary attempts
in psychotherapy to be in touch with the "here and now," the
distinctive characteristic of *vipassana* practice is a *particular
attitude* toward ongoing experience: a centered attitude,
comparable to that which we have discussed in connection with
the awareness of daily life; a neutral attitude of making space for
whatever is there, an attitude of panoramic availability of
attention. More deeply, yet, it is an attitude of not grasping for
anything and not rejecting anything—an attitude of openness
and non-attached equanimity.

Perhaps the most important thing I can say to anybody
who has followed me thus far by putting into effect my
suggestions is to go beyond self-study, self-awareness, and self-
insight proper, to an increasing measure of confession in regard
to the understanding thus far gained of the personality. This may
have come about spontaneously—for what we learn about
ourselves tends to come into our communication, yet there is
something that may be cultivated to the extent that we
understand that not only is truth compatible with a successful
life but also shared truthfulness (in certain chosen relationships)
can be a path by itself; and conversely the inability or

unwillingness to be genuine, at least in such chosen relationships, contributes to the perpetuation of our self-imprisonment in the world at large.

An alternative to a resolution to increase transparency in regard to self-insight in the life of one's individual friendships and family relations may be an association with like-minded people interested in going further through these ideas. To such a group my main recommendation would be to share, not only in general terms, but to quote specific pages of journal writing with freedom to censor and an acknowledgment of what censorship was introduced. Sharing alone, I can anticipate from past experiences of groups, will be a significant stimulus to the ongoing work, from the moment of the group formation on. Another piece of advice is to use the time of being together as an occasion to practice meditation together and also a psychotherapeutic exercise in couples best carried out with changing partners throughout successive sessions. This is an exercise consisting in the alternation between what I call a "free monologue" (more exactly, a free monologue in meditative context) and a retrospective commentary on the same in terms of interpersonal roles, character traits, and manifestations of resistance. While the former exercise is conducted in couples, it is useful to carry out the retrospective discussion in groups of 4 or 6 (where two speak at a time, in the presence of the others). I quote the following description of the free monologue from a joint meeting with E. J. Gold under the auspices of the Melia Foundation, in Berkeley, California:[4]

"I'd like you to close your eyes, and make yourself comfortable and relaxed, but with a straight spine. Make like a column, letting gravity pass through it. Let your body be relaxed, and let your mind be as it wants to be. Feel your body; feel your breath. In a couple of minutes I'll ask you to open your eyes in such a way that that doesn't change anything of your internal state."

(The pairs sat quietly for a few moments.)

"When it is time to open your eyes, look not at your partner's face, but at their belly. Just let the visual impressions

---

[4]Naranjo, C., in "Transformation and the Human Potential Movement," *Talk of the Month* journal, no. 85 (Nevada City, CA: Gateways Books, 1990).

come in: see without looking. Watch yourself without interfering, be aware without an agenda, and if you find yourself getting into thinking or body tension, you can close your eyes again and try once more from zero. Now, open your eyes and stay in zero.

"So with your eyes open, there you are, sitting in the presence of somebody else, and still you don't have to think. You don't have to do anything about being in the presence of somebody else. Allow yourself just to be, or, as the Taoist instructions for meditation put it, allow yourself to be like an idiot—which is a little more difficult in the presence of somebody.

"Now, very slowly start moving your gaze upwards to your partner's chest, continuing to sit with a silent mind and a relaxed body. Continue going up, very slowly, until you rest on your partner's throat. Feel if there is a different taste; a different quality to being there. Finally, your gaze arrives at your partner's mouth. While one of you continues to be attentive to the simple presence of their partner, the other will begin to speak. The words are given no significance by either party, they are merely sounds.

"The rules of the game will not be those of psychoanalysis, which is to say letting the mind go where it wants to go, nor those of the awareness continuum (i.e., expressing what your ongoing experience is). If you are a speaker, you are absolutely free. There is no rule about what you talk about. You just talk. The only rule is that you continue to observe yourself, that you are aware of yourself. And every now and then, as a recommendation, throw in some of your awareness of yourself into what you are saying."

For any group that has come thus far in implementing these suggestions, another step could be a measure of supervision, for which I find myself in a position of recommending a number of people that have trained at it under my direction during the last ten years or so.

This, in turn, could be a transition to the second stage of the work—which focuses on the cultivation of the higher feelings or virtues, and the selective inhibition of the most destructive conditioned responses—a subject that goes beyond the compass of the present volume.

Since after many years of teaching the material in this book to psychotherapists I consistently have seen how significantly it has affected their clinical practice, I cannot help feeling that the impact of this book—making these ideas available to a much wider professional audience—will make itself felt in the still wider community of those undergoing psychological treatment. This, naturally, contributes to my satisfaction in releasing this volume, and also causes me to want to say something specifically to those among my readers who are psychotherapists.

I want to address myself very briefly to a question that I have often been asked: "How should one apply these ideas in psychotherapy?"—only to say that it may not be the most fruitful question to ask. Though I have shared some observations which have arisen from my own practice as a gestaltist at the second International Gestalt Conference in Madrid (1987),[5] and might write someday how I have implicitly used the same information working with therapeutic communities (where a considerable portion of the benefits derive from the friction between different personalities and from the occasions with which individuals are provided to see things through each other's eyes), now rather than attempting to produce any set of notions as how to apply the understandings in this book to psychotherapy, I want to say that I, personally, never endeavored to apply them intentionally, and that I also feel like recommending to others to let the ideas "work by themselves"—that is to say, to let them seep into their practice in an organic and spontaneous way.

It is my conviction that a sharp perception of character is one of the best supports of effective psychotherapeutic intervention, whatever its modality, and since I also believe that character constitutes the skeleton of neurosis, I am convinced that a character-focused therapy is necessarily more to the point than one concerned with symptoms and memories only. Consequently, with the trust that this knowledge will be illuminating, orienting, and inspiring in creative ways to those who are assisting others in their healing and growth, I think that

---

[5]Naranjo, C., "Gestalt and Protoanalysis" in *Gestalt Therapy: The Attitude and Practice of an Atheoretical Experientialism* (Nevada City, CA: Gateways Books, 1993).

it only remains for me to emphasize the distance that mediates between intellectual and experiential understanding, and to suggest that the best that any professional may do by way of applying these ideas will then be to verify them in himself or herself—for the rest will follow naturally.

REMARKS FOR THE DIFFERENTIAL DIAGNOSIS AMONG SOME PERSONALITY TYPES

I/III:

Though alike in regard to self-control and formality they differ in that E I is restrained and serious while E III is expansive and cheerful. Also, E I is more tradition directed; E III, other-directed.

I/V:

Though both are controlled and perfectionistic they differ in that they identify more with the dignified or the guilty sub-self, respectively, and E I is assertive and straightforward while E V shy and inhibited in expression.

I/VI:

The predominantly dutiful variety of E VI may be difficult to discriminate from E I; one difference lies in the greater assertiveness of the latter; another, the greater difficulty of the fearful in coming to decisions. Also, E I is more active.

II/III:

Though both share the concern for personal appearance and the thirst for attention, E II is comparatively free and spontaneous, while E III controlled, fearful of letting-go. Also E II tends to be invasive, E III more mindful of limits.

II/VII:

Though both are seductive and hedonistic, E II is a truly emotional type, while in E VII a warm amiability exists in the context of a greater independence and in a background of cool non-involvement.

II/VIII:

Though the proud can be impulsive, arrogant and disdainful, E II is definitely emotional while E VIII is active. E II is predominantly seductive, E VIII more oriented to power and explicit dominance.

II/IX:

While sometimes I have seen E IX and E II confused in view of their generous disposition, no character could be called less histrionic and less egocentric than E IX, while E II is minimally resigned or routine-oriented, and E IX is consciously disinterested while E II is manipulative and self-centered in his giving. Also, E IX is patient; E II, impatient. E IX "matter-of-fact;" E II, romantic.

III/IV:

As in the case of the distinction between II and III, that of III and IV involves the contract between over-control and emotional expressiveness. If the stereotype of E III is Barbie Doll, that of E IV is a ballerina. Most distinctively, there is the contrast between the E III elated disposition and a greater contact with sadness in E IV—which echoes good and bad feelings about themselves, respectively. Though both can display an interference with spontaneity, this takes in E III the form of formality and in E IV that of affectation. Also, comparatively speaking, E III is more intellectual and E IV more emotional.

III/V:

These are difficult to confuse since E III is efficient and V, in its otherworldliness, inefficient and impractical. Both can be called narcissistic in that sometimes E V, just as E III, seeks being and love through performance, but their style is different in that E III is more social and confrontive than the schizoid, while the latter avoids confrontation and social contact.

III/VI:

These may be difficult to distinguish in some instances since E VI can display much vanity and E III may be prone to anxiety. The content of this anxiety is usually different, however--more in connection to self-disclosure and separation in E III; more in relation to making mistakes or not knowing what course of action to follow in E VI. Even though E III can be highly intellectual, his intellectual orientation is that of needing rational support for practical action, whereas E VI generally is more interested in theoretical and metaphysical issues, beyond the practical. Perhaps more striking than the introversion-extroversion contrast between the types is the inner-directedness of E VI vis-a-vis the other-directedness of E III.

III/VII:

These may be confused in that E VII usually regard themselves vain and extroverted. Frequently the motivation to achieve is stronger in E III, while in E VII it is tempered by a self-indulgent aversion to effort. Also while E III may regard him or herself as an enjoyer, E VII is more exactly a hedonist in that the desire for pleasure exists in the context of true permissiveness and little concern for social conventions. More decisive still is the contrast between them in terms of discipline vs. control and in that of permissiveness vs. control vis-a-vis others.

III/VIII:

These can occasionally be confused in that the E III individual may be aware of having developed self-assertive competitiveness in a vindictive manner, and may be both dominant as well as competitive. The main difference, as in the distinction between III and VII, is the impulsiveness and rebelliousness of E VIII in contrast to the typical self-control and conformity of E III.

III/IX:

While the contrast between these may be striking in terms of perceived achievement motive, both can be workaholics and both live on the surface of their being. Also, E IX can be as unemotional as E III seems to be, and E III as affectionate as E IX typically is. One difference between them is that E IX is the most tradition-directed of characters, while E III the most other-directed; also E IX character exists in the context of viscerotonia while E III in that of a somatotonic background. While both are practical, the former is relaxed, and the latter energetic and direct—not only in physical but psychological posture.

IV/V:

E IV and E V, sharing the bottom of the enneagram, share the under-dog identification that implies feelings of inferiority and guilt as well as a submissive tendency. While E IV hangs on to relationships in face of frustration, however, E V gives up, and while the depression typical of E IV is—in line with its emotional background—one of grief, weeping and self-accusation, the depression of E V is a dryness and hollowness, a forlorness in which grief seem to have been buried under a layer of resignation. On the whole, we may say that E IV is intense, E V the least intense of personalities after E IX.

IV/VI:

Perhaps the most striking difference between these types is the emotionality and expressiveness of E IV, in contrast to the intellectual centeredness and inhibition of E VI. They are not easy to confuse.

IV/VII:

The contrast here is between depression and elation, and also between guilt and the feeling of "being OK". E IV also has more of a super-ego characteristic than E VII. In most cases E IV expresses more anger than E VII, who is compulsively gentle.

IV/VIII:

Though these types have much in common, there is a more emotional intensity in the former, and an intensity of the active life in the latter. Also anger in the former lasts longer, while in E VIII it is dissipated through its explosive expression. More important yet is the contrast between the impulsiveness of VIII, that goes after what it wants, and the inhibition of E IV, whose strong desiring goes hand-in-hand with self-prohibition and an inward condemnation of over-desiring. As a consequence E VIII invades, E IV complains or manipulates through suffering.

IV/IX:

The one feature in common between these characters is that they can constitute the background for depressive states.

Even in these cases, however, E IV goes together with a "claiming type" of depression, while in E IX there is a depression of pure grief and passivity, in which we do not sense the dramatic element and the attention need of the former. Though both have received the label "masochistic", E IV is emotional and hypersensitive, E IX practical and long-suffering, E IV histrionic and E IX phlegmatic.

V/VI:

May be confused in virtue of the schizoid features of E V as well as the sad moods of the more avoidant subtype. Also E V can be, as E VI, distrustful, yet the distrust is more avoidant than even in the avoidant or phobic E VI who is more dependent, more affectionate and generous, both in terms of availability and in the quality of being good hosts. Also E VI is comparatively more disciplined, and takes external authority more into account, both in terms   of submissiveness to conventional or actual authority, and dominance towards those lower in the authority hierarchy.

V/IX:

It is possible to confuse these characters, for, in spite of the contrast between the hypersensitive introvert and the "undersensitive" extrovert, in both we may speak of resignation and self-forgetting. The difference is that between a resignation away from people (isolation) and a resignation with participation (contactfulness) which implies the contrast between a non-generous and an abnegated characteristic, respectively. Most characteristic, however, is the contrast between generosity of E IX and the limited availability, cooperation and support volunteered by E V.

VI/VII:

E VII is much more likely to be charming than E VI and considerably more adaptable. The experience of anger, in the other hand, is more prominent in E VI. Most striking is the difference in regard to guilt as characteristic in the latter by its presence as it is in the former by its absence. Whereas E VI has a hierarchical view of relations E VII approaches people as equals and is little intimidated by authority. While E VII is, in a broad sense of the word, a fear type, he is not prompt to anxiety as E VI, and fear is only a psychodynamic aspect behind compulsive gentleness.

VI/VIII:

The distinction here is quite clear in terms of unassertiveness vs. over-assertiveness, and manifest fear vs. manifest fearlessness—except in the case of one of the subtypes of cowardliness, the counter-phobic character, in which the pursuit of strength and pugnacity may simulate the phallic-narcissistic character. One difference between them is the greater intellectual orientation of E VI—which contrasts with the anti-intellectual orientation that is more frequent in E VIII—and also the greater presence of guilt and concern for intellectual authority, as well as a measure of introversion of the former, and the greater impulsiveness and indiscipline of the latter.

VI/IX:

One difference here is that of introversive-extraversive characteristic. Another related to the above, the predominance of an intellectual and sensory-motor orientation, respectively. While E VI orients itself to hierarchy, E IX rejects a hierarchical perspective. Also, while E VI, together with E V, is the most inner-directed, E IX is the most pure expression of tradition-directedness.

VII/VIII:

The difference between these two characters may be conveyed in terms of the contrast between tender-mindedness and tough-mindedness. Though both are impulsive, the former is intellectual, the latter active. Also, while E VII tends to be submissive, E VIII is dominant.

VII/IX:

These may be confused, because the passive and lazy characteristics, sometimes present in E VII, are interpreted as an expression of the E IX ruling passion. One difference is that the intense fantasy life of E VII contrasts with the lack of interiority of E IX. Another, the foxy astuteness and subtlety of E VII which contrast to the lack of subtlety and the naiveté of the "Sancho Panza" syndrome. Furthermore the self-indulgence of E VII contrasts markedly with the capacity of E IX to postpone his desires and to over-adjust to the milieu. Furthermore, while gluttony leads to psychological complexification, however, psychological laziness leads to over-simplification.

BIOGRAPHICAL NOTES

Claudio Naranjo studied medicine, music, and some philosophy in Chile, where he also was a resident at the University of Chile Psychiatric Clinic under Matte-Blanco. He taught psychology of art at the Catholic University and social psychiatry at the School of Journalism, University of Chile, and served as Director of the Center for Studies in Medical Anthropology.

After coming to live in the United States, Dr. Naranjo was among the staff of the early stage of Esalen Institute, where he became one of the three successors to Fritz Perls. Later his life's pilgrimage brought him in contact with various spiritual masters including Swami Muktananda, Idries Shah, Oscar Ichazo, Suleyman Dede, H.H. the XVIth Karmapa, and, most decisively, Tarthang Tulku Rinpoche. Also, he was at one time Research Associate at the Institute for Personality Assessment and Research on the Berkeley Campus and associate of Raymond Cattell at the Institute of Personality and Ability Testing. He has taught comparative religion at the California Institute of Asian Studies, humanistic psychology at the University of California in Santa Cruz, meditation at Nyingma Institute in Berkeley, California, and he was the founder of SAT Institute, an integrative psycho-spiritual school.

Dr. Naranjo is the honorary president of two Gestalt Institutes, Fellow of the Institute of Cultural Research in London, and member of the U.S. Club of Rome. He is considered one of the pioneers of the Human Potential Movement, and his introduction of "Fourth Way" ideas to psychotherapy is an instance of his work as an integrator at the interface between psychotherapy and the spiritual traditions. At present he is primarily dedicated to an integrative and transpersonal education of psychotherapists in various European and South American countries.

Claudio Naranjo's published works include *The One Quest* (Viking Press, 1972), *The Psychology of Meditation* (Penguin, 1972), *The Healing Journey* (Pantheon Books, 1974), *La Vieja y Novísima Gestalt: Actitud y Práctica* (Editorial Cuatro Vientos, 1990), *Ennea-type Structures* (Gateways Books, 1991), *Gestalt Therapy: The Attitude and Practice of an Atheoretical Experientialism* (Gateways Books, 1993), *Gestalt After Fritz* (published by Era Naciente, 1993, as *Gestalt sin Fronteras*), *The End of Patriarchy and the Dawning of a Tri-une Society* (Dharma Enterprises, 1994, and Kairós, 1993, as *La Agonía del Patriarcado*), *The Divine Child and the Hero* (to appear through Sirio, 1994, as *El Niño Divino y el Héroe*), *Ennea-types in Psychotherapy* (Hohm Press, 1994) and *Los Males del Mundo, los Males del Alma* (*The World Problematique and the Love Crisis*, forthcoming from Planeta).

INDEX

Abraham, Karl, 18, 44, 153
Abstraction, 86
Abulic psychopath,
in Schneider, 247
Accidia, 245
Adaptation, 5, 7
Adorno, T.W., *The Authoritarian Personality*, 53, 236
Adultomorphic
(of psychoanalytic view of infancy), xxxv
Agoraphobia, 70
Albert, Totila, xxiii
Alcohol(ism), xvi, 123, 217
Alienation, 84
Allport, Gordon, xvii, xxv
Anal axis
(of the enneagram), 22
Anal personality, 42 ff.
Anankastic(s), 42-43, 71, 82
Anger,
as passion, Chapter One,
as trait, 52
Anti-intraceptive, 42
Anxiety, 231
Apollonian, 223
Arcipresta de Hita,
Book of Good Love, 126
Arete (virtue), 223
Arica (Chile), xxix, 30,
Institute, xxxii
Arieti, Sylvano,
on "claiming," 114, 249
Arsenicum,
as perfectionist, 50-51
Asch, Stuart S.,
on masochistic
personality, 120

Aschaffenburg, 100
Audience(s),
of this book, xxxviii
Authority, 34, 234, 241
Authoritarian, 139, 171, 236
Authoritarian Personality, The
(T.W. Adorno et. al.), 236
Autobiography, 273
Avarice,
as passion, Chapter Two
Avoidance,
of inwardness, 128,
of life, 94
Avoidant personality, 34, 224
Awareness continuum, 279

Bad faith, 26
Barron, Frank, Preface, xxi,
The Interpersonal Diagnosis of Personality, xix
Behavior modification, 272
Being, xxxv,
inauthentic, 26,
loss, 64,
search for, 37-38
Being-scarcity, 63, 75, 125
Benjamin, Lorna,
Interpersonal Diagnosis and Treatment of Personality Disorders, 251
Bergler, Edmund,
on oral pessimism, 101
Berne, Eric,
Games People Play, 103
Birth trauma, 4

Bleuler, 100
Book of Good Love
    (Arcipresta de Hita), 126
Borderline, definition, 105
Bosch, Hieronymus,
    "Seven Deadly Sins," 201
Boundary disturbance, 259-
    260
Breastfeeding, 111, 120, 170
"Breast Feeding and
    Character Formation"
    (Frieda Goldman-Eisler),
    100-101, 120, 170
Buddhism, 3, 276
Butler, Samuel, 177

Calcarea,
    as ennea-type IX, 253-254
Canterbury Tales, The
    (Chaucer), 65, 152, 175
Carcinosin,
    as perfectionist, 51
Cathexis, 163
Cattell, Raymond B., xvii,
    xxiv ff., 12
Center for Studies of
    Personality, xxv, xxvi
Cerebrotonia, 70, 89, 120
Character,
    core of, 7,
    definition of, 6-7,
    disorder, xxxviii,
    masculine, 23,
    masochistic, 18
Charlataneria (the fixation),
    30

Charlatan(ism), 177,
    as fixation, 152, 165-166
Chaucer, Geoffrey, *The
    Canterbury Tales,* "The
    Parson's Tale," 65, 152,
    175
Chief feature, 12, 31
Chile, xv ff., xxix, xxxiii,
    University of, xxiii, xxv
Christianity, 174,
    esoteric, xxviii
Christian, 243,
    charity, 49,
    ideal, 223,
    tradition, 11, 28, 151, 201,
    271
Chutzpah, 187
Cinderella, 194
Circumplex models, 14
Claiming, 114, 119, 249
Cleckley, H.,
    on psychopathology, 130
Compulsive, virtue, 55
Confluence, 260-261
Conscious suffering
    (Gurdjieff), 274
Consciousness,
    degradation of, 2 ff., 197,
    perturbation of, 258
Cooper, Arnold M., (with
    Allen J. Frances and
    Michael H. Sacks),
    *Psychiatry, Vol. 1: The
    Personality Disorder and
    Neurosis,* 14, 59, 92, 120,
    169, 192, 216, 261
Coulter, Catherine R.,
    Portraits of Homoeopathic

Medicines, xxxiii, 50-51, 80-81, 109-110, 138-140, 159-160, 183-185, 207-209, 229-231, 253-254

Counter-identification, 146

Counter-introjection, 146

Cyclothymic, 68, 99, 103, 248

Dante, *The Divine Comedy*, 174, 246

Dark Night of the Soul (St. John of the Cross), 40

David Copperfield (Dickens), 257

Davidson, Roy, xxix

Deception, 32, 190, 200, as trait, 212

Defense(s), xxxviii,

Deficiency-motivation, xxiv, 2-3, 6, 24 ff., 36

Deflection, definition, 259

Dementia praecox, 69

Dependence, 184

Depression, 23, 106

Desensitization, definition, 146

Detachment, as fixation, Chapter Two, as trait, 83

Devil, 238

Diabolus (the devil), 238

Diagnosis, differential, among personality types, Appendix, 282-289

Dickens, *David Copperfield*, 257, Mr. Pickwick, 267

Dionysian, 31, 223

Disorders of Personality: DSM-III: Axis II (Theodore Millon), 46, 54, 77-79, 105-106, 130, 132, 155-157, 181

Divided Self, The (R.D. Laing), 76

Divine Comedy (Dante), 174

Doll House, The (Henrik Ibsen), 33

Dominance, as trait, 142

Don Quixote, 235, 240, 243-244

Donath, J., 43

DSM III (*Diagnostic and Statistical Manual of Mental Disorders* - 3rd Revised Edition), xxxiv, 15 ff., 44, 98, 104, 201, 219, anti-social personality, 131-132, avoidant personality, 224, compulsive personality, 46, 71, dependent personality, 250, histrionic personality, 181, schizoid personality, 77

Dysthymia, 100

Easser, R., on hysterical personality, 179-181

Ecclesiastes, 199

Ectomorphia, 70, 92, 120, 169

Ectopenic, 147

Ego, 9, weakness, 75, 244
Egocentrism, 195
Einstein, 125
Ellis, *Rational-Emotive Therapy*, 32
Emptiness, 38
Endarkenment, xxii, 2, 275
Endomorphia, 169, 192, 240, 261
Ennea-types, definition, 13
Ennea-type Structures (Claudio Naranjo), 10
Enneagram,
    courses, xxxi,
    diagrams of, in Introduction, 14 ff.,
    movement, xxxii,
    structure, 91,
    symmetry of, 23
ENTJ, 229
Envy,
    as passion, Chapter Three,
    as trait, 110 ff.
Envy and Gratitude (Melanie Klein), 102, 111
Epileptoid group, 16
Equalitarian, 162
Erikson, Erik, 41, 60
Eroticism, 175
Essence, definition, 10 ff.
ESFJ, 253
ESTJ, 49
Extraversion (extroversion), 23, 48, 137, 169, 182, 229, 249, 253
Eysenk, Hans, xxiv

Fairbairn, W. R. D., xxxvi, 3, 75, 84
Fear,
    as passion, Chapter Eight,
    as trait, 231 ff.
Fenichel, O., xxvii, 227
Ferenczi, S., on introjection, 117
Fernandez, Hector, xxvii, xxix
Fixation(s), 24, 29, 36
Fourth Way, The, xxviii, xxx, 11, 28, 276
Fourth way characterology, 17
Freud, Sigmund, xxvii, 3, 44, 90, 192, 232, 239, 269,
    denial, 146,
    instinct theory, 8,
    introjection, 117,
    neurosis, 4,
    reaction formation, 58,
    theory on masochism, 101
Freud, Anna, 89
Fromm, Eric, 60, 131,
    on cynicism, 143, "the marketing orientation," 17, 202-203,
    To Have or To Be, 268

Games People Play (Eric Berne), 103
Gestalt (Therapy), xxvii, 259,
    International Conference, 280

Giannini, H., 245-246
Gluttony,
  as passion, Chapter Five,
  as trait, 161,
  definition, 151-152
Gold, E.J., 278, *The Human
  Biological Machine as a
  Transformational
  Apparatus*, 272
Goldman-Eisler, Frieda,
  "Breast Feeding and
  Character Formation,"
  100-101, 120, 170
Gospel of St. John, 4
Grinker, R. R., 105
Guilt, 145, 236,
  as trait, 87
Guntrip, Harry, xxxvi, 37,
  "ego weakness," 244
Gurdjieff, G.I., xxiii, 7, 10,
  12, 274, *Meetings with
  Remarkable Men*, xxix

*Hallucinogens and
  Shamanism*, by Michael
  Harner, xviii
Hara (Karlfried von
  Durckheim), 275
Harlow, Harry, 5
Harner, Michael, xviii
Healing Journey, The
  (Claudion Naranjo), 170
Hedonism, 21, 152, 161, 173,
  197,
  as trait, 186

Hesse, Herman, *Siddhartha*,
  84
Hindu Kush, xxix
Histrionic (personality), 17,
  27, 177,
  as fixation, Chapter Six,
  as trait, 188
Hölderlin, 69
Homeopathy, 50, 80, 109,
  138, 159, 183, 207, 229,
  253, types in, xxxiii
Homosexual, 224
Horney, Karen, xxvii, 55,
  129, 197, 255, 269,
  *Neurosis and Human
  Growth*, xxxvii, 47, 72-75,
  107-108,
  (on narcissistic character),
  203-204,
  Our Inner Conflicts
  (on vindictive character),
  133-136
Hospitalism, 92
*Human Biological Machine as
  a Transformational Appar-
  atus, The* (E.J. Gold), 272
Hyperactivity, 214
Hyperaesthesia, 69
Hyper-intentionality, 232-
  233
Hypersensitivity, 70,
  as trait, 88
Hyperthymic, 132,
  in Kurt Schneider, 201
Hypochondriac, 178
Hypocritical, 55
Hypomania, 99

Hysterical personality, 179 ff., 197, 205
Hysteroid group, 16, 200

Ibsen, Henrik, *The Doll House*, 33
ICD-IX (*International Classification of Diseases*, 9th ed.), 44
Ichazo, Oscar, xxix ff., 7, 29, 40, 127, 141, 152, 200
Id (Freudian), 238-239
Idealization, 32, 34, 144, 167-168
Identification, 215, 218
Illusion(s), 36, 204
Imitatio Christi, 223
INFJ, 109
INFP, 109
Instinct, 5 ff., 57, distortion of, 13
Institute of Personality and Ability Testing (IPAT), xxvi
Institute of Personality Assessment and Research (IPAR), xv, xxvi
Interiority, lack of, 21
Internalization, xxi, 242
Interpersonal Diagnosis and Treatment of Personality Disorders (Lorna Benjamin), 251
Interpersonal Diagnosis of Personality (Frank Barron), xix

INTJ, 158-159
INTP, 79
Introjection, 102, 117, 119, 215
Introversion, 66, 71, 78, 109, 228, 251
ISTJ, 252

Jewish mother, 191
Jodorowsky, A., on sexuality, 220
Johnson, Stephen M., *Characterological Transformation*, 204
Jones, Ernest, on rationalization, 167
Jung, C.G., *Psychological Types*, xxxiv, 48-49, 78-79, 108, 137-138, 158, 182-183, 206, 228, 251
Jungian typology, xxxiv

Kaliyuga, 4
Keirsey, David, & Marilyn Bates, *Please Understand Me*, 49-50, 109, 158, 207, 229
Kelman, Harold, on masochism, 106-107
Kernberg, Otto, 17, 75-76, 98, 104, 169, 192, 205
Klein, George, xxxv

Klein, Melanie, *Envy and Gratitude*, 102, 111, 117
Koch, 130, 178
Kraepelin, E., 130, 178, 224
Kretschmer, Ernst, 16, *Physique and Character*, 68, 88, 99, 248

La Fontaine, on charlatanism, 152
Labile (character), 153, 180
Lachesis, as ennea-type IV, 110
Laing, R.D., 243, *The Divided Self*, 76
Language of Psychoanalysis, The (Laplance and Pontalis), 118
Lao-Tse, on Virtue, 63
Laplanche, J., and J.-B. Pontalis, *The Language of Psychoanalysis*, 118
Law of Three (in Gurdjieff), xxiii
Lazare, Aaron, 179-180
Leary, Timothy, xvii, xix, 14
Lesser, S., on hysterical personality, 179
Libido, 197, 266, theory, 196
Lilly, John C., "The Arica Training," 30
Love, deprivation, 92, 107, erotic, 108, defense against, 225, expectations of, 146, 230,

parental, 103, 121, 148, 168, search for, 148, 172, 175, 185, 195, 219, 243
Lowen, Alexander, *Narcissism*, 17
LSD, xvii
Lucifer, in *Divine Comedy*, 174
Lust, as passion, Chapter Four, as trait, 140, definition of, 127
Lycopodium, as ennea-type VI, 229-230

M.C.O., mutual comfort operation (Idries Shah), 176
"Marketing orientation" (Erich Fromm), 17, as fixation, Chapter Seven, definition, 202
Marx, Karl, 9
Maslow, Abraham, 2, 24
Masochist(ic), 57, 143, 249, 258, character (as fixation), Chapter Three
Matte-Blanco, Ignacio, xxii, 90, 167
MMPI, xvi
McClelland, David, xvii, xxv
Medea, 134
Meditation, 221, 276 ff.

Meetings with Remarkable Men (G.I. Gurdjieff), xxix
Melia Foundation, 278
Mescaline, xvi
Mesoendomorphs, 59, 147
Mesomorphic, 240
Metaphysical illusion, xxxv
Midas, story as descriptive of schizoid process, 94-95
Millon, Theodore, *Disorders of Personality: DSM-III: Axis II*, 46, 54, 77-79, 105-106, 130, 132, 155-157, 181, 226, 228, 250, 262
Molière, 164
Molina, Armando, xxxi
Moral anesthesia (Scholtz), 129
Motor isolation, 90
Murray, Henry, xxv, 191

Naranjo, Claudio, xv ff. (Preface), *The Healing Journey*, 170
Narcissism,
    as character, Chapter Five,
    as trait, 164-165,
    definition, 154
Narcotization, 255, 259
Nasruddin, Mullah, 36, 63, 150, 268
Natrum Muriaticum,
    as ennea-type IV, 109-110
Nature/nurture equation, 169

Neurosis, xxxvii,
    definition of, xxxviii
Neurotic Styles (David Shapiro), 226
Nietzsche, 223
Nux Vomica,
    as ennea-type VIII, 138-140

Object-relations theory, 8-9, 112
Oedipal situation, 102, 235
Ontic obscuration, xxxv, 27, 62, 94, 149, 244
Ontic insufficiency, 87, 173, 198
Optimism, 34, 168
Oral-agressive, 60, 170,
    axis, 22
Oral erotic, 108
Oral-optimistic, 18, 172
Oral-receptive, 18, 154, 165,
    axis, 22
Orality, 25
Organismic interference, xxxvi, 37
Organismic self-regulation, 9, 214
Orgasm function (Reich), 101
Oriental traditions, 2
Our Inner Conflicts (Karen Horney), 133-136
Ouspensky, P.D., xxiii, 13
Over-adaptation, 19,
    as trait, 255-256

Palmer, Helen, xxxi
Panza, Sancho, 255
Paranoid character, 18,
    as fixation, Chapter Eight
Passion(s), xxxvi, 7, 19
Patriarchal bias, 111
Penis envy, 103, 111
Perfectionism,
    as fixation, Chapter One
Perls, Fritz, 6, 8, 119, 166,
    disciple of Horney, xxvii
Personality,
    conditioned, xxxvi,
    definition of, xxi, xxxv,
    distortion of, xxxviii,
    research, xxv,
    syndromes, 12,
    type A, 205, 211
Peterfreund, E., xxxv
Phallic-narcissistic, 19, 129-
    131, 144-145
Phosphorus, as ennea-type
    III, 207-209
Physique and Character
    (Ernst Kretschmer), 68, 88,
    99, 248
Pickwick, Mr. (Dickens), 267
Please Understand Me (David
    Keirsey & Marilyn Bates),
    49-50, 109, 158, 207, 229
Pleasure, 17, 33, 57, 85, 140,
    163, 172
Polster, Erving and Miriam,
    on deflection and
    confluence, 259-261
*Portraits of Homoeopathic
    Medicines* (Catherine R.

Coulter), xxxiii,
    (see Homeopathy entries)
Poverty, 147
Pride, as passion, Chapter
    Six, as trait, 185
Protoanalysis, 30, 127, 175,
    193, 223
Proust, *Remembrance of
    Things Past*, 112
Prussian character, 234
*Psychiatry, Vol. 1: The
    Personality Disorder and
    Neurosis* (Arnold M.
    Cooper, Allen J. Frances,
    and Michael H. Sacks), 14,
    59, 92, 120, 169, 192, 216,
    261
Psychopathic Personalities
    (Kurt Schneider), 43
*Psychotherapy of Neurotic
    Character* (David Shapiro),
    xxxviii
Psylocybin, xvi
Pulsatilla,
    as ennea-type II, 183-185
Pyknics, 59

Questiones Disputatae
    (Saint Thomas), 39
Quevedo, Francisco,
    on the envious, 97

Rape, as paradigm, 149
Rational-Emotive Therapy
    (Ellis), 32

Rationalization, 167-168,
    212, 216
Reaction formation, 57-58,
    61, 191
Red and the Black, The
    (Stendhal), 112
Reich, Wilhelm, xxvii,
    xxxvii, 4, 44-46,
    hysterical character, 179,
    masochistic character,
    101,
    phallic narcissistic
    character, 129-131, 144-
    145
Remembrance of Things Past
    (Proust), 112
Repression, 58, 190
Retentiveness, 68,
    as trait, 82
Retroflection, 119
Riesman, David, 17, 55
Rigidification, 63
Riso, Don, xxxi
Robotization, 26, 257
Romantic (orientation), 185

Sadistic character,
    as fixation, Chapter Four
SAT Institute, xxx ff.
Sargent, Tony, xvii
Sayers, Dorothy,
    on *accidia*, 246
Schizoid, 20, 27, 67 ff., 93,
    group, 16
Schizothymic, 68
Schneider, Kurt,
    Psychopathic Personalities,

43, 67-68, 98, 129, 153, 178,
    201, 225, 247
Scholtz, F.,
    on moral anesthesia, 129
Schreber case, 224
Schulgin, Alexander, xviii
Scripts People Play (Claude
    H. Steiner), 104, 205
Self-accusation, 239
Self-deception, 160
Self-forgetfulness, 256
Self-idealization, 167
Self-invalidation, 223, 237
Self-observation, 275
Self-realization, 172, 198
Self-study, 270 ff.
Sepia,
    as ennea-type V, 80
Seven Deadly Sins, 40, 151,
    174, by Hieronymus
    Bosch, 201
Sex-appeal, 220
Sexual, attraction, 103, 212,
    desire, 3,
    needs, 134
Sexuality, 154, 204, 220, 230
Shah, Idries, 176
Shakespeare, 216
Shapiro, David, xxxv,
    Neurotic Styles, 226, 238,
    *Psychotherapy of Neurotic
    Character*, xxxviii, 206,
    on impulsive character,
    157-158
Sheldon, William H., xxiii,
    *The Varieties of
    Temperament*, xxiv, 70-71,

on somatotonia, 136-137,
on viscerotonia, 248-249
Siddhartha (Herman Hesse),
84
Silica, as ennea-type V, 81
Somatotonia, 59, 240,
in childhood, 147,
traits of, 136-137
Spanish Royal Academy,
127
Spontaneity, 41, 84, 116
St. John of the Cross, *Dark
Night of the Soul*, 40
Steig, William, 17 ff.
Steiner, Claude H., *Scripts
People Play*, 104, 205
Stendhal, *The Red and the
Black*, 112
Strindberg, 69
Sufi(s), xxii
Suffering, 34, 143,
dramatization of, 11
Sullivan, Harry S., 84
Sulphur, as ennea-type VII,
159-160
Summum bonum, 152
Superbia (pride), 201
Super-ego, 87, 117

Tao(istic), 54
Tartuffe (Molière character),
164
Taxonomy, 1
Thomas, Saint, *Questiones
Disputatae*, 39
Tillich, P., 232
To Have or To Be

(Erich Fromm), 268
Toilet training, 59
Traits, system of, xxi
Transactional Analysis, 205,
250
Transcendence, 25
Transformation, 28, 271,
of neediness, 58
Type A personality, 205, 211
Typology, xvi

Under-dog, 6, 88, 145

Vagina envy, 111
Vanity, as passion, Chapter
Seven,
as trait, 209,
definition, 199
Varieties of Temperament, The
(William H. Sheldon),
xxiv, 70-71, 136-137, 248-
249
Vindictiveness, 27
Vipassana meditation, 276 ff.
Viscerotonic, 192, 240, 248-
249, 262
Von Durckheim, Karlfried,
Hara, 275
Von Franz, Marie-Louise,
251-252
Von Gebsattel, V.E., 43, 71,
82

Winnicot, 3, 10
Womb, 22

Dear Reader of *Character and Neurosis*:

As the author writes in his Foreword and final chapter, he intends this book to be used as an introduction to an effective and proven method of work on self. It can also serve as a handbook, a diagnostic tool, or a teaching manual for professionals in this field.

We at Gateways would like to encourage you to apply Dr. Naranjo's analysis to your own character and test out this method for yourself. As with all genuine knowledge, it cannot be properly judged or verified intellectually. It *must* be empirically tested with one or more live subjects in the laboratory of *your own life*. Once you have begun this research for yourself, you may find that you have more and more data to analyze and share with others, whether you are a novice or a professional on this path.

Dr. Naranjo's workshop and training offerings are currently sponsored and conducted by various organizations in Europe and Latin America. If you are interested in these activities, contact Gateways for referral to his SAT office in Spain or to his correspondence secretary.

For further books, study materials, audio and video-tapes of Claudio Naranjo and others, you may contact Gateways at the address and phone below with no obligation to purchase. Ask for a free catalogue of current resources.

Gateways Books & Tapes
P.O. Box 370-E
Nevada City, CA 95959
Phone: (800) 869-0658 or (916) 272-0180
Fax: (916) 272-0184